Wolves Among Lambs

My Story of Sexual Abuse
& Cover-ups in the Church

Stacey Shiflett

SUREWORD
PUBLICATIONS
surewordpublications.com

Wolves Among Lambs

Copyright © 2019 SureWord Publications
Second Edition – March, 2, 2019
ISBN: 9781797029221

By Stacey Shiflett

Printed in the United States of America

All rights reserved solely by the author. The author guarantees all contents are original and do not infringe upon the legal rights of any other person or work. No part of this book may be reproduced in any form without the permission of the author.

All Scripture references are from the Authorized King James Bible.

Table of Contents

SECTION ONE
My Story

Part 1 – The First Time
Chapter 1 - Molested ………………………………….25
Chapter 2 - Justice …………………………………….36

Part 2 – The Second Time
Chapter 3 - Job Offer …………………………….....45
Chapter 4 - Grooming ……………………………....51
Chapter 5 - The Proposition ……………………….64
Chapter 6 - Green Light ……………………………75
Chapter 7 - Confrontation ………………………….80
Chapter 8 - Reinforcements ……………………….84
Chapter 9 - Going Public …………………………..89
Chapter 10 - Alone With God ……………………..93
Chapter 11 - Vindication …………………………...98
Chapter 12 - The Rest of the Story ……………..105
Chapter 13 - Blacklisted …………………………..110

Part 3 – National Headlines
Chapter 14 - Earthquake …………………………..116
Chapter 15 - Fact-Finding Mission ……………....127
Chapter 16 - My Promise …………………………137

Chapter 17 - Ripple Effect 153
Chapter 18 - Tidal Wave 159
Chapter 19 - Tsunami 163
Chapter 20 - Aftermath 170
Chapter 21 - Calling Out the Hypocrisy 182
Chapter 22 - IFB Paradigms and Paradoxes 212

SECTION TWO
Restoring Our Credibility

Part 4 – Responding Biblically
Chapter 23 - A Clear Position on Sexual Abuse 235
Chapter 24 - Reality Check 253
Chapter 25 - The Real Problem 276
Chapter 26 - When Allegations Surface 282
Chapter 27 - False Accusations 294
Chapter 28 - Analysis versus Paralysis 300
Chapter 29 - Open Door Policy Re-examined 313
Chapter 30 - An Environment of Transparency 331

Part 5 – Safeguards
Chapter 31 - Common Sense Preventions 340
Chapter 32 - Implementing Ministry Policies 360

Part 6 – Hope and Healing
Chapter 33 - Victory for the Victim 376
Chapter 34 - Ultimate Healing 387

~ Acknowledgments ~

* * *

Grace, thank you for being the most wonderful wife a man could have. I love you and thank God for you.

I want to thank my five children for your loving support. I am grateful for your understanding and patience. I love all of you more than you could ever know.

I am thankful for the members of Calvary Baptist Church in Dundalk, Maryland. Your unwavering support during this project was such a blessing. Thank you for helping me keep the wolves away from the lambs in our church.

I appreciate all those that helped with the proofreading and editing. Your labor of love is humbling!

I am grateful for the pastors and godly ladies that read the original manuscript. Thank you for your insight, constructive criticism and words of encouragement.

Lastly, I am thankful to the Lord for allowing me to finally tell my story. I am a testimony of His grace.

~ Dedication ~

This book is dedicated to every man, woman, boy or girl that went to church sometime in their life and became a victim of sexual abuse.

I pray that God will heal you, and that He will bring your abuser to justice.

~ Prologue ~

Ezekiel 22:25-27 There is a conspiracy of her prophets in the midst thereof, like a roaring lion ravening the prey; they have devoured souls; they have taken the treasure and precious things; they have made her many widows in the midst thereof. Her priests have violated my law, and have profaned mine holy things: they have put no difference between the holy and profane, neither have they shewed difference between the unclean and the clean, and have hid their eyes from my sabbaths, and I am profaned among them. Her princes in the midst thereof are like wolves ravening the prey, to shed blood, and to destroy souls, to get dishonest gain.

In this passage of Scripture, Ezekiel paints a vivid picture. The people of God have been victimized by corrupt leadership. The poetic phraseology used in this description is amazing in its accuracy. I could not help but notice the alliteration that Ezekiel uses to set up the characters. He names the Prophets, the Priests, and the Princes. Further down in verse 29, He also blames the People of the land. It is a group effort. The attacks on the innocent were coming from every side.

The tragedies he described are much like the assaults we are facing now in many of our churches. Like Ezekiel, we are dealing with a conspiracy among our prophets. They are working together behind the scenes to devour the souls; the treasures and the precious things (our children). The priests (and pastors) have violated God's laws and have profaned the holy things. They show no distinction between the holy and the profane. They have shown no preference between the unclean and the clean. The princes (leaders) are in the midst of the flock, ravening the prey, shedding blood, destroying souls and profiting from it all at the same time.

God's solution for this terrible plight was to search for a man to make up the hedge -- a man to stand in the gap for the sake of the flock. Verse 30 reveals the outcome of God's solution. He found not a single man to secure the flock. He looked for, but did not find a single man who was willing to do what was needed to provide safety to the people. Because of their apathy and weakness, God consumed them with the indignation and fire of His wrath. He recompensed upon their heads "their own way." They did nothing to stop it, so it destroyed them. The conspiracies and victimization of God's people went uncontested, so it prevailed. Not a single man stepped up to be the barrier between the people of God and destruction. God's appeal for a leader to make a difference was disregarded. His search for a man to protect the flock, expose the conspiracies and thwart the lions and the wolves came up short.

In 1993, I surrendered to be that man. This book is my latest attempt to make up the hedge and stand in the gap.

There are wolves among our lambs. When Jesus commissioned His disciples in Luke 10:3, He said, "Go your ways: behold, I send you forth as lambs among wolves." This statement was made to prepare these humble men of God for the bloodthirsty crowd that they would encounter on their mission to spread the Gospel.

However, what we are witnessing today is a complete reversal of the original description of God's servants. Instead of being lambs, too many in the church today are actually wolves. Somehow, they have infiltrated the flock of God and are systematically destroying our little lambs, one at a time. This has been going on far too long. It must end. We must make it a priority to do everything within our power to discover the wolves, point them out and eradicate them from the flock.

The very lives of our little lambs depend on it.

Matthew 7:15
Beware of false prophets, which come to you in sheep's clothing, but inwardly they are ravening wolves.

~ Introduction ~

"But whoso shall offend one of these little ones which believe in me, it were better for him that a millstone were hanged about his neck, and that he were drowned in the depth of the sea."
Matthew 18:6

✳ ✳ ✳

I will be the first to admit it. The topic of sexual abuse is repulsive. Any decent person will cringe when confronted with this subject. Yet here we are. Sexual abuse in our churches has been in the headlines a lot recently. The unchurched and the unbelievers seem to be the loudest voices in this fight. For too long, many of the leaders and the laymen have remained silent on this issue.

The time has come to speak up. Someone has to say something. Someone has to be a voice for the victims. Not just those that have already been victimized, but the ones that may be hurt in the future. I have stood by for months and watched pastors, editors, evangelists and authors weigh in on their blogs, newspapers, and their devotionals with their opinions and analysis. Now it is my turn.

I have the joy of being the senior pastor of Calvary Baptist Church in Dundalk, Maryland. We are located just east of the Baltimore city limits. Recently, we experienced a public sexual abuse scandal at our church. I deal with this nightmare in Part Three. In summary, the former pastor of our church was publicly accused on Facebook of sexual abuse by a woman who once was student of our Christian school.

As of the writing of this book, the allegations are still under criminal investigation. As a result of that, I will be somewhat restricted with many of the details. The victim would have been sixteen years of age at the time of the alleged crimes. No official charges have been made and no arrest has been made. Gathering the evidence of a twelve year old alleged crime takes time. The State of Maryland also has some complicated laws pertaining to the statute of limitations on certain sex crimes.

This book will address many of the issues that we faced in our church. I will refer to these allegations throughout this book. We are still navigating it because it has yet to be resolved. We are prepared for the possibility that it may never be, and have turned it over to God if that ends up being the case.

My goal is not to exploit this situation. I simply want to use it as a guide to help others. Because the accused was the president of a prominent Bible college, this quickly became a highly publicized scandal. In my response to the gross mishandling of this situation, I made a video and uploaded it to my YouTube channel. The feedback was overwhelming. Many people were dumbfounded that an independent Baptist pastor would do what I did. I agree that my methods were unorthodox. Looking back, I believe more than ever that I did what needed to be done.

I believe that most people had given up on the hope that someone -- anyone -- would publicly and honestly address this issue. My inbox was literally flooded with letters from hurting victims, angry mothers of victimized children, frustrated staff members and dis-enfranchised church members. I was inundated with requests from pastors and parents to please do something to help stop this madness.

Several churches that were without a pastor asked me to pray about taking their church. They were desperately seeking strong, biblical leadership to help them navigate the stormy waters of a scandal in their own congregations. They wanted a pastor who would address it rather than dodge it.

I lost count of the evangelists, missionaries, Bible college staff and pastors from all over the world who reached out to me. It was overwhelming. I listened to details about cover-ups of unimaginable atrocities that made my heart break. I read emails written by weeping parents telling of their child being raped or molested in the church nursery or church restrooms only to be shamed and run off from their church for involving the police. I took phone calls from preachers' wives who had been abused by their pastors as teenagers and never told anyone. I listened to a missionary's wife and her husband as they sat in my office and shared the pain of abuse from her pastor when she was a teenager.

I read letters from adults who opened up to me about the sexual abuse they endured from their dads who were leaders in the church and nobody would believe them. I had church members in my own congregation who confessed to being sexually abused as children and had never told a soul. I spent days on the phone listening to frustrated, hurting and hopeless people who, after seeing my passionate response, felt a small glimmer of hope. They had a spark of optimism that maybe, just maybe, someone would give them a voice. They had prayed for someone to make enough noise so that this horrible reality of sexual abuse and cover-ups might be exposed and stopped.

A few preachers went on the offensive, claiming it is really not as bad as I made it out to be in my video. I have concluded that any preacher who downplays or minimizes the extent of this problem is either oblivious or disingenuous. Or both. Or an abuser himself.

I did not ask for this heartbreaking scandal to happen in my church. I did not ask for this platform that has in all actuality been forced upon me. I could not turn my head and walk away. As the priest and the Levite did in the story of the Good Samaritan, I could not pass by on the other side, ignoring what I had witnessed. I could not ignore the pleas of the hurting. I could not defend the actions of my friend who was accused.

This alleged abuse happened -- in my ministry, my church, my school, and my office. It involved the granddaughter of one of my assistant pastors. Deflection was not an option. Resorting to politics and the cronyism that is the normal reaction in the IFB movement was not in my DNA.

Let me be clear. There are multitudes of pastors and churches that take a stand on this issue. They take the right stand. They want to do what is right. They love God, they love the Bible, they love their people and they would do anything to protect the truth. In my passionate response, I do not want to give the impression that nobody is handling these situations correctly. I would never want to make it sound like everybody is guilty of covering up sin and that everyone is protecting the abusers. That is far from the truth. I know of hundreds of men in leadership who would fight tooth and nail for truth and justice. I want to establish that up front. I have drawn much encouragement from these men and am challenged to continue to fight because of them.

But there are far too many preachers who simply do not "get it" when it comes to this subject. Their philosophy has been skewed either by their mentors or their training. They were exposed to warped theology or badly misguided influences that have tainted their ability to deal with this subject correctly. It is my prayer that this book will help the victims get clarity and healing, and help church leaders who have a teachable spirit to make the effort to handle these situations properly should they encounter them in their church. As the church, we need to do better in how we handle sexual misconduct and abuse!

The vicious cycle when an allegation surfaces cannot continue. The ducking and diving of the leadership in the church, and the ostracizing of the victims has to stop. It is time we put our foot down and declare that our churches will no longer be a sanctuary for perverts and pedophiles. We must work together to expose the wolves and get them away from the lambs.

As you will see in Section One, I have been a victim of sexual abuse and sexual harassment. I spend a lot of time in this book telling my story because it is so unbelievable. What happened to me was so extraordinary that by sharing it, I pray others in similar situations can relate and get closure. I have some insight on this issue, both as a victim and as a pastor who has had to deal with this topic multiple times in my ministry. I am not an authority on this subject, but I have some things I must say. I hope this book will help clarify things and as a result, we will see positive changes brought about.

My story is painful, but if it will help someone else who has been hurt, it will have been worth digging up the suppressed memories. I cannot begin to describe the inner turmoil I have faced in the decision to write this book. The shame and the stigma that is associated with being an abuse survivor never goes away. When people see you or think of you, that event is always attached to you. I'm aware that by telling my story, it will forever affect how people think of me. I am prepared to pay that price if it will help other victims find the courage to come forward and help stop these perverts.

I have done my best to keep it discreet. I apologize in advance if reading my accounts of what happened causes you to blush. This is a nasty topic. It is ugly and repulsive. But it happens. We can no longer turn our heads away. One of the biggest reasons that abuse victims do not report what happened to them is because it is so embarrassing. Being victimized is degrading and humiliating. In my effort to help victims, I tell my story.

In my desire to help non-victims understand the seriousness of this, I tell more details than some may be comfortable with. This is an uncomfortable topic. To take the edge off of the crime and to dilute the facts would only minimize the terror and trauma associated with sexual abuse. The abuse is real. The pain is real. Therefore the details of what happened to me and what happens to thousands of people across our country is to keep it real. Please bear with me.

I have chosen to write this book in plain English. This will not be a formal textbook or a coffee table picture book. I did not spend years researching other people's stories and I have not collected boxes of evidence and statistics. This is simply my story and my thoughts on how we can fix this. I am just a country boy. I am a matter-of-fact, tell-it-like-it-is man. I don't water it down or worry about offending someone. I have written this book in the same way that I speak and preach -- plain, passionate and with as much biblical support as possible.

At times my tone may come across as angry. I am not angry. I am highly motivated. There is a difference! I will be honest with you. If this subject does not make you angry, you might be part of the problem. If we are so spiritual and gracious and loving that it doesn't grind our gears when our children and teenagers are targeted by pedophiles, we might be a little too "spiritual!"

We need more Christians, more dads, more moms, more church members and more leaders to get some fire in the belly, make some noise, and help put a stop to this perversion. We've got to stop handling pedophiles with kid gloves. There is no nice way to decapitate a wolf. It's messy and it's nasty, but somebody has to do it.

Not Just an IFB Problem

Let me be clear about several things. This problem is not specific to any single group of churches or denomination. The Catholics are in the news almost weekly. The Independent Fundamental Baptists (IFB) have been in the news a lot recently. Sexual abuse spans all faiths and creeds. This plague has affected every church, every denomination, and every religious group in the country.

Don't be fooled. Just because it is not in the news does not mean it is not happening.

I am a fifth-generation Baptist preacher. My experiences, my opinions and my interpretation of scripture are going to be coming from that perspective. Nevertheless, this problem spans doctrinal boundaries. Sexual abuse knows no ecclesiastical limits. It is everywhere. And it must stop. Or I should say it must BE stopped. That will require some major changes in our attitude and response.

Let's be honest. What we've always done and how we've always handled this is not working out for us very well. We've got a mess on our hands and it is up to us to fix it, with God's help. All children and teenagers need to be protected. All of those who walk through our doors should be a priority. Whether it is the little girl in the Catholic school, or the little boy at the Charismatic youth camp, they both deserve protection from this insatiable monster. The Mennonite children need safeguards as well as the Mormon kids. From the Amish children to the Anglican teenagers, this issue is real and is ruining many little lives. It doesn't matter if you are Baptist or Buddhists, we have to agree on this one thing. Our children are worth protecting!

We must take ownership of this fiasco and turn it around if we are to maintain any level of credibility in the world. We can argue theology and doctrine until the cows come home, but one thing is undeniable – the victims of sexual abuse deserve to be heard and vindicated. We must protect our lambs; not the wolves.

This book was written to accomplish several goals. I pray that God will help them come to pass.

1. I am giving my personal account of the two times that I was targeted by sexual predators. I hope my story will embolden other victims to come forward and deal with their pain. I hope that by doing so every sex offender who has gone undetected will be found and dealt the measure of justice they deserve.

2. I chose to go into great detail in order to create a connection with victims. Many feel their circumstances are unbelievable or unique. Sex offenders have a very specific mode of operation, and if you are a victim, chances are you are not their first. Others share your pain, your shame and your desire for healing. Someone may read this book and not even realize that they are being groomed for sexual abuse. Many predators work for years to prep their next target. It happens every day. Hopefully, my story will expose the devious techniques that are used by predators everywhere.

3. I chose to name names because these people have been granted anonymity long enough. It is time to shine the light on them and their evil deeds. May God have mercy on their wretched souls! "Now I beseech you, brethren, <u>mark them</u> which cause divisions and offences contrary to the doctrine which ye have learned; <u>and avoid</u>

<u>them</u>. For they that are such serve not our Lord Jesus Christ, but their own belly; and by good words and fair speeches deceive the hearts of the simple." (Romans 16:17, 18)

    4. The purpose of Section Two is to help us rethink the way we have always looked at this subject. Too often we have turned our heads away and swept it under the rug because we are disgusted by it all. We cannot continue to do that. We must have a strategy, a plan, and a prescribed course of action that we defer to when this tragedy takes place in our ministry. I believe we can turn the tide with proper preventive measures, solid accountability protocols, a bold, righteous indignation toward the perpetrators of these crimes and a harsh, swift response.

~ SECTION ONE ~
My Story

✳ ✳ ✳

PART ONE
The First Time

* * *

1

Molested

"O my God, I trust in thee: let me not be ashamed, let not mine enemies triumph over me."
Psalms 25:2

* * *

I thought I was dreaming. It's normal for teenage boys to dream of intimate moments, even if they've never experienced them.

I awoke to discover that I was *not* dreaming. It was real. It was not my imagination. In that brief moment as my sleepy mind began to focus, it started to dawn on me what was happening.

My eyes opened and slowly adjusted to the dark. Then I saw him. He didn't know that I was awake. I couldn't move. As the realization slowly seeped through my mind, my heart was filled with terror. I was so scared I froze. What was he doing? Why was he doing this? Why did he do this to me? What made him even think of doing this? How long had he been doing this?

I remembered what I thought was a dream. Dream experts say that a dream can last from five minutes to up to as long as fifty minutes. How long had I dreamed? How much of the dream was real? How long had this been going on? How much of it really was a dream?

I squirmed and rolled over. It had only been a few seconds since I woke up, but it seemed like an eternity as the magnitude of what had just happened sank in. The man backed away and laid down beside me very still. He still had no idea that I was awake. My heart was pounding. My blood felt like ice water in my veins.

Our family had met John Batchelor when we were serving in Hawaii as missionaries during the late 1980s. His parents were well known on the island of Oahu. His dad was the pastor of a Baptist church and we had been to their church and in their home on several occasions. I don't remember much about John. He was several years older and I can't recall having had much interaction with him during any of our visits. We lived on the western end of the island between Makakilo and Nanakuli. We were pretty busy trying to start a church so opportunities to fellowship and interact with other pastors and ministries were few and far between.

One day in September of 1990, John, who was now twenty-one years old and studying at Bob Jones University in Greenville, South Carolina, called and told us he was in the area and wanted to come by for a visit. At the time, we were living in Buford, Georgia. Being the hospitable Southern folk that we were, we invited him to dinner. After finding out he was not in a rush to get back to campus, my parents invited him to spend the night. Our house there in Buford, Georgia only had three bedrooms. My parents and my sister each had a room, and my brother and I shared a room.

That night, for some reason, instead of putting John on the couch downstairs, it was decided he would sleep with me in my full-sized bed.

The terror I was feeling began to turn into guilt. I must have done something wrong. I had to have done something wrong. There is no way a man would do that to me unless I had done or said something to make him feel he had my permission. I must have in some way given him the impression that it was ok for him to do this. I suddenly felt very dirty and very guilty. I laid on my side for probably a full minute or two before I could even think of what to do next.

My first thought was that nobody would ever believe what had just happened to me. I had never even heard of anything like this happening to anyone before. I had never in my life imagined anything like this happening to me. I had just experienced it; I had just witnessed it and even I couldn't believe it had happened. But it had. This had actually happened.

I slowly got up and left the room. I walked down the hall to the bathroom and went in and locked the door. I felt dirty. I had never felt so filthy. I experienced emotions and feelings that I had never felt before.

Nothing had prepared me for this. No one I had ever known had ever mentioned something like this happening to them. Nobody had ever taught me or prepared me for what to do in a situation like this. I had never felt so alone in all my life. I had never felt so vulnerable. I had never felt so violated. My brain was scrambling to answer the question, "Now what?"

I could not stay in the bathroom all night. I definitely could not go back to my room. He was there. He knew I was awake. And he knew I was spending a long time in the bathroom. Then the feelings of guilt turned into fear. I was scared out of my mind. It dawned on me that he was probably feeling like a caged lion. He was in my room and he was no doubt wondering what I was going to do. Was he violent? Did he have a temper? Would he come look for me and try something else? Would he try to threaten or hurt me?

I was seventeen years old, but I was 5' 7" and weighed about 120 pounds. I was no match for him physically. At this moment, I wouldn't have been a match for anybody. I was scared. I was an emotional and mental wreck. Fighting back was the last thing on my mind. I was as weak as a dishrag. I wanted to get as far away from him as I possibly could.

I opened the bathroom door and crept down the hall to my parents' bedroom door. It was directly across the hall from my bedroom door which was open. I tried their doorknob, and it was locked. I panicked. I needed to get in their room and tell them, but the thought of this man coming out of my room and confronting me in the dark hallway made my knees weak. I was being as quiet as possible, but he was still lying on the bed, and I was just a few feet away from him, trying to open my parents' locked bedroom door.

I went back into the bathroom and shut the door and locked it. I turned on the light and found a bobby pin in the drawer next to the sink. I had learned how to pick the locks on the bedroom door sometime back. It never occurred to me to turn on the hall light and start banging on their door and hollering and making noise. I had such tunnel vision about the possibility of him coming after me that I was literally scared out of my mind. I turned off the light, opened the bathroom door and walked back down the hall to my parents' bedroom door.

How I was able to unlock their door in the dark with that bobby pin, with me as scared as I was, is nothing short of a miracle. The door unlocked with a loud CLICK and made my heart stop. I quickly opened the door, slipped inside and shut the door behind me. I remember distinctly walking into my parents' dark bedroom. My mom stirred and sat up.

"Son, what is it?"

I remember verbatim what I said. I will never forget it.

"He messed with me."

I remember saying it. I remember my parents' reaction. I remember the instant feeling of relief that I was safe. I remember the immediate knowledge that this man cannot and will not ever do this to me again. I was aware in that moment that the crisis was over and that he would be held responsible for what he did. My parents were wide awake.

"What happened?" Her voice was filled with concern.

"You said he messed with you?" My dad's voice was tight.

"He bothered me while I was asleep." That was all I could say. My dad immediately got up and went out into the hallway and turned on the hall light. Then he walked into my bedroom and turned on the bedroom light.

"Get up and get your stuff and get out of here right this minute."

The tone in his voice was not a tone I'd heard my dad use very many times when talking to other people. My dad was a mild mannered and an easygoing man. But that night, his voice sounded like gravel. Within a matter of minutes, John had thrown his belongings together. I heard him scurry down the hall, down the stairs, out the front door and leave the house. He got into his car and pulled away. I breathed a sigh of relief. He was gone. I was safe.

I went downstairs where Dad was locking the front door. The conversation that took place is a bit hazy in my memory. I do remember Dad asking me what had happened. I was ashamed to tell him. To say that he had "bothered me" was bad enough. To actually describe what had been done to me was extremely embarrassing. I felt like an idiot.

Even though I cannot recall the exact conversation, I will never forget the emotions that I experienced that night. Every imaginable feeling on the spectrum coursed through my heart and soul that night.

I have a Type A personality -- at least I do now. I do not recall that alpha-male persona fully developing until I was about twenty-two years old. I'll get to that eventually. But that night, I was not an alpha-male. I had been victimized in my own house; in my own bed and had done nothing but run to Mama and Daddy. I felt like a baby, powerless and scared. I was embarrassed. I was confused. I had so many questions. Why had he felt that he could do that to me? How had I not picked up on his tendencies? Why was a man I barely knew allowed to share a full-sized bed with me? What were my parents thinking?

As Dad and I talked, I managed somehow to tell him what John had done to me. The look on his face went from concern to anger. He told me that we would call the sheriff first thing in the morning and report it. My dad did not realize the seriousness of the crime when he told John to leave. However, as it turned out, we knew where John was headed, so finding him didn't seem to be much of a concern. Dad and I talked a little bit more and he went back upstairs. I found my Bible and started reading. I had no desire to get back into the bed after that. I remember reading my Bible until the wee hours of the morning.

What God did in my heart that night was unbelievable! I somehow found myself reading in Ephesians chapter 6. Those familiar verses spoke to me in a powerful way that night. Over and over again I read and mediated on those verses. They came alive to me. God used that passage to begin immediate healing and a mental recalibration of what had just transpired in my life. I underlined the entire passage that night and circled several key words. I still have that Bible that God used to calm my heart.

Please allow me to share with you the verses that helped me then. God used His Word to move me past this tragic event and very soon after, I rarely even thought about it again.

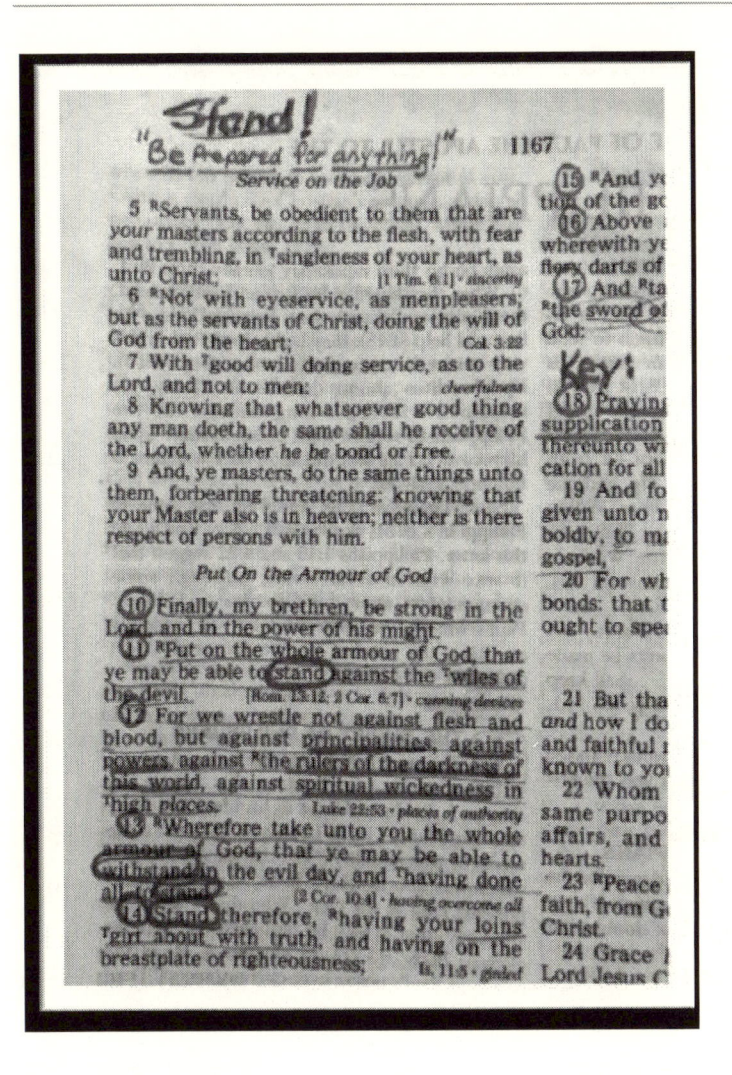

Ephesians 6:10-13

- *10 Finally, my brethren, be strong in the Lord, and in the power of his might.*
- *11 Put on the whole armour of God, that ye may be able to stand against the wiles of the devil.*

- *12 For we wrestle not against flesh and blood, but against principalities, against powers, against the rulers of the darkness of this world, against spiritual wickedness in high places.*
- *13 Wherefore take unto you the whole armour of God, that ye may be able to withstand in the evil day, and having done all, to stand.*

These verses reminded me that even though I was not strong enough to handle what life throws at me, I can be strong enough in the Lord and with His power. What a comfort! I also learned that I had a defense against the wiles, or tricks and traps of Satan.

It was verse 12 that did me the most good that night. I had enough discernment to recognize that my fight was not with a human being, or with people generally. My fight was with Satan. It was the devil that had marked me for destruction, not John Batchelor. John had a problem. I just happened to be a convenient, quick, easy way for him to feed his wicked lusts. However, it was Satan that had long-term plans for my destruction. It was Satan that I needed to be on the lookout for.

The passage went on to tell me how I could *"withstand in the evil day."* I was no Bible scholar, but I was pretty sure that being sexually assaulted in your sleep met the criteria of an "evil day." I realized that night I could withstand the fiery darts of the wicked. I had been hit, but I did not have to let it take me out. I did not have to let this event redefine who I was and create life-long issues and scars. God assured me that I was not the guilty one. I had done nothing to ask for, or encourage, this assault.

Little did I know that awful night in 1990 that God would take that painful experience and uniquely equip me to help other people who had experienced similar situations. God was preparing me for a life of ministry. It reminds me of SEAL training, where they drown-proof you. God knew that I could handle that sexual assault, so He permitted it to happen to me. He didn't cause it to happen. He didn't make it happen. He didn't order it to happen. But He allowed it to happen because He had a plan.

I prayed and read my Bible for a long time that night. When I finally went back to my bed, I was fine. I wasn't afraid. I wasn't angry. I did not blame God. At the time, I didn't realize the lasting impact this night would have on my life.

2

Justice

*"Touching the Almighty, we cannot find him out:
he is excellent in power, and in judgment,
and in plenty of justice: he will not afflict."*
Job 37:23

* * *

The next morning, my dad called the sheriff. They sent out a couple of officers to take my report. I remember how embarrassed I was describing in detail what happened to me the night before. They asked very specific questions, and I answered each one. For me as a seventeen-year-old boy, talking to complete strangers about this was mortifying. My dad sitting there made it even worse. We didn't talk about this kind of stuff in our house. Ever.

We grew up strict. We were homeschooled from the time I was in fifth grade. Before that, we had only attended Christian schools. We didn't have a television. We didn't go to the movies. We didn't tell dirty jokes. We didn't even tell shady, off-color jokes. We didn't cuss. We were not allowed to use slang words.

To say I was sheltered was an understatement. Modesty was ingrained in us from little kids. We didn't run around in the house in our underwear. We didn't come out of our room with our shirt off. We didn't go mixed-bathing. We were taught to be modest. We were taught to pursue holiness and godliness and that meant to abstain from nakedness and anything unbiblical.

Now here I was, sitting in the living room of our house and describing to these two complete strangers and my dad the explicit details of my sexual assault. To say I was squirming would be putting it mildly.

The discomfort of that interview will forever be etched in my mind. I was glad when it was over. One of the most unsettling aspects of the whole meeting was when I was asked if I would be willing to testify in court as to what happened. I didn't hesitate. Even as a kid, I knew that if those who know something say nothing, the bad guy wins. The statistics tell us that the average sexual offender gets away with it 117 times before being caught. That is a lot of people who did not step up and speak out! It is not easy, and it is embarrassing, but I knew I had no choice but to see this through. I agreed to testify if it was necessary.

As it turned out, I didn't have to testify. The Gwinnett County Sheriff's department put out a warrant for John's arrest. He was picked up on the Bob Jones University campus in South Carolina the next day and was extradited

to the jail in Gwinnett County. Once confronted with the accusations, he pled guilty. I didn't have to go to court. I didn't have to see him. I was so relieved -- and grateful.
God had moved mightily. I had no proof. I had no evidence. There was no way in the world to prove that he did to me what I said he did. If he had vehemently denied it, I do not know what would have happened. It would have just been my word against his. But God fought my battle for me.

    I can honestly say what happened to me that night, as bad as it was, did not affect me as badly as it would have had I not told anyone. Had I kept that secret, only God knows what it would have done to me. It would have eaten me from the inside out. I would have had to deal with guilt, fear, shame, worry and countless other negative emotions. No doubt it would have altered my personality, my attitude, my viewpoint about biblical sexual intimacy, and a thousand other things. It could have made me suicidal. It could have made me violent. Who knows? Because I immediately told my parents who confronted my abuser, the psychological scars and the emotional pain were significantly reduced. I was able to begin healing literally within the hour of the abuse.

    Waiting to tell only makes the pain worse. If you have been sexually abused, please – I beg you – go tell. If you are a young person, tell your parents immediately. If you are a wife and you were abused as a young woman, find someone who you trust like a pastor or counselor to tell. If you are a man and you've been the victim of a predator, you really should tell someone. The relief that floods your soul is priceless. Don't live with that shame anymore!

John Alfred Batchelor was sentenced to two years in prison for aggravated sodomy and had to register as a sex offender. He can be found today online if you do a search. His crime is now a matter of public record. I have not seen or heard from him since that night. To be honest with you, I have no desire to.

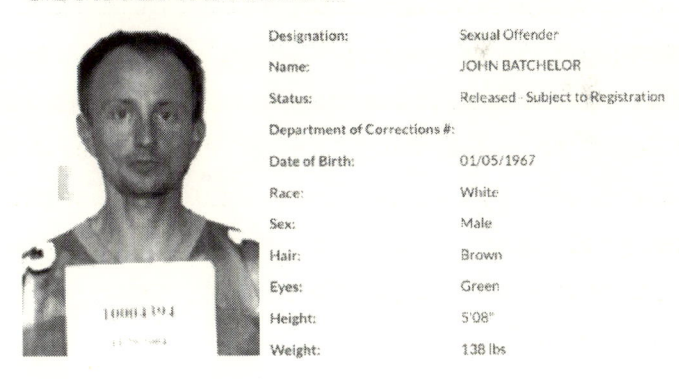

JOHN BATCHELOR

Designation:	Sexual Offender
Name:	JOHN BATCHELOR
Status:	Released - Subject to Registration
Department of Corrections #:	
Date of Birth:	01/05/1967
Race:	White
Sex:	Male
Hair:	Brown
Eyes:	Green
Height:	5'08"
Weight:	138 lbs

FDLE
FLORIDA DEPARTMENT OF LAW ENFORCEMENT

Aliases
John A Batchelor, John Batchelor

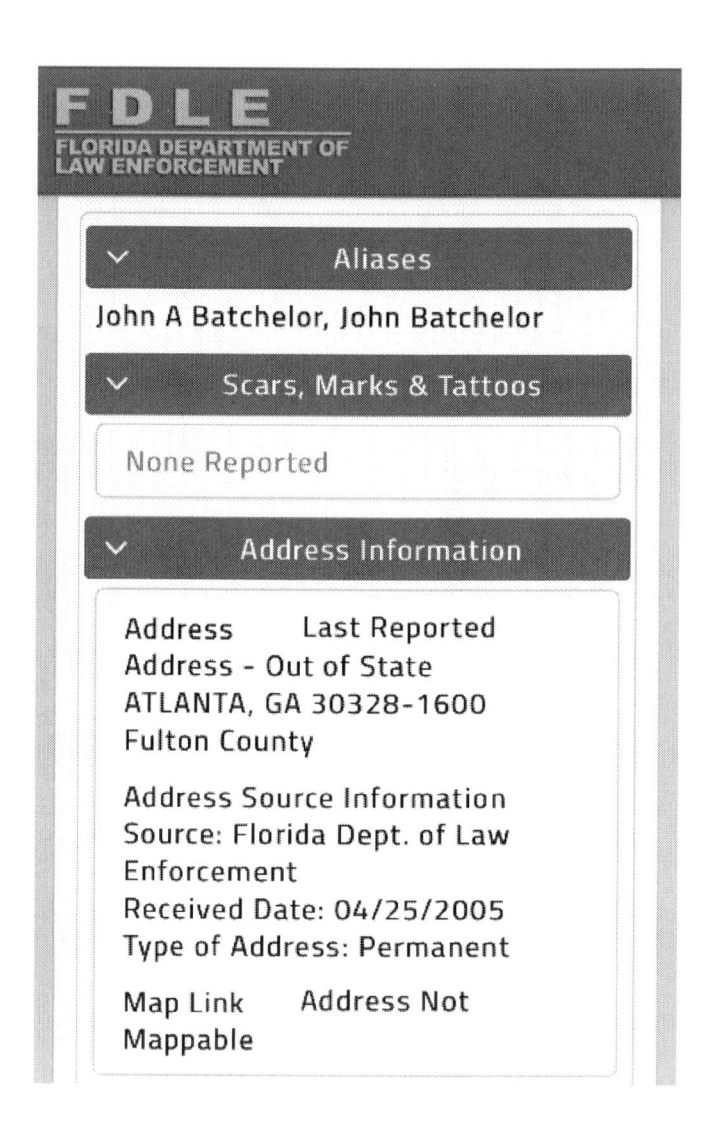

Scars, Marks & Tattoos
None Reported

Address Information

Address   Last Reported
Address - Out of State
ATLANTA, GA 30328-1600
Fulton County

Address Source Information
Source: Florida Dept. of Law Enforcement
Received Date: 04/25/2005
Type of Address: Permanent

Map Link   Address Not Mappable

Crime Information – Qualifying Offenses

Adjudication Date   09/14/1990

Crime Description   SEX OFFENSE, OTHER STATE (AGGRAVATED SODOMY)

Court Case Number   90-B-642-3

Jurisdiction & State   Gwinnett, GA

Adjudication   Guilty/convict

Victim Information

Gender   Male

Minor   Yes

We were shocked to later discover two very disturbing things. First of all, John apparently had been involved in some kind of incident the previous summer at a youth camp somewhere. The details were sketchy, but he had done something inappropriate and it had been told to someone at Bob Jones University. The second disturbing thing was being told that John had apparently been undergoing "counseling" at the school for his homosexual tendencies and past inappropriate conduct.

Looking back, I can't help but realize that had his past deeds been properly dealt with, I may not have been a victim. Had the camp directors notified the police? Had he abused or violated a child or teenager? If so, had their parents been notified? Did John's parents know about it? How was he still a student at BJU if this was true? If he had not been allowed to stay at the university, he would probably not have been in a position to come by our house. I don't know.

I've wondered many times what could have been done differently. I wonder if he had committed any previous crimes that were not reported. Was I the first person he had violated? I am almost certain that I was the first one that had involved law enforcement.

I will never know what he did prior to molesting me, but I can't help but think that several people could have done more to stop him before he ever showed up at my house that fall night in 1990. Maybe if someone had done more, he would have never had the opportunity to hurt me.

From all indications, his sexual crime against me was his last. As far as I can tell, he's not been arrested again.

I'd like to think that by my saying something, I possibly kept a number of other people just a little bit safer.

PART TWO
The Second Time

* * *

3

Job Offer

*"The wicked have laid a snare for me:
yet I erred not from thy precepts."*
Psalms 119:110

* * *

To this day I do not know why she told him. Twenty-five years later I am still perplexed. It was a year later and we had moved from Buford to Conyers, which is east of Atlanta. My parents had decided to enroll us in Philadelphia Christian School, a ministry of Philadelphia Baptist Church.

The pastor was Dr. James Kelley, whom we had known in the late '70s when he was the pastor of Bemiss Road Baptist Church in Valdosta, Georgia. My dad had pastored Victory Baptist Church, also in Valdosta, during that same time. I had attended first grade at Lowndes Christian Academy, a ministry of Bemiss Road Baptist Church.

For some unknown reason during the enrollment process, my mom felt the need to tell Dr. Kelley about my recent molestation in Buford. Saying something to the school administrator would have made more sense, though still unnecessary. But she met with the pastor of the church and told him that I had been molested the year before. I found that out later from him. She never told me that she'd said anything to Dr. Kelley.

Up to this point, the incident back in Buford had stayed in our family. There was no need to tell anybody since John Batchelor had confessed and was serving his two-year prison sentence. I had pretty much put it behind me and moved on. I was grateful that it didn't have to become public news. I was grateful that people who knew me would not think about that every time they saw me. Some things you'd rather people just not know. Being sodomized in your sleep by another man is definitely one of them.

If my mom had known what would come of that meeting, I'm sure she never would have told James Kelley what happened to me. I do not know what she thought it would accomplish telling him about it. I do not blame her for what happened, but it turned out to be a key contributor, which is the only reason I am mentioning it.

One thing is sure. He was the wrong man to tell. From that day forward, I was marked. The clock started ticking and I was on his radar. It would be just a matter of time before that bit of information would germinate in his mind and start a series of events that even to this day I find absolutely nauseating.

We transferred from Philadelphia Christian School halfway through my junior year of high school to Trinity Baptist School, a small A.C.E. school on the other side of town. My younger brother was having difficulty adjusting to the Abeka curriculum that was used at Philadelphia. We had been homeschooled for years using the A.C.E. curriculum. This new school had a more familiar classroom arrangement than the traditional setup. In order for him to transfer to Trinity Baptist School, I had to transfer as well. I was the one that drove us both to school and so I didn't have much say in the matter. Though I really enjoyed the atmosphere and had made many new friends at Philadelphia, I did not complain. After being homeschooled for the past five years, I enjoyed being in a school with thirty students! I do not recall having any interaction at all with James Kelley during my time at Philadelphia.

I graduated from Trinity in 1992 and then enrolled at Pensacola Christian College. In July of 1993, I surrendered to preach and did not feel impressed of the Lord to return to PCC where I had been studying business administration and computer science. I began working with a local construction company and continued seeking God's direction for my life.

It was in the spring of 1994 when I got the phone call from Dr. James Kelley.

He had taken a small church north of Atlanta in Forsyth County. Fellowship Baptist Church in Cumming, Georgia was a relatively new ministry made up of a group of people that had come from several different churches.

They had somehow managed to lure Dr. Kelley away from a church running hundreds of people with a large Christian school. Even then I wondered how they had been able to accomplish that.

James Kelley had pastored for thirty years and had climbed to the top of the ladder, so to speak. He was on the Executive Advisory Board for Macedonia World Baptist Missions in Lawrenceville, Georgia. For him to leave that large church in Conyers and take a brand-new church up in the country with fewer than a hundred people was odd, even to me as a young preacher. Things that I found out later about what he had done at Philadelphia in Conyers might have had something to do with it.

Not long after he got there, he called me and offered me a part-time position as a youth pastor and music director. I was blown away. I had not been to Bible college. Granted, I had grown up in the home of a pastor and a missionary. I had a solid foundation, thanks to my upbringing, but I had not been preaching for even a full year. To be offered a staff position at the age of twenty-two, unmarried and with no formal Bible training was unheard of. I talked with my pastor, and after much prayer, we both agreed I should move up to Cumming and take the position.

The arrangement was fantastic. I would live in the furnished basement of an elderly couple in the church. Earl and Lucille Gilstrap were precious people. Earl was either a deacon or a trustee; I can't remember. They were leaders in the church that I began to trust and look up to. Earl had run a grocery store in town for years and was retired. He knew more about the grocery industry than anybody I had ever met. I loved to hear him talk about it. He was also very involved with the Gideon's International Bible ministry. Lucille was a social butterfly and was always going out for brunch with her friends and to different functions. Their house and yard were immaculate. They had a fervent passion for the Lord and for people. I liked them and I liked living there.

    I ate supper with them nearly every night. Lucille did my laundry. I worked for the church Thursday through Sunday. Saturday was my day off. I worked Monday through Wednesday as a carpenter on a framing crew for Joe Bridges, a builder who attended the church.

    Looking back, I had it made! I was making $7 an hour working for Joe those three days a week. Put that with the $400 a week the church was paying me, and I was doing pretty good. I was making almost $600 a week in 1994! The Gilstraps asked for a ridiculously low amount for room and board. Lucille's cooking was incredible. I ate like a king! With Lucille doing the cleaning, the cooking and my laundry, I was living the life.

    I drove the 160 miles to Dearing, Georgia every other Saturday or so to see my girlfriend, Grace Young. I would then stop by and see my folks on the way back to Cumming.

Life was good. I started thinking about getting married. I even started looking for a small house to purchase.

But James Kelley had other plans.

4

Grooming

"When my spirit was overwhelmed within me, then thou knewest my path. In the way wherein I walked have they privily laid a snare for me."
Psalms 142:3

* * *

Not long after I got there, I started noticing things -- small things you just couldn't quite put your finger on. But it was there.

Growing up sheltered and protected, I was admittedly naïve. Not stupid, but naïve. I trusted people, especially the pastor - God's man. I had grown up in the ministry and even though we had seen pastors do unethical things and things we didn't agree with, it was ingrained in me to trust and follow the pastor.

So when James Kelley did something unusual or out of character to me, I just wrote it off as I'd been sheltered and was not up to speed on what was socially acceptable. I had definitely not had the opportunity to be around a lot of older preachers. I had not spent a lot of time with many adults outside of my small circle of church family. James Kelley would often talk about things so casually and easily that I thought it was just me, and that me being a "prude" was the problem.

Looking back now, I know that what he was doing was "grooming" me for himself. I didn't recognize it then, but over time he began to cause me to become desensitized to the topics he would bring up. It got to where it didn't startle me or disturb me like it did at first. When it first started, I was shocked that a white-haired man in his fifties with grandchildren would discuss things of a sexual nature with his young assistant pastor, a single man no less. It seemed so off-base, that at first, I'm sure I locked up and acted weird. He never seemed to notice. He would talk about people he'd counseled. He would go into details about their love life (or lack of it). He talked about things he had done before he got saved. He even shared intimate details about his own wife and their marriage. He made it sound like he was "training" me for the pastorate, and he made it sound logical to a degree. I realized that I had a lot to learn, and just took it in stride as "part of the ministry."

It was extremely awkward for me at first, and I was very uncomfortable. I would attempt to change the subject or act disinterested. But I was always afraid to cross the line of rebuking or correcting my pastor. I just assumed he was right, I was wrong and I needed to chill. So, over time, I became more and more accustomed to his improprieties. Even though I never enjoyed it, it got to the place where I just figured that was how he rolled and I went along with it.

He was just getting started.

Over the next few months, his "grooming" became more and more intense. I'll never forget the day we were driving someplace and he asked me my shoe size. I told him. He asked me if I happened to know my shirt size, and I told him. He asked me if I knew my pants size, and I told him. He asked me what size hat I wore and I told him. Then he looked straight at me and asked me the size of my privates. I blinked and looked away.

"You know the size of everything else. Why don't you know the size of your ---- ?"

I remember being extremely uncomfortable. "What difference does it make?"

He asked me again. "What size is it?"

I was in shock. He was serious! "I don't know! Who cares?"

Then he got serious and started "teaching me" about how wrong it was to know so little about your own body. Then he lectured me on how wrong I was to be ashamed to talk about it. Man, was I squirming! He went on and on about how that for some reason, talking about one's body and the natural course of things was considered taboo, and how that God never intended for one's physical attributes and normal desires to be "off limits." He made it all sound so convincing. Sort of.

I was shell-shocked. My pastor – my boss – the man of God was asking me to describe my private parts to him? Was this normal? Just how sheltered had I been anyway? He dropped the subject and that was the end of that. For the time being.

Another time, we were in the car and he pulled over into a parking lot. He reached into his Bible and pulled out a handwritten letter and a photograph. He handed me the letter and told me to read it. The letter was written by an anonymous person. In the letter were accusations of serious improprieties against me. The letter was written to Pastor Kelley to warn him that I was not who he thought I was. The letter went on to describe all kinds of immoral conduct that the writer was aware of "firsthand". The letter described me as some kind of pervert and sex fiend and warned Pastor Kelley that I had no place in the ministry. The letter closed by saying they had enclosed "proof" that I was the kind of person that they had described in the letter.

I remember looking up from the letter with a feeling of disgust and great anxiety. Who had written this? What did they think I had done? My brain was racing to try and figure out who would do this to me. The letter was obviously a pack of lies, but how could I prove it? I looked at my pastor and just stared. Finally, I spoke.

"I have no idea what this is, but none of this is true."

He looked at me for a long time before finally saying, "Well, they have the proof right here."

He pulled the photo out of the envelope, but hid it from me.

"Proof? There's no way they have any proof because there is not a shred of truth to anything in this letter!"

"They have the proof, and it is very bad."

Again I spoke, this time getting angry.

"There's no way they can have any proof because I've never done those things! Here, let me see it."

"Are you sure you want to see this? It is very convincing."

"Give it here."

I took the picture out of his hand and looked at it. I took one glance at it and quickly handed it back to him. I exhaled for a long time and then snorted. It was a snapshot of a nude man but his head was not in the picture. He was standing in someone's living room facing the camera. I had no idea who it was or where it was taken, but if this was the "proof" of the anonymous letter writer, it was without a doubt the worst "proof" anybody ever had. Relief flooded my soul.

"That's not me. Trust me. That's not me. I have no idea who that is or where that was taken, but trust me; that is not me, and I have never been in that house before."

He stared at the picture for a while before speaking.

"How do I know that is not you?"

I looked at him in disbelief.

"Because I'm telling you that is not me."

"Prove it."

There it was. This was what this whole thing was about.

"Prove it? What do you mean prove it? How am I supposed to prove that is not me in the picture?"

"There's only one way you can prove it is not you. It won't take you but ten seconds to prove this is not you in this picture."

I stared at him in shock. Was he for real? Oh yes. He was for real. I laughed nervously and shook my head.

"Well, you can forget it. I don't have to prove anything. Just take my word for it; that is not me. I don't know who sent you this letter, or who that is in the picture, but it is not me."

He seemed genuinely disappointed. In retrospect, that was a pretty clever scam. I'm convinced now that he wrote the letter and I don't even want to know where or how he got that picture. But it was a pretty convincing act and a very well-orchestrated plan. Obviously, it didn't work. But he was wearing me down. I think back now to the entire conversation and how many ways he tried to "trigger" me or "break" me just during that one incident.

Waving that pornographic picture around in my face was one way for him to test my reaction. I was repulsed to say the least, but he was grooming me. And the whole time it was hidden under the guise of something that on the surface seemed very legitimate and necessary.

Most young men in my position would have probably felt they had no other choice but to clear their name. And like he said, it wouldn't have taken but a few seconds. He had done his best to blackmail me into exposing myself to him in his car that day. It never crossed my mind to do it, but how many other young people would have felt they had no other option?

It didn't occur to me until years later that the whole way that went down should have told me everything I needed to know about him. In a real life situation, an anonymous letter of this nature would have required immediate and serious attention, but not like this. If the letter had been real, why didn't he confront me in his office, with a witness if he had any suspicion that his youth pastor was some kind of sexual deviant? Why approach me alone, in a car? What was his plan if I had confessed to the accusations? He wouldn't have even had any witnesses. Would he have attempted blackmail? This was wrong on so many levels that I don't even know where to start to point out the ridiculousness of it all.

For weeks after that he hounded me to prove that the headless model in the snapshot was not me. I would always just tell him to forget it. At one point I told him that if he thought that letter was true, he should just fire me. He didn't want to do that.

I spent days trying to figure out who had sent him that letter. Why would someone do that to me? Who could hate me so bad that they would make up such terrible lies about me? I racked my brain for the longest time trying to figure it out. I was so naïve that it never occurred to me that the entire thing was fabricated.

I won't elaborate on all the times and ways that man tried to break me. He was relentless. Once on my day off I had managed to pick up a few hours of extra work at a cabinet shop. The owner went to our church and knew I was handy with wood and tools. He needed some extra help, and it was a Saturday that I did not have plans to go see Grace, so I agreed.

I remember that day while I was working, James Kelley showed up unannounced and unexpected. That in and of itself was not all that odd. It was just a random visit, but again, I guess there was nothing abnormal about that. What struck me as very strange was what he was wearing. He had on a western-type shirt, brand-new blue jeans and a nice pair of cowboy boots.

Now I had been working with him for months. We had spent hundreds of hours together, and I had NEVER seen him in a pair of blue jeans, much less a pair of cowboy boots. I was the one who wore cowboy boots. I've worn boots as far back as I can remember. I love horses, I love anything western, and I had numerous pairs of cowboy boots. I had casual boots, as well as nice dress boots that I wore to church. But he had never worn a pair of boots as long as I had known him.

Seeing him in that getup was such a jolt that I actually said something to him about it. I will never forget his question. It was downright nerve-wracking!

"Do you like them?" He put his hands in the pockets of his jeans and posed. I looked up at him like he had lost his mind.

"I didn't even know you owned a pair of boots. Why don't you ever wear them?" I stammered to cover up the awkwardness of the moment. What was he doing here?

"I've had them for years. I wear them on special occasions."

"Special occasions?" What was I missing? Was he going somewhere? Was the church having a rodeo?

"Yes. I came by here to check on you." That was the special occasion? It was my day off. I was standing ankle-deep in sawdust, running ¾ inch plywood through a table-saw. There was nothing special about that. What was he up to? He stood around a while and watched us work and then said goodbye and left. It was just another one of many "red flag" instances.

Again, it was so subtle and so slick that even though it was inappropriate, somehow I always felt like it was my fault. I was too sheltered. I was reading too much into it. I was guilty of thinking he was doing something wrong, when there was *no way* he could be doing something wrong. He was the pastor. He was God's man. He had thirty years in the ministry. It was so out of character for a man of his stature and position that I refused to believe it was him that was wrong.

I chided myself for being so critical of him. I caught myself feeling sorry for him. Here was a man who had extended an amazing opportunity to me -- an untrained, untested, single guy -- and my thanks to him was to think he was some kind of weirdo?

I did my best to do as the Apostle Paul wrote in Ephesians 4:1, "I therefore, the prisoner of the Lord, beseech you that ye walk worthy of the vocation wherewith ye are called..." I so desperately wanted to walk worthy of this new vocation. I kept telling myself that I just needed to grow up; loosen up; stop being so uptight about everything and get with the program. I did not want to fail in this new endeavor as a staff member. I had so much to learn. I was just grateful for the opportunity to be mentored by such an experienced and well-seasoned man of God.

I worked hard to please Dr. Kelley. In the six months I served at that church, not once did he ever come to me with a complaint, a rebuke or a suggestion of anything that I could do better or do different.

I organized the youth activities. I had never done anything like that before. In fact, I had never even had a youth pastor at any church I had ever attended. I don't think I had ever even met a youth pastor. I had no clue what that position involved. I just dove in and figured it out.

I taught the teen Sunday school class. I had never done that before, either. I led the singing, scheduled the special music and led the choir. I was so far out of my comfort zone it wasn't even funny, but I stepped up to the plate and gave it my best shot. As a twenty-two year old young man, I conducted myself in a way that earned me the respect of the entire church. I sat on the front row during the services and did my best to say "Amen" during the preaching.

I was more accustomed to a fire-and-brimstone type of preaching. His style was far more subdued. Looking back, I have to admit that the content was good. He was considered by many to be a good preacher, so I supported him as much as I knew how. I had only been preaching for a year and he'd been doing it most of his life. Who was I to say he was doing it wrong? As a matter of fact, he had an honorary doctorate from Tabernacle Baptist Church in Greenville, South Carolina. I had attended both the church and the day school at Tabernacle back during the early '80s. If Dr. Harold B. Sightler, the man who baptized me as a young boy, thought James Kelley was good enough at what he did to honor him with a doctorate, who was I to judge?

I noticed he never preached much on the subject of sin. When he did, he didn't name it. It would be generalizations rather than specifics. As the youth pastor, I would go to him about things that I felt he should preach on in order to help the teens. His response was that it was my place to teach and train the teens; not his. I told him that I was not comfortable dealing with some issues, but that if he would preach on it, I would take it and run with it in Sunday School class and discuss it further. He never did. I was pretty much on my own in the sin-preaching department. It was not easy trying to be a mentor to teenagers when I was barely in my twenties. Looking back, it made no sense.

The truth is, he didn't ask me to come up there to be the youth pastor. He didn't ask me to come serve because he needed a song leader. In fact, he already had a good one when I got there. Brother Wheeler did a fine job prior to my coming. When I arrived, he had to step down. I know that must have been hard on him, being a much older man, but he never complained. He moved from the choir director lectern to the tenor section of the choir and yielded to my inexperienced leadership. What character that man must have had! He never interfered or did anything to make me look bad, though I am sure he could have.

We went soulwinning every Thursday and Friday for hours. For those who may not be familiar with that term, it comes from Proverbs 11:30, "The fruit of the righteous is a tree of life; and he that winneth souls is wise." We take this verse to mean that it is wise if we can be used of God to help "win" a person's soul to Christ.

However, James Kelley didn't ask me to move to Fellowship Baptist Church to win souls to Christ. He didn't invite me to serve the church or because I had a specific skill set that I could contribute. He got me there for himself. I just didn't know it at the time.

The Christmas of 1994 was one to remember. I will never forget how bad I felt. I believe I gave my pastor and his wife one of my paintings. I'm not positive, but I do know I gave them something for Christmas. I'm sure it was nice, but not anything extravagant. On the other hand, what I got from my pastor was over-the-top ridiculous.

To be honest with you, I don't even remember what all he gave me. It was crazy. I'm not talking about a nice gift or two. I'm talking about a ton of presents. It was so crazy that I remember my girlfriend was astounded when I told her what all he gave me. I was beyond embarrassed. I was mortified. And very confused. Was this normal? Each gift was wrapped in the nicest paper. Every gift was extravagant and very personal. I had no idea how to respond.

There was no telling how much money he spent on me that Christmas. He had several grown children and a few grandchildren! I remember wondering what *they* got for Christmas. I felt like a fool for not doing more for him, and said so. He assured me that it was fine, and that he just wanted me to know how much I meant to him.

5

The Proposition

"The wicked have drawn out the sword, and have bent their bow, to cast down the poor and needy, and to slay such as be of upright conversation."
Psalms 37:14

* * *

The culmination of his well-laid plans occurred one night in a hotel room after the first of the year. Let me set the stage for how we ended up in a hotel room in Cumming. The circumstances were so bizarre that even now I can't believe I didn't see it coming. I was such an idiot!

He approached me one day about a prayer and fasting retreat. He asked if I thought it would be good to get away for a couple of days and spend some time praying, fasting and planning church events. I was new to this staff member thing, but it sounded like a good idea. He recommended a cabin up in the mountains. Who in their right mind was going to turn that down?

At first, it was going to be him, his wife, me and maybe another person or two, even though I was the only staff member. So we made plans and set a date.

When the day of the staff retreat came, he informed me that his wife wouldn't be able to go. She was sick or something. He told me that the others weren't going to make it either, so it looked like it was going to be just the two of us. I was fine with it. We were going to be praying and fasting, so I didn't care who all went.

When it came time for him to pick me up for the retreat, he called me. He told me some story about how the retreat accommodations had fallen through and that we wouldn't be able to go to the place he had booked. I asked him what we were going to do. He said that it didn't make sense to drive for a couple of hours to a place in the mountains when we could just get a nice hotel room in town and fast and pray and plan there. Made sense to me. So I asked him where he wanted me to meet, and I drove to the hotel.

We arrived at the same time and checked in. I remember feeling weird standing next to another man in a hotel lobby and checking into a hotel room, knowing we lived fifteen minutes away. I was so stupid!

We checked in and unpacked. He sat down on his bed and started reading his Bible. I piled my pillows up against the headboard and got comfortable and started reading my Bible too. We talked a little bit, but not a lot. We were just reading and marking stuff in our Bibles and would occasionally jot down a note or two.

So far, the staff retreat was off to a great start! The pastor and I were reading our Bibles together. It doesn't get much better than that. And to think I was getting paid to do this! The ministry is rough and difficult at times, but it's not all bad. Sitting there on that nice hotel bed, kicked back, reading my Bible and enjoying a much needed retreat was pretty cool. The ministry definitely was the way to go!

He eventually mumbled something about needing a shower and headed toward the bathroom. After his shower he came out in his bathrobe and sat down on his bed and went back to reading his Bible. It felt a bit awkward, but I squelched any ideas of impropriety. I had never stayed in a hotel room with another man before, so maybe this was normal.

After a while, he started talking about needing to share a very important prayer request with me. Apparently, he had some health issues that he wanted me to help him pray about. I'll spare you the details, but I'll tell you this; he was setting his trap. He went into this spiel about some very personal health problem. He had been to a lot of doctors and none of them could help him. It was difficult to follow him.

He went into a very detailed description of the medicine he was taking and how it wasn't working properly. He explained how his body was rejecting it and how it was affecting him in other ways. He rambled on and on and on.

It was all I could do to act interested. He was losing me. Let's just pray about it and get on with our Bible reading already!

He wrapped up his long and boring health history with a very plain and specific request. He asked me if I would let him perform a sexual act on me. It startled me back to reality.

I was floored, completely caught off guard. So that is what this whole "prayer request" monologue was about? I was dumbfounded. Our staff retreat, that had started out so great, had just tanked. Fast.

I will never forget the next two minutes if I live to be a thousand years old. I just stared at him in disbelief. Did he just ask me to do what I thought he did? There is no way I heard him right. This could not be happening. My mind must have wandered off. I had to be daydreaming. But no. Who daydreams about what he just said? I sure don't! I looked over at him with a blank, stupid look.

"So will you do it?"

He turned from leaning against the headboard of the bed and faced me. I looked at him disbelievingly. I felt like I was in a time warp.

"You've got to be kidding me!? There is no way I'm doing that!" I was flabbergasted.

His response took the cake. It will go down in my opinion as one of the most unbelievable statements to ever be spoken. He looked at me, almost pitifully, and said, "Well, I was hoping you would at least pray about it."

I was numb. And speechless. My pastor had just asked me if he could perform a homosexual act on me, and when I said no, he wanted me to pray about it?

My entire world exploded in that moment. My life, my ministry, my job, my reputation, my name, my call to preach – everything became one huge question mark. What would my parents think? What would the church think? What would my girlfriend think? I had not the foggiest idea what they would think because I didn't even know what to think. My mind was racing to absorb the insanity of the moment. How in heaven's name did I get here?

In that moment, everything began to make sense. The isolated comments, the random innuendos, the disjointed remarks and months of red flags all came together to form a very clear picture. My pastor, the highly respected, white-haired Dr. James Kelley, was a homosexual. And not *just* a homosexual, but a homosexual predator who had no problem wielding his power over the people under him to get what he wanted. He was a con-artist. And a very experienced and calculated one at that. He was a patient, methodical and diabolical man.

It all became crystal clear to me that my being in that hotel room was no accident. In fact, my being in Cumming was no accident. The last six months of my life had been one long con game and I was the mark. This had been his plan from day one.

It suddenly dawned on me just when "day one" was. I recalled him randomly telling me of the time that my mom had come into his office at Philadelphia Baptist Church prior to my junior year of high school. I remembered him casually mentioning to me that he knew I had been sexually assaulted as a teenager. I remembered asking how he happened to know that, and he offhandedly mentioned that my mom had met with him during the enrollment process and told him about it. I had been surprised that he knew, and confused as to why he had needed to know that. I remember at the time wondering why he would even bring something like that up.

Now it all made sense. He must have thought I was vulnerable. Because of that terrible event in my past, he must have thought I would be an easy target. He may have even had a suspicion that there was more to my sexual assault story than I had led people to believe. Maybe in his dark and wicked heart he hoped that I had initiated it, or gone along with it, or enjoyed it. He must have thought that as an older and more mature young man I might now be willing to experiment or explore. What he had asked to do to me was the same thing that John Batchelor had done to me in my sleep.

I don't know what he was thinking. Whatever it was, he had me pegged wrong. Either way, he apparently forgot the part where my dad called the sheriff and had the pervert locked up.

James Kelley stood up and walked toward his clothes hanging on the rack. He looked old and tired in his bathrobe. His shoulders were slumped over dejectedly. His plan had failed. His years of scheming and months of grooming had been for naught.

I had said, "No."

That is the last thing a sexual predator wants to hear.

"No."

Two letters. One small word. But a huge word to a pervert.

"No" is their worst nightmare. "No" means they failed. "No" means they picked the wrong mark. "No" means they now have to start all over with someone else. "No" means all their plans, their fantasies, their efforts were in vain.

And I had said, "No."

He got dressed and mumbled something about how he was just going to go home. He told me that since the room was already paid for, I might as well stay the night. He packed and left me there. I just sat there on the bed in shock, alone, and scared out of my mind.

I grappled with how this was going to play out. I couldn't go back to the Gilstraps' house because they knew I was supposed to be at a staff retreat. If I just showed back up, there would be a lot of explaining to do, and I had zero answers. I couldn't believe what had just happened. How would anybody else believe it? I didn't even want anybody to know about it.

I decided to stay at the hotel. I remember turning the TV on just for company, but I wasn't at all interested in what was on the television.

I spent an agonizing night trying to figure out what to do. If I called my dad, I knew what he would say. He would insist that I come back home. Not that I was opposed to that idea, but there was no way that I was just going to skip town. I could not walk away with this disaster unresolved. I knew if I ran from this, there would be a cloud over me forever. How could I stand and tell my home church and my pastor that it was God's will for me to move up to Cumming, to just come running back home six months later with my tail tucked between my legs without a reason?

I know that God had given me direction to go to Fellowship. My pastor and I had both been in full agreement on that point. God had put me here. But why? For what? For this?

For the time being, my best move was to clear my head and get some direction from God about how to proceed. I prayed fervently that night; more fervently than I had ever prayed in my life. I confessed my utter ignorance to God and begged His forgiveness for ignoring the months of red flags. I begged him to forgive me for anything I may have said or done that would make this man think I would go along with something this wicked. I begged for wisdom, direction, boldness, courage, for my name to be cleared and my ministry not to be ruined before it even got started.

I went back home to the Gilstrap's the next day. I tried to act like we had to cut the retreat short for some reason or another. I don't remember what all I said, but later Lucy would remember thinking when I came back early that something was wrong, but she never said anything. I went back to my normal routine, which was anything but routine after that night.

To say that things were weird at church the next service would be an understatement. I couldn't believe I was still there. I couldn't believe he was still there. He couldn't believe I was still there. It became a Baptist version of a Mexican standoff. Neither one of us knew what to do. We couldn't decide what we were going to do until the other one made a move. I had no direction from the Lord on what to do, so I did nothing. And because I did nothing, he did nothing. I could not involve the law because as far as I knew at the time, he had done nothing illegal. Even if I had called the sheriff, I had no proof.

This situation would have to be handled in-house. I was sure of that. But how to go about it was something far less certain.

I became withdrawn and conflicted. My whole world had been shattered. And I couldn't tell a soul. I started questioning everything I had ever been taught. I questioned the Bible. I questioned God. I questioned my upbringing. I questioned the ministry. I grappled with basic ministry philosophies. I questioned literally every single aspect of everything I had ever been told or taught.

If this was what the ministry consisted of, what had I gotten myself into? If this man could rise to the top of the ministry totem pole being a sexual predator and a pervert, what was I doing even thinking about being in the ministry?

This was no place for me. I didn't belong here. This is not what I signed up for. Not at all.

Grace noticed the change in me. She knew something was wrong, but didn't know what it was. There was no way I could tell her what had happened. So I bore my cross alone, waiting for wisdom and clarity.

I stayed the course for a few weeks. I was on auto-pilot. Life was a blur. I do not remember anything about that span of time. I was a carpenter Monday through Wednesday. I was a staff member the rest of the time.

My time with James Kelley was almost like an out-of-body experience. I did not want to be there. I went soulwinning with him. I went to church with him. I went out to eat with him. I went to visit people in the hospital with him. I listened to him preach.

I led the singing. I worked with the choir. I taught my Sunday school class. But I was a hollow and lifeless machine. I had been taught to be faithful. I had been taught to do what was expected of me because that is what God wanted me to do. I had been trained that a servant of God doesn't just work when they feel like it; they work whether they feel like it or not. God said in Ephesians 6:6, 7, "Not with eyeservice, as menpleasers; but as the servants of Christ, doing the will of God from the heart; With good will doing service, as to the Lord, and not to men:"

For the last six months I had worked to please my pastor. Now, I just wanted to please the Lord. Sometimes that means doing what we are supposed to do even when we do not feel like it. That means doing what is expected of us under difficult and adverse circumstances. So I plodded on.

    I somehow managed to keep the nightmare I was living a secret. I kept praying for wisdom and waiting for a green light from God on how to proceed. There was no question in my mind that I would make my move. I just knew that I did not want to do it in my own flesh and power. I needed God to tell me what to do.

6

Green Light

"Lead me, O LORD, in thy righteousness because of mine enemies; make thy way straight before my face."
Psalms 5:8

* * *

It was about a month after the hotel room proposition when the answer I had been praying for finally came.

It came to me while I was driving back to Cumming on a Saturday after visiting Grace. I was headed west on I-20 in Atlanta listening to a preaching tape. The preacher was talking about sin in the ministry. He told that many times it gets covered up, but that God will always pull the cover off.

During the message, the preacher gave an illustration of a pastor in Texas who had been caught engaging in illicit activity with his male staff members. As he told that story, he made the statement that after the scandal broke, that pastor's wife confessed that her husband had not touched her in years. Their marriage was a sham, and nobody suspected a thing.

It was during that message that I realized what had happened to me, had also happened to others. I was not the first. This was not an isolated incident. As unbelievable as it had seemed to me, there was someone, somewhere who would believe me because this had happened before.

As I drove through Atlanta and headed north up GA 400, God flooded my soul with peace and the promise that He would vindicate me through this nightmare. I purposed in my heart to confront my pastor about this sin on Monday as soon as Sunday was over. I had enough respect for the Lord's Day, and for the fate of the souls in the service, to not deal with this at church on Sunday.

I still marvel at the wisdom that came only from God. There is no way I could have thought out a more efficient way to handle this. God was leading my steps. He was guiding my thoughts. He helped me at every turn. My actions were not motivated by anger or vengeance. I had been very angry at first, but it had been reduced to a low smolder and was greatly suppressed. That was the only way I could function. My decision to go public was not based on personal vendettas. It wasn't about revenge.

My biggest concern was for the welfare of the church. The precious people at Fellowship Baptist Church had no idea that the man they listened to every service was a sexual predator. They had no clue that the man they called "Pastor" was trying to seduce the youth pastor. They had not the foggiest inclination that their "man of God" was a cold, calculating homosexual with a wicked, personal agenda that was an affront to God, the Bible, the church and everything we stood for. He had to be confronted. His true colors had to be revealed.

My second concern was to stop Kelley from ever targeting someone again.

It was a distasteful task; a thankless job, but somebody had to do it and for the moment, that lot fell to me. In fact, I was the only person on the planet who could do it. This mess had fallen into my lap. I was the one who had been targeted and groomed. I was the one who had witnessed these despicable conversations and been manipulated into that hotel room under false pretenses. I was the one who had been propositioned. I was the one.

Nobody else could do what had to be done. It was up to me. And I couldn't do it alone. I was in way over my head and I knew it. I called on God to help me, and just as His Word promised, He came through.

On Monday, as soon as I got home from the construction site, I picked up the phone book and looked up the number for Dr. Don Richards.

Don Richards was the senior pastor at Corinth Baptist Church in Stone Mountain, Georgia. He was also the president of Macedonia World Baptist Missions, the same mission board where James Kelley served as an advisor. I had met Dr. Richards a time or two, but we were not close by any stretch of the imagination. In fact, we had never had a conversation to my knowledge. He had been to Fellowship for a special service or two while I was on staff, but that was about the extent of our interaction.

I still marvel at the leadership of the Holy Spirit in guiding me to reach out and involve this pastor I barely knew. With my heart beating double-time, I dialed his number.

"Hello, this is Pastor Richards. How can I help you?"

"Brother, you know me, and you know my pastor. But I am not going to give you my name. I am going to tell you something, and I want your unbiased opinion as to how I should deal with this. God told me to call you, so that is what I am doing. Will you give me some counsel, please?"

"Ok. What is it you want to tell me?"

"Brother, what I am about to tell you is the God's honest truth. It is far-fetched and it is despicable. But it is the truth and I need to know how to deal with it. This involves my pastor, who is my boss. I am on staff at his church. You know me and you know him. What he has done cannot go unresolved. I am going to deal with this one way or another, but I need advice."

"What has he done?"

That question opened the floodgates. I spent about twenty minutes telling him the whole story, starting with the isolated grooming incidents, and finished my story with my pastor's indecent proposition in the hotel room. I left nothing out. He listened without saying much of anything. The whole time I was talking, I was begging God to please help this man believe me. I'll never forget his next statement.

"Son, I don't know who you are or who you are talking about, but one of two things is very clear to me. Either you need to be writing scripts for Hollywood, or this pastor you're telling me about is a disgrace to the ministry."

"Brother Richards, I assure you, I'm not writing scripts for Hollywood!"

"I don't think you are either. I believe what you're telling me, and you were right to call me. I want to help you get this resolved. Have you told anybody any of this?"

"No Sir, I have not told a soul. You're the first person I've told. I was waiting on direction from the Lord, and He led me to call you."

"Son, are you willing to confront your pastor with these accusations?"

"Absolutely. I will do it tonight if you think I should."

"You go call him and set up a meeting, and then call me after you're finished and let me know what happened. I'll be praying for you."

"Ok. I'll do that right now. I'll call you in a little bit."

7

Confrontation

"And he led them on safely, so that they feared not: but the sea overwhelmed their enemies."
Psalms 78:53

* * *

I picked up the phone and called James Kelley. He answered the phone. "Hey, this is Stacey. I need to meet with you right now at the church."

"Can it wait?"

"No. I need to talk to you right now. I'll meet you there in fifteen minutes." I hung up the phone.

I got to the church before he did. I had my own set of keys, so I let myself in and walked down to the front of the sanctuary. I was leaning up against the communion table with my ankles crossed and my arms crossed when he walked through the double doors in the back. My body language was unmistakable. I was in charge. I pointed to the front right pew.

"Sit down."

He walked down the aisle and sat on the end of the front row right where I had pointed. The look on his face was of a man that knew his time was up.

Looking back, only God could have orchestrated the outcome of this situation. I was just a kid. Green as a gourd. I was still wet behind the ears. But that afternoon, it was David and Goliath all over again and Kelley didn't stand a chance. He was dealing with a preacher boy who had waited on the Lord, sought godly counsel, and was led by the Holy Spirit. He had no idea how to deal with that. Looking back now, he was the one who was in over his head. He was in unchartered waters.

"What is this about?" He asked me like he had no idea what was coming down.

"I just wanted to look you in your God-given eyeballs and let you know that you are nothing more than a stinkin' pervert. The only reason you brought me here was to break me down and take advantage of me to satisfy your filthy, rotten lusts. You ain't nothing but a stinkin' sodomite and YOU'RE DONE PAL! It's over! Now either you can tell the church what you are, or I will. It don't make any difference to me, but one way or the other, you're done. You're outta here. You're finished!"

He didn't flinch. He didn't blink. He didn't move a muscle. He just looked at me. After a moment, he spoke.

"Well, if I tell you I'm sorry, then you have to forgive me. And you have to forgive and forget."

I shook my head in disbelief at the gall.

"I might forgive you one day, but I will NEVER forget what you did to me, and I'm telling you that you're done here. The church will know what you are. Now do you want to tell them, or do you want me to tell them?"

"I'm not telling them."

"So you want me to do it?"

"No. I want you to forgive me like the Bible says you're supposed to do and let's just forget about it."

"Wrong answer. Looks like it's my move. I'll keep you posted."

I walked past him and out the back door. I drove back to my room and called Dr. Richards.

"Brother Richards, it's me again. I just talked to him."

"And what did he say?"

I told Brother Richards what had happened. He still had no idea who I was or who I was talking about. I knew when he found out he would be shocked. I wanted his unfiltered counsel, and I was getting it. I will always be grateful for how that dear pastor handled this scandal.

"Brother Richards, I need your advice on what to do next. Do I call the deacons? I really believe that God led me to get your opinion, and I'll do whatever you tell me to do. This thing is bigger than me."

"Well, I appreciate that, Son. This thing is bigger than both of us. Let me ask you a question. What about your dad? Is he a Christian?'"

"Yes, sir. Actually, he has both pastored and served as a missionary."

"Why haven't you called him?"

"Because I know what he will say. He will tell me to pack up and come home. And I plan to do that right after I deal with this. I can't leave that man in that church without saying something. People need to know what he is."

"Call your dad right now and bring him up to speed on what's going on and see what he says. I'll be praying for you."

8

Reinforcements

"And he answered, Fear not: for they that be with us are more than they that be with them."
2 Kings 6:16

* * *

I put the phone down and dialed my parents' house. Dad answered the phone. I told him the whole story. He was in shock. He understood why I had not called him earlier and agreed with me that he would have told me to pack up and get out. I told him that I could not with a clear conscience walk away from this without dealing with it.

He advised me to call my former pastor, Terry Brock, who was also my parents' pastor. So I did. Pastor Brock listened while I told him the story, and I will never forget what he said to me that night on the phone. I had been going to that church since we moved to Conyers back in 1991. He loved me like a son. He took a tone of voice with me that night on the phone that I had never heard from him.

"Son, you'd better be telling me the truth. You'd better not be lying to me."

"Preacher Brock, I promise you. Everything I told you is true, and I didn't even tell you all of it. There's a lot more."

"A lot more? A lot more of what?"

"Just things he said and did in the last six months that I should have picked up on, but I ignored them for one reason or another."

"Here's what I want you to do. I want you to get a notebook and write down every detail you can think of. Every conversation. Every single inappropriate comment or incident. Write it all down. You're going to need it before this is over with."

"What are you going to do?" I knew my pastor well enough to know he wasn't going to throw me under the bus, but I wanted to know what was going to happen next. I was glad to finally have some reinforcements.

"I'm going to call Dr. Richards and set up a meeting. I'll call you back in a little bit."

I was glad to pass the ball off to someone else. Having him willingly, and quickly, get involved in my crisis was a relief.

"Don't tell him who you are," I said. "He may figure out it's me. I don't want him to know it is James Kelley we are talking about. Stay anonymous."

"OK. I will. In the meantime, I want you to pack up your things and go back home to your parents' house. You do not need to be up there any longer. He may try to stop you."

I felt very vulnerable. I had just confronted the senior pastor and threatened to expose him to the whole church. It was like the walls in that basement apartment were closing in on me. I couldn't get out of there fast enough. I threw some of my clothes into a suitcase and told the Gilstraps that something came up and I had to go home. By now it was well after 10 p.m. and they knew something was amiss, but had enough respect not to ask any questions. I assured them I would let them know what was going on later but that I had to go.

I tossed my stuff into my car and headed toward home. In the meantime, Pastor Brock called and set up a meeting with Dr. Richards for the next day.

The next morning I met with my dear pastor, Terry Brock. I distinctly remember the seriousness with which he responded to this situation.

Affectionately called "Preacher Brock" by those of us in the church, he was just a country preacher. My home church, Light of Calvary Baptist Church in Conyers, was located in the suburbs of east Atlanta, but it was still a country church. We were plain and simple folk. We didn't have a nice manicured campus. We didn't have fancy facilities. We didn't have any staff members. It was just Preacher Brock and the church people.

To be thrown into a scandal of this magnitude involving these pastors with doctoral degrees and big churches was not something Preacher Brock would have ever wanted or asked for. Yet here he was, up to his eyeballs in this mess, and so far, all he had to go on was the word of a preacher boy out of his church.

I still get a knot in my throat when I recall just how far my pastor had to stick his neck out on my behalf. I cannot describe the feeling of value and worth that it gave to me for my pastor, first of all, to listen to my story, and secondly, for him to believe me. I had absolutely no evidence. I had not a shred of incriminating proof to offer to anybody. All I had were personal accounts, personal conversations, personal experiences - of which not a single soul was a witness. It was the ultimate "he said, he said" scenario.

I was very well aware that I did not have a leg to stand on other than my word. I was also aware of the fact that a man with a thirty-year track record in the ministry (with an impeccable reputation) was being accused by a kid that nobody knew. I knew the risks that Preacher Brock was taking just by believing me and getting involved.

My love and appreciation for Preacher Brock grew exponentially during that crisis. He was available for me, he listened to me, he treated me like I mattered and that what had happened to me mattered. He didn't treat me like a young preacher boy in his church; he treated me like an equal.

It was during that crisis in my life that I was once again reminded of the importance of having a personal testimony of faithfulness and integrity. I also realized the pricelessness of having a close and personal relationship with one's pastor. My pastor stuck his neck out for me, not just because he believed me, but he believed IN me.

In the years I had been a member there, I wasn't just a face in his church. I wasn't just a body that filled a space on a pew. I was involved, and had taken the time to build a friendship and relationship with my pastor that was about to prove invaluable. He knew me. He had watched me grow from a seventeen year old teenager to a young man with a heart for God. I had spent hours at his home and had worked with him and done things with him.

Preacher Brock was more than just my pastor; he was my friend. He had confidence in my walk with God and he had confidence in my decision to confront this mess rather than to run away from it. Having him on my side was priceless.

As we talked that Tuesday morning, I filled in as many of the gaps as I could to bring him up to speed with what the last six months of my life had entailed. Cumming is about an hour's drive from Conyers. Though I had not been far away, I had not been to any of the services at Light of Calvary since taking the position at Fellowship Baptist. It was good to get caught up on what was going on in my home church and to spend some time with my pastor.

Those few days that Preacher Brock dedicated to helping me were such a blessing. He dropped everything and focused entirely on this crisis and helping me follow it through.

9

Going Public

"Fear them not therefore: for there is nothing covered,that shall not be revealed; and hid, that shall not be known. What I tell you in darkness, that speak ye in light: and what ye hear in the ear, that preach ye upon the housetops."
Matthew 10:26, 27

* * *

We set up an appointment to meet with Dr. Richards later that afternoon after my dad got off work. Together, my dad, Preacher Brock and I walked into Dr. Don Richards' office at Corinth Baptist Church in Stone Mountain.

I will never forget the look on his face when he saw me. He stared at me for a minute trying to place me, and then stated matter-of-factly:

"You're with James Kelley."

I nodded.

"And the things you told me were about him?"

Again, I nodded. The look on his face when he realized the magnitude of this situation revealed a mixture of disappointment and disgust.

"Have a seat." He motioned to a conference table nearby and after introducing him to my dad and to my pastor, we sat down. I could tell immediately that Dr. Richards was intent on getting to the bottom of this. I realized at once that looping this pastor in on this situation was the right move. I filled in a few more of the blanks and presented my case that James Kelley had to go, and I would not leave that church until the members knew what he had done and the kind of person he was.

Not once did Dr. Richards ask me to reconsider my decision or try to talk me out of moving forward with this. Not one time did he act like he didn't believe me or hint that I was making up any part of the story. He listened with intense soberness and I could tell he was 100 percent on board with what had to happen next.

In fact, his next move took me by surprise and humbled me all at the same time. He walked over to his desk, sat down and picked up the phone and dialed a number.

"James, this is Don Richards."

There was a short pause.

"James, I've got a young man who is on your staff sitting here in my office, along with his dad and his pastor. He has come to me with some very serious allegations and I need you to come down here and let's talk about this."

Another pause.

"James, you can't avoid this. He's committed to seeing this through, and if you don't come down here and face these accusations then you are going to give me no choice but to go to the deacons of your church. I'd much rather you come down here and let's deal with this, and the sooner the better."

Another pause as he listened.

"Well, I hope you will reconsider and agree to come meet with this young man. I have been asked to help facilitate some kind of resolution to this situation, and I'm pleading with you to come face this. It is in your best interest and in the best interest of the church to hit this head on."

Another pause and the conversation ended. Dr. Richards hung up the phone. The look on his face was grim.

"What did he say?" I was dying to know.

"He said he isn't coming. He said he has no desire to talk to you or any of us about this."

"What did he say when you told him that you would go to the deacons of the church?"

"He pretty much told me to do whatever I wanted to do, but he wasn't going to come down here."

"Does that sound like a man who is innocent to you, sir?"

"No. It doesn't. If he was innocent he would meet us right now and try to clear this up. I believed you before, but it's obvious to me now more than ever that he is guilty of what you're accusing him of. This doesn't look good for him at all."

To make a long story short, after a series of phone calls to the deacons and the trustees of the church, they were informed of the situation and agreed to meet with us at Dr. Richards' office on Thursday night. We thanked Dr. Richards for his help and after a word of prayer we left his office that Tuesday afternoon.

I knew that the real battle was less than forty-eight hours away and we needed God to intervene in a big way. If He didn't, I realized that this thing could go sideways fast and I would pretty much be toast. To say that my dad, my pastor and I were stressed out for the next two days would be a gross understatement.

On the way back to Conyers that night, Preacher Brock told me he did not want me to come to church on Wednesday night. He didn't want people asking why I was there, and he didn't feel like saying anything to the church about the situation until after the meeting on Thursday.

10

Alone with God

"Though he slay me, yet will I trust in him: but I will maintain mine own ways before him. He also shall be my salvation: for an hypocrite shall not come before him."
Job 13:15, 16

* * *

I will never forget that Wednesday night as long as I live. One reason is because for the first time in my life, I did not go to church, on purpose, without being sick. That was nearly twenty-five years ago, and it is still the one and only time that I have not been in my place at church for a church service without being sick or providentially hindered. My whole family went to church without me and left me at home alone. I have gone to church for Sunday School, Sunday morning, Sunday night, mid-week service, revival services, mission's conferences, you name it – I have been to every service my church had from the day I was born until now. But that night I stayed home because my pastor told me to.

It felt weird missing church. How people do it on a regular basis is beyond my comprehension. The Bible says in Hebrews 10:25, "Not forsaking the assembling of ourselves together, as the manner of some is; but exhorting one another: and so much the more, as ye see the day approaching." The Bible is clear; we are commanded not to forsake the assembling of ourselves together. If the church that I am a member of has scheduled an assembling, I'm commanded to be there. Plain and simple. But that night, I stayed home. I will never forget it.

The second reason I will never forget that night is because of what God did in my heart while I was home all alone. I remember as my family pulled out of the driveway there in Social Circle and headed toward church, I sat down with my Bible and began to read. I was overwhelmed with the magnitude of my situation. The weight of my decision to confront this wicked man, and to bring him before the church was almost more than I could bear. I had never done anything like this before. I had never even met anybody that had done something like this before. I was dealing with so many emotions and thoughts that it was almost more than I could handle.

I say "almost" because God was with me. I was reminded of the similarities in my situation and the Apostle Paul when he wrote, "At my first answer no man stood with me, but all men forsook me: I pray God that it may not be laid to their charge. Notwithstanding the Lord stood with me, and strengthened me; that by me the preaching might be fully known, and that all the Gentiles might hear: and I was delivered out of the mouth of the lion. And the Lord shall deliver me from every evil work, and will preserve me unto his heavenly kingdom: to whom be glory for ever and ever. Amen." (2 Timothy 4:16-18)

Though I had my dad, my pastor and Dr. Richards on my side, this pending meeting would be a showdown between a veteran pastor with an honorary doctorate and a rookie preacher boy who wasn't even qualified to be on staff in the first place. Paul prayed to be delivered from the mouth of the lion. I echoed that prayer. If anybody had ever "had the lion by the tail," it was me.

I slid off of the couch and sprawled out face down on the floor. I began to weep. It was like a dam broke. I have never in my life wept as hard and as long as I did that night. I remember grabbing a box of Kleenex off the coffee table, and as I prayed and wept, the used tissues grew into a pile on the floor.

I poured my heart out to God that night. I begged him to please protect me from this scandal; to help me come through victorious and unscathed. I prayed as Paul did to deliver me from every evil work, and to preserve me; that by me, the preaching of Christ might be fully known. I pleaded for God to put His hand on me and to give me a holy anointing for the work He had called me to do. I begged His forgiveness for doubting Him, for doubting His word, for doubting the truth I had been exposed to and taught my whole life. I asked God to not let a few bad apples in the ministry turn my heart away from the highest calling in the world, and that is to preach the Gospel to lost and dying souls.

I begged Him to give me a backbone as big as a saw log. I prayed for power, courage, the guts, the integrity, the stamina and the will to stand and fight. I pleaded for God to use me in His work. I begged Him to help me to never become a hireling or a fake or a phony. I asked Him to make me a true man of God; not in title, but in reality. I wanted all of God and I wanted Him to have all of me.

That night, lying on the floor of the house I helped my dad build on the side of a dirt road, God came down and met with me. He put His hand on me, and that night, Stacey Shiflett was forever changed!

I cannot explain it. The Pentecostals would say that I received "the second blessing." The old-time Baptists would say that I was "filled with the Spirit." I won't argue theology here. I believe in far more blessings than just two. And I believe being filled with the Spirit is not an experience, but rather a daily yielding and obedience to the Holy Spirit. Regardless of what you want to call it, that night was the night that I went from being a flailing little staff member to a man of God – a man that God could use.

I died to self that night. I got up off the floor a new person. I had used about half that box of tissues. I was physically exhausted from praying and weeping. I was no longer a boy. I was now a man. And I was ready for the confrontation that was about to happen. I was as spiritually, mentally, and emotionally ready as a person could be. I was ready to get this over with. The alpha male that had been hiding in the deep recesses of my psyche rose to the surface that night.

Never again would I be a victim. Never again would I be a sheep. I was a sheepdog now. The wolves had better beware. I had been an obedient and submissive follower my entire life. My time had come. It was time for me to lead.

11

Vindication

"My defence is of God, which saveth the upright in heart."
Psalms 7:10

* * *

The next night, we all arrived at Dr. Richards' office about the same time. The meeting consisted of me, my dad, Preacher Brock, Dr. Richards, three of the deacons and trustees and James Kelley. At first he had refused, but somehow the men of the church had persuaded him to attend.

I was surprised. I never expected him to show up and face his accuser. Men in his position rarely do. They protest from a distance and insist on their innocence but rarely do men in his predicament have the gall to face the charges. The fact that he came caught me slightly off guard, but I was glad. I had a few things I wanted to say to him.

Dr. Richards started the meeting off with prayer. He then asked James Kelley if he had anything he wanted to say. He got a bit sarcastic and replied that he had come to listen to me. He said that since I had so much to say, that I should go first.

That was a mistake. I recall a story where a giant taunted a young man that was facing him. He mocked him and laughed at his stature and his choice of weapons. I also recall that giant never knew what hit him right between the eyes.

I opened my notebook and took a deep breath. I was glad now that Preacher Brock told me to write it all down. I had a list of about two pages of inappropriate comments and incidents. I will never forget how we were seated at the table. Dr. Richards was at the head of the table. On his right sat my pastor, then my dad, then me. On his left sat two deacons and directly across from me sat James Kelley. Another man from the church sat at the end of the table to my right.

I started down that list with the question:

"Do you deny saying…?" I rattled off one of the inappropriate comments he had made.

"No."

I was taken aback. I wasn't ready for that answer. I continued.

"Do you deny making this comment…?"

"No"

"Do you deny going into detail with me about you and your wife and your intimate relationship?"

"No."

I went down that list systematically. His answer was the same. He didn't deny a single accusation that I had written down. Not one! The more he admitted to them, the bolder I got. The more he didn't deny anything, the more amazed I was at God's glorious intervention. The more he admitted his actions, the more vindicated I was. I was not fighting this battle. I was just slinging the stones. God was directing this meeting. In my wildest dream I never imagined that James Kelley would admit to being a sexual predator in a room filled with the church's leadership and his colleague, Dr. Richards. I couldn't believe what was happening!

The more I questioned, and the more he admitted, you could feel the air being sucked out of the room. I don't think anyone there was prepared for this. It was like he did not have the ability to resist or deny a single charge made against him. It was incredible!

I couldn't help but notice the look of shock and pain on Dr. Richards' face. Even though he had believed me, I'm sure he was hoping that somehow this was all just a big misunderstanding. I'm sure that he had hoped and prayed that this pastor who had served with him on the Executive Advisory Board was not the person I had accused him of being. But he was. Here he was admitting to every accusation in plain English in a room with six other men besides me and him.

As the conversation continued, I noticed the deacon sitting beside Kelley started shifting in his chair.

"Do you deny propositioning me the other night in that hotel room?"

"No."

There it was. A full and unmistakable confession. By the time I was finished with that list, the deacon had turned in his chair with his back completely to his pastor.

The downcast eyes and disbelief in the faces of those deacons and trustees will always be in my mind. Their world had just come crashing down. I knew the feeling. I had that same experience a month prior. The truth was out and it was ugly. The cat was out of the bag and there was no putting it back in. I had done what I had to do and God had done what only He could do. He was guilty by his own confession, and I was vindicated.

Dr. Richards spoke up.

"James, I cannot tell you how disappointed I am. When this young man came into my office and I realized that the story he told me involved you, I desperately didn't want to believe it. But you have admitted to every accusation here tonight. My heart is broken. What do you have to say for yourself?"

James Kelley fidgeted in his chair and offered up one of weakest, most pathetic excuses I've ever heard.

"Well, I brought Stacey to our church to work with our young people. He was inexperienced and he was untested. I wanted to make sure that he was the right man for the job and that he had the character to be in that position. I said and did those things as a test to see what he would do."

I glared at him across the table. Did he say "test?" Are you kidding me? That was the best he could come up with? I leaned forward.

"A test? All of this was just a test?" I shoved the notebook across the table. My blood pressure was rising. Fast.

"A test? Seriously? Well, answer me this. Did I pass the test?"

"Yes. You did. You handled yourself correctly and you passed the test."

I snorted angrily. "Let me tell you something. When I take a test, I don't just want to pass it. I want to make a hundred on it. I didn't make a hundred on this test. Because what I should have done the other night in that hotel room was picked up a chair and busted your head wide open with it! That would have been making a hundred on the test!"

I had raised my voice considerably and was getting madder by the minute. A test?!

My dad put his hand on my arm.

"Calm down, Son. Calm down. You've said enough."

I leaned back and stared at Kelley. Now I knew how David felt when he saw Goliath fall on his face. That was a good start. But that was not enough. David drew Goliath's sword and made sure he never got up again. Kelley had fallen. Big time. Right in front of God and everybody. But I wasn't finished. Not yet. It was time to end this for good.

"The only reason you called me and asked me to come on staff was because you thought I would be vulnerable and easy. You knew about my previous incident where I was molested and you thought I wouldn't be able to say no. Well, I did! I said 'no'! You didn't get me. You're nothing but a filthy, stinkin' pervert."

He just sat there. He looked like a whipped puppy. I turned to the deacons. They still had their faces turned away from him. I felt sorry for them. I don't know what they expected this meeting to be about, but I'm pretty sure they weren't ready for this. They were extremely uncomfortable. I looked over at the chairman of the deacon board and spoke up.

"James Kelley hired me, but I'm not turning in a resignation to him. I'm turning in my resignation to you men tonight. I'm gone. I'm out of here. I'm going back home. Now you've got a decision to make about what to do with him. Either way, I won't be there to see it. Earl, I'll be coming by tomorrow to get the rest of my stuff. Tell Lucy that I appreciate everything."

I stood up and was ready to go. I looked at Dr. Richards.

"Thank you for your help. I hated to drag you into this, but I needed advice. God answered my prayer. I have been vindicated and His church will now be protected from this wolf in sheep's clothing. If you need anything else from me, just call."

Dad and Preacher Brock and I left the meeting. I was in a state of shock. God had brought a miraculous victory. Never in my wildest dream did it occur to me that James

Kelley would admit to what he had done. If he had denied the allegations, I could have left that meeting looking like a fool, a traitor and a liar. I had not one iota of proof of a single allegation against that man, yet God orchestrated the situation to where he admitted every bit of it.

My faith in prayer grew substantially that night. My God loved me and He heard and answered my prayer. What a mighty God we serve!

Hear my cry, O God; attend unto my prayer. From the end of the earth will I cry unto thee, when my heart is overwhelmed: lead me to the rock that is higher than I. For thou hast been a shelter for me, and a strong tower from the enemy.
Psalm 61:1-3

12

The Rest of the Story

"We are troubled on every side, yet not distressed; we are perplexed, but not in despair;"
2 Corinthians 4:8

***

This story does not have a happy ending. In fact, it is still a frustration to me at the way things worked out.

I cleared my belongings out of Earl and Lucille Gilstrap's basement and moved back home. The deacons worked out an exit strategy for James Kelley that consisted of some incredible conditions. He made three very specific demands:

1. Three months' severance pay
2. A letter of recommendation to another ministry
3. To never refer to him as a homosexual

For some unknown reason, they agreed to every single one of his conditions. He packed up and left town and nobody ever really knew what all happened. People whispered, but as far as I know, there was no official statement to inform the church of why he left. Or why I left.

One thing is certain. I didn't get any severance pay OR a letter of recommendation.

James Kelley was removed from the advisory board at Macedonia. I do not know the details of how. I don't know if he resigned or was kicked off. I also do not know if everybody associated with the board ever knew why, but he was not on the board anymore. I've got a feeling that was kept on the down-low as well.

James Kelley moved to Greenwood, South Carolina and joined East Side Baptist Church where E.A. Cooper was the pastor. He became the administrator of the church's Christian school. I learned later this was his home church when he was a teenager.

As soon as I found out where he landed, I called and set up a meeting, and then drove up to meet with Pastor Cooper. I took my dad and Preacher Brock with me. It is a two-and-a-half-hour drive (150 miles), but we drove up to inform Pastor Cooper of what had just happened.

We sat in his office for well over an hour and relayed the story of what had transpired back at Fellowship Baptist Church in Cumming. One thing that I thought was odd was James Kelley's wife, Judy, was in the meeting. Pastor Cooper had invited her in to hear our story. She sat there and heard everything. I handed him a list of every man who was in the meeting that night in Dr. Richards' office. I had included their phone numbers. I begged Pastor Cooper to call and verify my story. His next statement to me was unforgettable.

"Son, I have no reason to doubt what you're telling me is true."

To my knowledge, he didn't call a single one of those men. He didn't fire James Kelley. He allowed an admitted sexual predator to run his Christian school. It blew my mind then. It still blows my mind. What in the world was he thinking? Did he refuse to deal with Kelley because of his wife? Did he feel sorry for her and was protecting her? I'll never know.

After the story leaked out, my phone began to ring. This was back before Google, social media, websites, and cell phones. This was 1994. But people found me. They found my phone number. I got calls from men that had been on Kelley's staff as far back as the '70s. The stories they told me would curl your hair.

One man opened up to me about how James Kelley had groomed, seduced and molested him as a young staff member. He wept as he told me of his inability to stand up to him. He told me how Kelley had used his position of power to manipulate, intimidate, abuse and violate.

The stories would have been impossible to believe if I had not experienced them myself. One man called to confess that as a young staff member, he had allowed James Kelley to "help" him rub calamine lotion all over his private area when he got poison ivy. His pastor had offered to help him and he didn't have the wherewithal to tell him no.

Another young man called to let me know that he too had been molested by James Kelley at Philadelphia Christian School in Conyers when he was a teenage student in the high school. He had told his parents, but nobody did anything about it. Now a student at Bob Jones University, he wanted to thank me personally for standing up to Kelley and putting a stop to him.

The problem is, I have no assurances that he ever stopped. He was the administrator of the Christian school in Greenwood from 1994 until 2000. How many boys or teenagers did he molest or groom or abuse during those six years? People like him don't stop. He had been doing that kind of stuff for nearly thirty years. That's who he was. That's what he did. And I was the first person to confront him publicly.

"The only thing necessary for the triumph of evil is for good men to do nothing."
- Edmund Burke

In 2000, we were on deputation as missionaries on our way to South Africa. We were in Arkansas that summer when I received a phone call from a dear pastor in Liberty,

South Carolina. He had heard of the allegations and wanted to talk to me about it. I will never forget that conversation.

The pastor who called me was very upset at the fact this had been hidden from people. He informed me that his grandchildren were attending the Christian school at Eastside Baptist Church in Greenwood where James Kelley was the administrator. He wanted to know how this could happen if it was true. I assured him it was true, and that I could provide him a list of men who were in the room when he admitted it. I furthermore informed him of my meeting with Pastor Cooper in 1995 to tell him about it, and how he chose to ignore my warnings.

The pastor became livid at the lack of inactivity on the part of Pastor Cooper. He told me that he was going to drive to Greenwood, walk into Cooper's office and demand that Kelley be fired. I told him to go for it.

Kelley eventually left East Side and went across town and started a church. Oddly enough, he named it Fellowship Baptist Church; the same name as the church he'd pastored in Cumming. He pastored that church until he died.

13

Blacklisted

"I looked on my right hand, and beheld, but there was no man that would know me: refuge failed me; no man cared for my soul."
Psalms 142:4

* * *

It is sad that not a single pastor called me during that time. They didn't call to check on me. They didn't call to tell me they were praying for me, or that they were proud of me for standing up and doing the right thing.

I stayed in touch with the Gilstraps via phone calls and Christmas cards down through the years, but I never heard from Fellowship Baptist Church after that. One or two people reached out, but I heard not a single word from most of the church members. The only pastor who ever commended me or cared about me was my pastor, Preacher Brock.

I learned early in my ministry that people don't like whistleblowers. Even if somebody is molesting children, being a whistleblower, in certain circles, is a no-no.

One might think I would get some kind of acknowledgement from the parents of the youth group thanking me for my actions, and for trying to protect their kids. All I heard was crickets. It was as if I had the plague. Here I was, a twenty-two-year-old preacher boy who had just had to deal with a scandal of epic proportions, and had handled it with wisdom and discretion. I had handled it biblically and ethically. I had recruited and relied on every biblical authority that I had to help me. I had come through this nightmare unstained and untarnished. I didn't get a single "Atta boy" from the brethren. The silence was deafening.

Of all the men who found out, not a single one tried to hire me. I didn't get a job offer, an interview, a consideration. I didn't get a recommendation, a referral, a speaking engagement – nothing.

Looking back, it is incredible how that by standing up to a sexual predator and an admitted homosexual deviant, I essentially burned my bridges. Because I did what nobody else wanted to do or had done, I was benched. Because I was looking out for the local church and the people and families in the church rather than my own career, I was toast.

I got married in July of 1995 to Grace Young and moved to her dad's church in 1996 to attend his Bible institute. We surrendered to go to Africa in 2000.

For five years after the James Kelley ordeal, not once was I ever approached about being on staff, serving in a church or anything. I started a construction business in '96 and served the Lord in my local church while I got my formal Bible training.

From 1995 until I surrendered to missions, I never got offered another staff position. I was not hired by any church or ministry. I had essentially committed ministerial suicide.

I had a mark on me that wouldn't go away. Nobody wanted anything to do with me.

I can count on one hand the places where I preached outside of my local church in those five years. That's OK. David was anointed by God to be king in 1 Samuel 16, but he didn't become king of Israel for another fifteen years (2 Samuel 5:3.)

God had me right where He wanted me. I had no regrets. I learned early on in my ministry that doing the right thing is its own reward. To seek any other reward would be setting yourself up for disappointment.

I'm praying that if nothing else comes from me telling my story, it may give other people that James Kelley abused the courage to come forward and deal with it and get healing.

James Kelley died in 2010. I looked online and found his obituary. Even though it is a matter of public record, for this book I edited it and omitted the names of his family members.

James Kelley Obituary

KELLEY, SR. Dr. James Franklin Kelley, Sr. went home to be with his Lord on Tuesday, August 10, 2010, at Emory University Hospital in Atlanta, Ga. from complications resulting from Pulmonary Fibrosis and surgery. He was 68 years old. At the age of 16, he accepted Christ as his Savior at East Side Baptist Church in Greenwood, SC and upon graduation from Greenwood High School in Greenwood, he went to Tennessee Temple University in Chattanooga, TN, and graduated with a Graduate of Theology Degree in 1966. Accepting the call of God in his life to preach, his first pastorate was Philadelphia Baptist Church in Atlanta, Ga. which he later relocated to Conyers, Ga. Realizing the need of Christian Education for children, he led the church in beginning Philadelphia Christian School in Conyers. His other pastorates included Bemiss Road Baptist Church in Valdosta, Ga., Fellowship Baptist Church in Cumming Ga. and East Side Baptist Church in Greenwood, SC. He completed his ministry of pastoring with starting and shepherding Fellowship Baptist Church in Greenwood. On his pulpits he often placed the verse "Sir we would see Jesus" and that was his heart's desire. Because of his faithful service and love for souls, he was honored with an honorary Doctor's degree from Tabernacle Baptist Church and Schools in Greenville, SC. He was the son of ----. In addition to his wife and helpmate of 48 years, he is survived by his sons, 7 grandchildren; a sister, and a brother. He also leaves behind his very close father-in-law. Preceding him in death in addition to his parents are two brothers, and 2 grandchildren. Funeral Services will be held at East Side Baptist Church in Greenwood, at 2:00 PM on Friday, August 13, 2010. The family will receive friends from 12:00 PM to 2:00 PM at the church before the service. Because of his longtime service for his Lord in the Atlanta area, a service will be held on Saturday, August 14, 2010 at 2:00 PM at Hope Academy, the former location of Philadelphia Baptist Church- 2360 Old Covington Highway, Conyers. The family will receive friends from 12:00 PM to 2:00 PM at the church before the service. Burial will follow at Corinth Memorial Gardens in Walnut Grove, Ga. on Hwy 81. Tim Stewart Funeral Home, 670 Tom Brewer Rd. Loganville, Ga. 30052.

I disagree with the first sentence of his obituary. I doubt very seriously that James Kelley was a saved man. It is my belief that he died and went straight to Hell. But that's just my personal opinion. God is his Judge.

According to Scripture, he wouldn't be the first preacher to go to Hell. "Many will say to me in that day, Lord, Lord, have we not prophesied in thy name? and in thy name have cast out devils? and in thy name done many wonderful works? And then will I profess unto them, I never knew you: depart from me, ye that work iniquity." (Matthew 7:22, 23)

PART THREE
National Headlines

✷ ✷ ✷

14

Earthquake

"Then the earth shook and trembled; the foundations also of the hills moved and were shaken, because he was wroth."
Psalms 18:7

* * *

"Pastor, I need to talk to you."

It was Friday morning, May 11, 2018. It has been my practice for years to meet with my assistant pastors, business manager and our Christian school administrator for morning prayer. We meet upstairs in my study, which is separate from my office. The pastor's office is not quite big enough for all of us to meet comfortably. The study is upstairs in a room which is adjacent to the men's changing rooms and the church baptistery.

This room is perfect for staff meetings and deacons' meetings. If I need to pray, or to study without being disturbed, I go upstairs to the study. There I am away from the phones and people knocking on my door because no one ever goes up there. All of my books are also up there.

As we finished up the 7:45 AM staff meeting, one of my assistant pastors, Philip (Bud) Hall, pulled me aside.

"We need to go to your office. It is urgent."

His voice was strained. I got a bad feeling. We walked down the stairs, across the hallway and into the wing that houses the Church Administrative Offices. I greeted my financial secretary, and then we walked into my office. The look on his face made my stomach knot up. I shut the door and we sat down.

"Ok. What is it?"

He sat down and looked at me with the weight of the world on his shoulders. He then began to share with me that he had received a phone call from one of his granddaughters early that morning.

She had shared with him that while talking with her sister, Sarah, the night before, she had opened up to her about an affair she'd allegedly had with the former pastor. Sarah Jackson, Sarah Hall back then, was sixteen years old at the time and a senior in the Christian school. This would have been twelve years prior. The details were a bit hazy, and my assistant pastor was very distraught. It had been all he could do to wait until after the staff meeting to tell me.

Needless to say, this revelation rocked my world. I immediately comprehended the magnitude of these allegations. The earth under me began to quake. I felt as though I was falling into a chasm.

The former pastor, Cameron Giovanelli, was a personal friend of mine. He had recommended me to the church after he resigned. He was moving to take a leadership position at Golden State Baptist College (GSBC) in Santa Clara, California. He had called me on a Saturday in June of 2014 and asked if he could give my name to the pulpit committee. I agreed to let him do that, and to make a long story short, God moved us to Baltimore in August. We become friends and spoke from time to time on the phone.

Giovanelli was soon promoted to president of GSBC. He preached for me multiple times whenever he was on the East Coast. He had invited me out to preach in the chapel service at GSBC. I had been out to North Valley Baptist Church (NVBC) where Giovanelli was on staff, multiple times for their annual conference. I played the piano and sung in several of their meetings. They allowed me to set up my product table and sell my books and preaching CDs there.

I developed friendships with some of the members and the staff. I always stayed in the home of Giovanelli's parents whenever I went out there. They are precious people and we always enjoyed such sweet fellowship during my visit. Giovanelli had family members still attending my church. Our lives were intertwined in many ways. We had half a dozen of our young people attending GSBC. My oldest daughter, Marissa, was enrolled there finishing up her third year of studies.

Upon hearing the allegations, I was devastated. My first reaction was the same as everyone else's. I thought,

"There is no way this can be true. I know this man! I just can't believe he would do something like this. Something else must be happening here."

I did not want it to be true. The magnitude of the impact this would have on me personally to even listen to this woman's accusations was staggering. The easiest thing for me to do would have been to ignore Sarah's accusations simply because I did not know her. If I had ever met her, I didn't remember it. However, I did know the man she accused, and I knew him well. Or so I thought.

It would have made my life much easier if I had just pushed her off to the side. If I could have chalked Sarah up as a disgruntled, former church member with an ax to grind, that would have been the easy route.

If I had suppressed the rumors she was spreading and defended my friend, life would have taken a completely different path for me, as well as a whole lot of other people. Trust me when I tell you that what little political capital I had went flying out the window just by my agreeing to listen to her.

But I had to listen. Even though I did not want it to be true, I had no choice but to hear her story and give an ear to the allegations. Why? Because kicking into "denial mode" is the wrong thing to do. Someone once said that there is no one as blind as those that will not see. Closing your eyes to the possibility is foolish. It is worse than naïve; it is extremely irresponsible.

It is also unbiblical. Proverbs 18:13, "He that answereth a matter before he heareth it, it is folly and shame unto him." The Bible is clear. For a person to say an allegation is not true before they even hear it out is foolish and shameful. The Bible also says in Proverbs 18:17, "He that is first in his own cause seemeth just; but his neighbour cometh and searcheth him."

Brother Hall did not know what to do. I asked him who all knew about this, and he had no idea. I asked him if he would reach out to Sarah. He didn't want to call her because he was hoping she would call him. Since her sister had been the one to tell him, he wasn't even supposed to know. Therefore, I wasn't supposed to know. But I did. And I couldn't wait much longer to get involved. This was huge.

I did not have to wait very long. It was around 2 o'clock on that Friday afternoon when Bud Hall's wife, who was teaching upstairs in the high school, got the phone call from Sarah. She had finally gotten up the nerve to call her grandmother.

Mrs. Hall was almost hysterical. She immediately found her husband and they came into my office. She did not know that either one of us knew because Sarah didn't know that we knew. Once she shared with us what her granddaughter had told her, we informed her of the early morning phone call from Sarah's sister.

"Do you believe her?" I know it is a crazy question to ask a grandmother, but I asked it anyway. I was hoping and praying that she would say no.

"Of course I believe her!" She wasn't angry with me for asking. Her answer was more of a confidence than I had anticipated.

"How can you be so sure?" Her quickness to believe these terrible things about her former pastor and former boss caught me off guard.

"How can I be so sure? I was his secretary! My desk was right outside this door back then. I distinctly remember him bringing Sarah into his office all the time and shutting the door. They would be in there for long periods of time with the door closed. How could I have been so blind?"

I looked at Bud Hall in shock. "Are you serious?"

He nodded. "We thought she was getting counseling."

Mrs. Hall spoke up again. "I remember asking her why she had to have so much counseling. I could never understand why such a young person would take up so much of the pastor's time."

My mind was reeling. This could not be happening!

I looked across my desk at Mrs. Hall who was weeping. Her husband was sitting in stunned silence. I asked her to call her granddaughter. She dialed her number on her cellphone and Sarah answered.

"Here. Hand me the phone." She gave me the phone without a word.

"Hello, Sarah? This is Pastor Shiflett. You do not know me, and I do not know you. But I just talked to your grandmother and I want to hear your story. Will you talk to me and tell me what happened?"

I put her on speaker phone and told her that both of her grandparents were in the room listening. She started telling her story. I could tell immediately that this was far more involved than I had originally anticipated. She wasn't being vague. She had specifics. Lots of them. She told me that she was debating whether or not to go public with her accusations on her Facebook page. I cringed. Big time.

"Please don't do that!" I begged her to wait. I will never forget my words to her.

"Putting it out on Facebook is like using a nuclear bomb. This is going to hurt a lot of people unnecessarily. Besides, if you are right in what you are saying, all you will do is give him opportunity to come up with a story to deny it. I prefer a surgical strike. If you will come in and tell me your story, I will go straight to Brother Giovanelli and his pastor, Dr. Trieber, with this. If you can give me something to work with, I will do my best to find the truth and make it known. If your story is credible, you have my word that I will not sweep this under the rug. But I need details, not just an allegation. You have to give me something to work with."

While talking with her, I couldn't help but notice her attitude. Normally, you would expect a woman in this situation to be angry and upset. Her tone and manner was not like that. She was kind, articulate, calm, collected and respectful. If she had been nasty and foul-mouthed, I may have not listened, but she wasn't. She did not know it, but the way she conducted herself on the phone with me did a lot to establish a baseline of credibility. She was not a ranting, raving, vindictive lunatic. She was a hurting human being who was just looking for peace, justice and closure. I knew how she felt. My heart ached for her.

She was leery of me. She did not know me, and did not trust me. I did my best in that short phone call to win her confidence, but she was very cautious. I asked her if she would come right then and meet with me and her grandparents. I learned that she was married and that she and her husband had a little boy. I invited her to bring her husband. I did everything I could think of to get her to come sit down with me.

She told me that she had made plans to be out of town for the weekend, but that she would meet with me on Tuesday, May 15. I was eager to get this over with, but meeting with her before Tuesday was off the table, so I agreed. I asked her in the meantime to write down every detail she could remember. I recalled my pastor's advice to me twenty-five years ago when I was the one making the accusations.

I urged her to write every detail, no matter how small or insignificant it seemed. She had mentioned having a cellphone on the church's group plan. She had mentioned exchanging emails. I told her to write down phone numbers, email addresses, dates, whatever she could recall and bring it to the meeting the next week. She said she would. I begged her to hold off on putting her accusations on

Facebook until after our meeting and she agreed. I was relieved at that news.

I asked her if she wanted to call the police since she had been a minor at the time. She said she didn't. She had told her parents about three years prior, but they were the only ones who knew it.

Her parents, former members of our church, were obviously livid and wanted to go public with it back then, but Sarah didn't want them to. She wanted to keep it private.

It was her understanding that the criminal statute of limitations may have expired, so going to the police wasn't her biggest concern. She did not want to go that route at first. It was her desire to put it behind her and move on with her life. But that was not possible. She was haunted by her secret.

Up to this point, I still did not know the exact nature of the allegations. I knew they were inappropriate and sexual in nature and had continued during her entire senior year of school, but that is all I knew. She did not elaborate on the details with me during this conference call and I did not ask. I was left with the impression that it was bad, but I did not know just how bad it was.

Not yet.

Because of her past hurts and violations, she had some major trust issues concerning pastors and church leaders. A few hours after we spoke, she made the decision to go public. She posted her accusations against Cameron

Giovanelli on her Facebook page. Apparently, she did not believe that I could or would help her. This alleged abuse had taken place nearly twelve years prior, and she was not very optimistic about justice ever being meted out in this situation.

I do not have a Facebook page, so I had no way of knowing she had gone public until my phone started ringing. People in my church were sending me screenshots of her Facebook post literally moments after it went up. I was getting bombarded with questions and text messages from my staff.

My strategy went up in smoke. I had intended to hear her story, get her journal and any corroborating evidence I could gather, and confront Giovanelli personally. By her putting her story on the Internet, it deprived me of the ability to manage the process -- or the confrontation.

Looking back, it all turned out for the best. I understood her lack of trust in me. I did not blame her for going public. If that was what she felt that she had to do, so be it.

One good thing came from her doing it that way. All I could do now was see where the facts led me. I did not have to wait for her meeting. I could immediately drill down on her story. And that is exactly what I did. Sarah's allegations became my number one priority.

I had to get to the bottom of this. I needed to know the truth. My family needed to know the truth. My church needed to know the truth. My community needed to know.

My internal review would either prove or disprove her allegations.

I was also very concerned about the collateral damage this would cause. In spite of all my efforts to disarm it, the nuclear bomb had gone off.

15

Fact Finding Mission

"Against an elder receive not an accusation, but before two or three witnesses."
1 Timothy 5:19

* * *

If they had a class on how to deal with things like this when I was in Bible college, I must have slept through it. I remember reading the Hardy Boys mystery books as a boy, but this was not fiction and I was no detective. I have no law enforcement experience. All I knew was this was happening, and it was happening to me.

In addition to recommending Sarah to pursue law enforcement's involvement, I also began to internally review the situation. I wanted to get to the bottom of it. I started asking questions and tried to verify things she told me had happened. It was my hope this would turn out to be nothing more than a false accusation that could easily be refuted.

One of the first things I did was to consult with my deacons. They needed to hear it from me, and they needed to hear just how committed I was going to be in getting to the truth. They expressed their full support.

My heart hurt for these men who had served under the former pastor. I cannot imagine the turmoil they had to contend with in their heart. They were as shocked and upset as I was at the allegations. No matter their personal feelings, they agreed with me that we needed to get to the bottom of it and deal with it accordingly.

One of my deacons was in Florida when the story broke. He was attending the graduation of a family member at Pensacola Christian College. He had not heard what had happened. I called him and assured him that I was handling it. He expressed his support and prayer.

I also consulted with our church's legal team. Their recommendation was to ensure that it was reported to the authorities, and they advised that our church support Sarah in whatever ways possible. As a part of this support, I was committed to finding the truth, but I was not oblivious to the fact if this proved to be true, our church or school might in some way be held responsible. I had no intentions of allowing that to cloud my judgment or my response, but I wanted to be up to speed on the process.

I was also aware of the media's propensity to grab hold of rumors like this and make it national headlines. That was the last thing I wanted. I desperately needed to get out front of this and find out what happened. I did not want some reporter doing my job. I had no desire to have a bunch of reporters shoving microphones in my face on camera asking me questions that I did not have answers to.

One of the first things I did was to send an email to my entire church and school staff on that Friday evening.

Here it is:

From: Stacey Shiflett <pastorss@cbcdundalk.org>
Date: Fri, May 11, 2018 at 6:47 PM
Subject: From Pastor Shiflett
To: Calvary Staff

Dear Staff,

It has come to my attention that things are being posted on Facebook about something that happened about 12 years ago here at our church. I was only made aware of it this morning and I am trying to gather the facts so I can deal with it biblically. Rest assured that I am seeking wisdom and trying to get to the bottom of it so I can keep our church free of distractions and reproach. I love you all and I covet your prayers.

Pastor Shiflett

PS. Please do not respond to people's questions other than that Pastor Shiflett is dealing with it. We will not let Satan rob our church of what God is doing right now!

It is amazing how reassuring it can be to a church when they hear their pastor say, "I am trying to get to the bottom of it." What an almost juvenile statement, but it said everything. I didn't know what had happened, but I was trying to find out. Without having met with Sarah, and without her notebook of details, I was left scrambling to piece together what I could from the few things she told me during the conference call with her grandparents. I only had a few tidbits of information, but it was enough to get started.

I am reminded of just how much trouble many churches go to in their efforts to hide the sin rather than to deal with it. I could have kicked into "self-preservation" mode and made a terrible mistake. That is what Adam and Eve did in the Garden of Eden. Instead of dealing with their sin, they made aprons of fig leaves (Genesis 3:7).

Do you have any idea what that involved? First of all, they had never seen garments of any kind. They had no idea how to do what they were trying to do. Secondly, imagine how crude their needle and thread had to be! Thirdly, can you picture just how ridiculous an apron made out of fig leaves must have looked?

I have thought about how much time they spent trying to cover up their sin, when the solution to their problem was right there. According to the words of God Himself, their vaccine or antidote for their sin was standing just a few feet away. The tree of life was right in front of them. All they had to do was to eat of that tree and they could have counteracted the curse of death. Their act of disobedience had brought about a deadly curse, but their healing was easily accessible. In fact, it was so easy to access that God sent an angel to keep them from eating from the tree.

Genesis 3:22-24

- *22 And the LORD God said, Behold, the man is become as one of us, to know good and evil: and now, <u>lest he put forth his hand, and take also of the tree of life, and eat, and live for ever:</u>*
- *23 Therefore the LORD God sent him forth from the garden of Eden, to till the ground from whence he was taken.*
- *24 So he drove out the man; and he placed at the east of the garden of Eden Cherubims, and a flaming sword which turned every way, to keep the way of the tree of life.*

Man's effort to hide sin rather than to confront it and deal with it is nothing new. It has been that way since the first sin man ever committed. Many ministries will exhaust themselves trying to cover, hide, deflect and refute rather than to simply look for the truth. Putting up a front and showering your people with "legalese" is one way to deal with a scandal. The other is to ask a few questions and see where it leads.

I decided to pursue the story. I started asking questions.

I was able to corroborate her story of being in the pastor's office for long periods of time with the door closed. I questioned a number of staff members, and each one confirmed that aspect of her story. The former school administrator called me from another state and confirmed that Giovanelli would take Sarah out of class and into his office for extended periods of time. He offered to go to court and testify to that fact if necessary.

It turns out that as a senior, Sarah had a free class period each day. She was given the title of "pastor's aide" and would be in his office for up to an hour at a time, almost every day of the school week -- with the door closed! She told how he would leave her in his office and go up to his study behind the baptistery to "pray." She would slip out the side exterior office door and make her way up and around to rendezvous with him in the upstairs study.

Brother Hall's wife confirmed that as secretary, she was required by the pastor to activate a small device on her desk called a "noise machine." It emits a constant white noise for the purpose of insuring confidentiality when the pastor is counseling or on the phone. Since her desk was literally next to his door, she kept it on whenever anyone was inside.

She remembers always having that machine on, so she was incapable of hearing anything, including anyone coming in or going out the side door of the pastor's office. She also recalled numerous times being given errands to run during these sessions.

She has repeatedly voiced her frustration over not being aware of what was happening and doing anything to stop it. I feel so sorry for her. I was devastated at the revelation of Giovanelli's office practices. At best, it was extremely naive of the staff to not even notice what was occurring. These actions were the evidence I needed to corroborate her story.

By digging around, I was able to confirm her story about having a personal church phone given to her by her pastor. Several staff members distinctly remembered having a conversation with Sarah about that very thing. They had asked her why a sixteen-year-old girl in the youth group had a church phone. She would avoid the question.

The staff remembers thinking it was odd, but apparently not enough to say anything to anyone about it. Later, when we got the phone number information from Sarah of that cell phone, we learned that it had been given to a staff member after she graduated.

Why would the church be paying for a teenage girl in the school to have a cell phone? Something didn't add up. This was getting worse by the hour.

Within just a few hours, I had already interviewed enough staff members and church people to confirm my worst fear. There was an unsettling credibility to Sarah's accusations. Many of the people I questioned did not know the details of the accusations. Her original Facebook post was very vague. But by my asking a few questions of people that were there during that time, the details came out.

The information that I was given by multiple people all formed a cohesive narrative.

To add to the already disturbing corroborations, Sarah sent to me more than a dozen screenshots of text messages from Giovanelli. The most recent one was the day before she went public on Facebook. It occurred to me that this man had been in California for nearly four years. It had been twelve years since she had been in school. Yet he was still texting her all hours of the night and early morning. Something was bad wrong here.

He texted her when he was alone and out of town. He texted her on her birthday. He texted her eight days before her birthday reminding her that her birthday was coming up. He texted her about his travel plans in the area. He texted about great memories of his time in Dundalk, especially at the church, complete with "wink" emoji's. He constantly used her full name, first and last, when texting her. It was personal and intimate. It made my skin crawl.

It was impossible now to deny that an inappropriate relationship had existed between the two of them. What was a married man doing texting another man's wife nearly three thousand miles away who he had not seen in almost twelve years? She had stopped coming to church not long after her senior year. Why were they still texting if nothing had been going on?

The next day, which was a Saturday, my phone rang. It was Cameron Giovanelli. He was extremely apologetic to me for what I was having to deal with. He also told me that he was innocent. It wasn't very convincing. He simply said, "What she's accusing me of, I didn't do it."

I told him that I was not going to allow our friendship to taint my objectivity nor my search for answers.

I remember being very honest with him. I told him of her account of being in his office alone him with the door closed for extended periods of time. He admitted to that. I told him of her claim to have been given a phone by him. His response was unsettling.

"There were a lot of cell phones floating around back then."

That was the wrong answer. I explained to him my intent to pursue the details in search of the truth.

"You know me well enough to know that saying you're innocent is not going to be enough for me. I do not have the luxury of taking your word for it. I will get to the bottom of it. I have to know for my own sake and for the sake of my church if these allegations are true."

His answer was simple.

"I know you will."

There was resignation in his voice. He had been in Seattle with a group of students on tour. Incidentally, they were all from my church. Once the Facebook post had been discovered, he was immediately put on administrative leave and had to come home. My heart was broken for his wife and children.

My heart was broken for the church in California and the college, both the faculty and the student body. I resented the position I had been put in. My past experiences had taught me that no matter how bizarre or unbelievable the accusations are, anything is possible.

If I had defaulted to the "he's-innocent-because-I-know-him" argument, I would have never asked the questions that I asked. I would have never listened to her story. I would have never received those damning text messages. I would have never checked the old phone records to verify the cell phone story. I would have closed my ears to anyone and everyone that had a story to tell.

Kicking into "denial mode" when accusations start to fly is a massive truth inhibitor.

16

My Promise

*"Better is it that thou shouldest not vow,
than that thou shouldest vow and not pay."*
Ecclesiastes 5:5

* * *

When I spoke to Sarah the first time, I asked her what she wanted. Her answer was simple. She emphatically stressed she did not want this man to be able to do to someone else what he had done to her. It was not her initial desire to press charges. She was not interested in creating headlines.

I asked her specifically what I could do. She asked me to please see that he was fired from his position as the president of GSBC to keep anybody else from becoming his victim. I assured her that I would do my best. I also assured her that under no circumstances would I allow this scandal to be swept under the rug.

In the short time that I had investigated her story, I found it to be disturbingly credible. I promised her that I would do everything I could to keep this from becoming a "cold case" that falls through the cracks and nothing happens. I was convinced her story was credible, and I could not pretend otherwise.

In multiple conversations with the people at NVBC, I repeated my conviction that these allegations were credible. I admitted that it was impossible to know if every accusation was true. The only ones who would know the truth about every accusation was Cameron Giovanelli, Sarah Jackson and God Almighty.

When a pastor takes a teenage girl into his office, shuts the door, and instructs those outside the door to drown out the noise, he then forfeits any claim of innocence. Her claims of being upstairs in the study, their multiple rendezvous at various locations around town, behind the shopping center, and other places would be nearly impossible to verify.

She claimed he would walk to church from the parsonage for the sole purpose of being able to talk to her on his cell phone. Multiple people, including the deacons, confirmed that the pastor would walk to church often during that time. The parsonage is about a mile from the church. Many of her specifics and details would be difficult to prove or disprove. I did not let that obscure the fact that enough of her story was verified by multiple people.

Not a single person I spoke with wanted these allegations to be true. Not a person in my church or on my staff had a personal vendetta against this man. They simply answered my questions with simple answers. The answers were given with no knowledge of anyone else's answers. They did not have the opportunity to assemble and collaborate. Yet each person I spoke with said the same thing.

On Sunday, May 13th, I gave a brief statement to our church after the morning service. I kept it simple and to the point. I mentioned there were allegations against the former pastor posted on social media. I assured the church that I was dealing with it, and once I found out more I would let them know. I encouraged them to pray for wisdom and guidance.

My church knows me well enough to know that when I say I am dealing with something, then that is exactly what I am doing. Our congregation was thankful we were supporting Sarah in these ways.

Early Monday morning, I began getting phone calls and text messages that indicated there were possibly other victims. When I use the word "victim" here, I am referring to women who were accusing Giovanelli of unwanted or inappropriate attention. This was going from bad to worse.

I remember telling my deacons when this all started that if Sarah's allegations were true, she would not be the only one. I remembered the long list of victims who had come forward after I went public with my own story. There are always more victims. My instinct proved to be correct. Between those who had reached out to Sarah in response to her post, and those who contacted me, it was evident this was not only credible, but much bigger and worse than we had originally thought.

I immediately began to track down these other women and listen to their stories. They proved credible as well. I was sent screenshots of late night text messages between Giovanelli and another young woman. It was so far out of bounds that I was astounded. The audacity! The feelings I had for my friend went from pity to outrage. The pattern of behavior that was uncovered was one of a deceptive, manipulating sexual predator.

Using as my intermediary, I began trying to convey the urgency and seriousness of what I had uncovered to the leadership at North Valley. I begged for someone at North Valley to take these concerns seriously. The message that I kept getting was that they believed Giovanelli's claims of innocence. He said he didn't do it, and they believed him.
I pleaded with them to call me and allow me to share my findings. No one did.

Later that day, I received word from Sarah that she was going down to the police station the next day and file formal charges. I called my deacons in for an emergency meeting.
I still did not have the notebook with all of Sarah's allegations. I felt like a sitting duck. I had done everything in my power to find out what happened, but this thing was far more involved than I had imagined.

It was during that deacons' meeting that Sarah and her husband called me. I put them on speaker phone and introduced them to my deacons. I again expressed our sympathy for what she had experienced. I asked her to please tell us what happened. She started telling her story.

For over half an hour, she told of the months of grooming. Their first kiss. The months and months of sexual activity. She named names, places, dates. Valentine's Day gifts; Christmas gifts. She provided a vast amount of details. I was taking notes as fast as I could but I do not know shorthand. I could not keep up with the flow of information. It was like sitting in front of a gushing fire hydrant.

I finally stopped writing and just listened. I watched the faces of the deacons go from pity, to disbelief, to brokenness and tears. We were all crying by the time she stopped. I looked at those men in my office. We were all physically and emotionally drained. I began speaking.

"Sarah, for what it is worth, I believe you."

I looked at the deacons. "What about you men? Do you believe her?" Each of them answered in the affirmative. I spoke again.

"What do you want me to do? What can our church do to help you?" Her answer was quick and simple.

"I want him fired. I do not want him to be able to do this again to another girl. I really do not want to go to the police. I am not trying to get him thrown in jail. I just want him out of the ministry. That is all I ask."

I was genuinely surprised at her request. After what she had just told me, I personally wanted to see him rot in prison. As a dad with teenage girls, and as a pastor, my outrage at the details she shared made me sick to my stomach.

"I really need you to meet with me or with one of the ladies on my staff. I need that notebook so that I can provide Dr. Trieber and North Valley with these details. They need to hear this. I assure you, if I have anything to do with it, he will be fired before this day is out. I will do my best to make sure that not only is he fired, but he will never be able to do this again. You have my word. This will not get covered up. This will not be swept under the rug. That is my promise to you."

She decided not to go to the police the next day. Her only reason for even thinking about doing it was she felt it was the only way to get him fired. I promised her I would convey the seriousness of the allegations to the leadership at North Valley Baptist. We hung up the phone.
The atmosphere in my office was heavy. One of my deacons was so angry that he was in tears.

"It happened!" He blurted it out forcefully. "This happened. Right here in this office."

I nodded my head. "I believe it did, too."

"Pastor, I have been in the interrogation room for many an interrogation, and I have never heard a witness who was more convincing than that woman was. You can mark it down. It happened."

We were all visibly shaken by the story we had just heard. They had been in full support of my pursuit of the truth from day one, but now they were adamant. This could not be ignored.

After they left, I received a call from informing me that Giovanelli had tendered his resignation from the college. I was relieved to hear that. I asked for a copy of the resignation letter, and I had it within minutes. I called Sarah to tell her that he was no longer on staff because he had resigned. She seemed content at the outcome. I was not satisfied yet.

I asked for confirmation from the leadership that his resignation had been accepted. They would not provide it. This was Monday afternoon, and I still had not been contacted by anyone from the church or college. I asked for a phone call confirming that his resignation was final and not just a ploy. No one called.

I got suspicious. I had started to think this ordeal was over, but I was wrong. This was not over. Not by a long shot.

Our legal representation wrote an official press release in case the media called me for a statement. So far, I had not been contacted by anyone and was grateful. I did not want to try and explain what happened and why. I did not want to be put in the position of having to apologize for another man's sins. I just wanted our church to survive the terrible shame and stigma that would be attached to us because of this. More importantly, I wanted Sarah to finally be able to put this mess behind her.

On Tuesday afternoon, I texted Pastor Jack Trieber and asked him to call me at his earliest convenience. He didn't respond. You must understand. I had no problem with this pastor. He was a victim of circumstances just like I was. He had no more control over what had happened twelve years ago than I did. We had both been blindsided by these allegations and were just trying to navigate the storm.

However, the longer they went without contacting me or the victim, the more frustrated and upset I became. I was dealing with a scandal of epic proportions and I could not even get a courtesy call that they were praying for us.

I was not just some pastor on the other side of the country. Our church supported that college for one hundred dollars a month and had done so for a long time. We had sent students there for years. I had flown out there and hired their graduates. We had six students enrolled there, including my own daughter. I could not believe the complete disregard for my repeated requests for a phone call.

My promise to Sarah Jackson proved to be a far greater challenge than I had imagined. On Wednesday morning, I texted Giovanelli and asked him to call me. He did. He told me that he had tendered his resignation, but that Pastor Trieber wanted him to fight these "false accusations" and defend his reputation.

I told him he had no choice but to step down. In no uncertain terms, I assured him that my deacons and I were confident that enough of the allegations against him were credible that there was *no way* he could fight it. I told the leadership that he needed to resign immediately, and I would not let this be another cover-up.

He assured me that he had resigned two days prior and that he had no intentions of fighting it. He told me that he would tell them what I said.

I was still upset that nobody had called me. What were they doing out there? This scandal had gone public on Facebook on Friday of the previous week, and here it was six days later and nobody out there had made any effort to contact me, my deacons, the victim – anyone.

I could not get over the lack of initiative. I told him if they tried to cover this up that I would have no choice but to go public with everything I had learned. I was not playing around.

At 12:26 p.m. Eastern Standard Time my phone rang. It was Dr. Jack Trieber calling me. Finally.

I spoke for nearly half an hour with him, his business manager and his attorney. I will simply say that my conversation was blunt and convincing. Before we got off the phone, I stressed to them that this could not be covered up. I urged them to deal with this in a very decisive and transparent fashion. I shared with them my confidence that this was credible.

By now, another woman had come forward with accusations. I became overwhelmed with the growing number of allegations. In my conversation with Dr. Trieber, distinctly told him that I was "one thousand percent committed" to this situation NOT being covered up. I emphasized that if they didn't handle these allegations to the satisfaction of the victim, I would.

They assured me repeatedly that they would be taking action immediately and that they would make an official statement following their evening service. Some accused me later of "threatening" that pastor. My only request was that they take a public stand against sexual abuse.

My phone rang about two hours later. It was my contact at who called to tell me that my phone conversation had done its work. Pastor Trieber had not only accepted Cameron Giovanelli's resignation, but had told him to leave the state and never set foot back on the property. They were appalled at the horrible nature of the allegations and what my investigation had uncovered. They were going to announce their decision to the church after the evening service.

I hung up the phone relieved that finally this nightmare was going to end.

I was wrong again.

That night, I watched the announcement that was aired on the church's livestream. What I witnessed was the biggest debacle I had ever seen. The layers of misinformation crammed into that brief public statement were incredible. Who wrote this thing? It was not only wrong, but it was purposefully misleading. I was flabbergasted.

Here it is in its entirety.

> **Official Statement**
>
> *It has come to our attention that allegations of inappropriate conduct have been made against Cameron Giovanelli, a member of our staff. Upon receipt of the notice of the allegations, we immediately placed him on administrative leave of all activities and responsibilities, to conduct a thorough and honest investigation. During the course of that investigation, Cameron Giovanelli tendered his resignation to the ministry and his resignation has been accepted. All responsibilities of any nature whatsoever were permanently and immediately terminated with receipt of his resignation. There were no allegations of wrongdoing of any nature that involved the ministries of North Valley Baptist Church or Golden State Baptist College. Please keep our ministry, the Giovanelli family and all others involved in your prayers.*

I tried to absorb what I was hearing. It was beyond belief. It was nothing like what I had been assured of on the phone just a few hours earlier. This was not only an attempt to downplay the scandal, but the outright deception in this statement was appalling.

Let me unpack this "official statement."

It has come to our attention that allegations of inappropriate conduct have been made against Cameron Giovanelli...

Inappropriate conduct? Allegations of inappropriate conduct? Could they possibly be any more vague? Could we not at least take into consideration that more than a year of alleged sexual activity between a pastor and a sixteen-year-old girl might qualify as significantly more than "inappropriate conduct"?

I would have been thrilled if they had simply said "allegations of immoral and possibly illegal conduct involving a minor." Inappropriate conduct can be pretty much anything from flirting with another man's wife to cussing someone out in the parking lot.

The meticulous downplaying of the event went on.

...a member of our staff.

A member of our staff? He was the president of the Bible college! Some believe he was being groomed to be the next pastor; who knows? But to call him "a member of our staff"? The spin was making me dizzy!

Upon receipt of the notice of the allegations, we immediately placed him on administrative leave of all activities and responsibilities,

This part of the statement was true. He did not even go to church on Sunday, which was a big deal, since he was the song leader.

...to conduct a thorough and honest investigation.

This is where my head almost exploded. An investigation? Seriously? It took them six days to call me!
Who conducted an investigation?
The victim assured me that she had not been contacted. Not a single person in my church had been asked a single question. I had only had that one conversation, but that was after getting the silent treatment for almost six days. There was no investigation. Period.
The only effort that I am aware of on their part was a phone call they made to one of my former deacons that lives out west. The man making the inquiry was looking to establish that Sarah was some kind of nutcase with an ax to grind. When that was immediately refuted by my former deacon, and my character and integrity were reiterated to the caller, the conversation ended. Whoever made that phone call was not looking for the truth. They were looking for dirt on Sarah Jackson.

There was no investigation – much less one that was "thorough and honest." The extent of their "investigation" appears to be simply asking Giovanelli if he did it. Of course he said he didn't. End of "investigation." There still has not been an investigation.

During the course of that investigation, Cameron Giovanelli tendered his resignation to the ministry and his resignation has been accepted.

Again, there was no investigation. Why did they have to keep saying that?

All responsibilities of any nature whatsoever, were permanently and immediately terminated with receipt of his resignation.

From all indications, this part of the statement was true. However, they conveniently left out the small detail that nearly forty-eight hours lapsed between the time when he tendered his resignation and the time that it was accepted. It appeared to me they were far more concerned about minimizing the fallout than they were about anything else.

There were no allegations of wrongdoing of any nature that involved the ministries of North Valley Baptist Church or Golden State Baptist College.

This was not true, and they knew it. I had told them during our phone conversation that Sarah, upon graduating from our Christian school, had attended their Bible College. The relationship she allegedly had with Cameron Giovanelli in Dundalk continued during her time at college, and after she came back home from the fall semester. She did not return to Golden State. But to say that these allegations did not involve the college was simply not true. She was a student there while it was happening. Just because the allegations were twelve years old did not mean that it did not involve the college.

Please keep our ministry, the Giovanelli family and all others involved in your prayers.

There was no specific mention of the victim or her family, unless she was part of the "all others involved." There was no mention of the credibility of these allegations. With the way the statement was worded, it sounded like the good guy was resigning. They looked like the good guys for not firing him. If not for those pesky "allegations of inappropriate behavior," none of this would be happening!

Once the official statement was read, a signal was given to the livestream crew. They cut the cameras and the pastor then proceeded to talk about how much he loved and appreciated the accused and his family. He talked about how much he owed him and how well the college was doing because of his fine leadership.

I was speechless. What I had just witnessed was the standard response by many ministries. Every tool in the toolbox was utilized in that misleading and inaccurate statement. It had been nothing but carefully crafted untruths for the consumption of their unsuspecting church members.

And I was one of the only people on the planet who knew it.

17

Ripple Effect

"The LORD on high is mightier than the noise of many waters, yea, than the mighty waves of the sea."
Psalms 93:4

* * *

The next morning, Sarah was scheduled to meet one of our ladies at a nearby restaurant to deliver the notebook. I had urged her to make detailed notes of her story. I told Pastor Trieber of the pending meeting with Sarah, and that I would deliver a copy of all her notes to them as soon as I had it in my possession.

I was sure that her notes would communicate her story was far more than just a random allegation. It would convey a pattern of deviant behavior that needed to be exposed.

What I did not count on was Sarah's reaction to the "official statement" that had been streamed online following the Wednesday night service. Her reaction was the same as mine. She could not believe what she witnessed. She decided the diplomatic route wasn't going to work. It was time to do something. And she wasn't playing. She smelled the same cover-up in the works that I did.

She was not having it. Her reaction was understandable. Sarah did what she had threatened to do from the beginning. She cancelled her Thursday morning meeting with us, and took her notes straight to the police. She had simply wanted her abuser to face the consequences of his actions and be exposed for what he was. Neither one of us had any confidence that would be the outcome after watching that fiasco of a public statement after that Wednesday night service.

She kept her notebook. I never saw it. I was unable to pursue any more of the allegations. I was unable to forward my findings on to the leadership at North Valley Baptist Church. They later tried to blame my failure to send it to them as justification for their inaction. They refused to accept the fact it was their fault that Sarah decided to go to the authorities with her story. After their botched attempt to "explain" what happened, she realized she had no other recourse.

The church had let her down. Again.

I was at a loss for words. I had promised her that this would not be swept under the rug. I had promised her that this would not become another "cover-up." But it had. Her abuser was getting the white-glove treatment, and she was the one getting the boot.

From all indications, she didn't matter to them. I didn't matter. Our church and our deacons agreeing that this was a legitimate story didn't matter. We were all expendable.

Forget that we were a supporting church. Forget that we had students enrolled there. Forget that we were friends and co-laborers in the ministry. We were all expendable.

The next morning, Friday, was a week after this storm had hit our church. I walked into the morning staff meeting frustrated at the turn of events. Sarah had rightly involved the police, and our church would now face the publicity of the actions of this man's sinful deeds.

We have a precious group of people here in Dundalk, Maryland. We are literally on the edge of Baltimore city. Our congregation is made up of a mixture of more seasoned saints as well as many new converts who are just learning what it means to be a Christian. The thought that our church would be in the newspapers, and on the evening news, turned my stomach.

All I could visualize were the Baltimore newspaper headlines: "Baptist Pastor Accused of Sexually Molesting a Minor." I could see the news reports with our church's name and reputation being dragged through the mud. I could see people mistakenly thinking it was talking about me. I envisioned news reporters broadcasting live from our parking lot. The thought of the repercussions made my head swim.

I did not want to think about where this was going to end. I have been around long enough to know that the church does not always get a fair shake when it comes to journalists and reporters. I fully expected to have the floor pulled out from under me by those in the unbelieving realm. I anticipated getting hammered by the outsiders that already do not appreciate what we are trying to do in their community.

What I did not expect was the opposition that was brewing from my own friends.

As we met for our morning staff meeting, it was brought to my attention that the rumors had already started swirling out in Santa Clara. The spin and the story being spread was that I had mishandled the whole thing. It was being told that I had falsely accused the former pastor and had provided no evidence. He was the victim, and I was the one who had brought all of this about.

I could not believe what I was hearing. This was all my fault? I had mishandled the situation? Are you kidding me?

My patience had run out. Giving others the chance to control the narrative had failed miserably. The part of me that did not want to make waves disappeared. The gloves were about to come off. It was time to go "scorched earth."

I had promised Sarah this would not be covered up, and I had to keep that promise. I prayed for a while to calm my nerves because I was devastated at the turn of events. How in the world did I turn out to be the bad guy?

I asked God for clarity and for direction. The only thing I could think of was to set up a camera and just speak from my heart. With articles and blogs, it is difficult to discern a person's true heart. I had something to say, and this was the only way I knew to say it. This was the only way I knew to say it like it needed to be said.

I called Sarah and told her I was about to make a video and post it, and asked if she was OK with it. She said she was. I called my deacons and told them that I felt I had no choice but to set the record straight in a big way. They agreed with me and gave me their full support. I felt I had no choice but to defend myself and my church. More importantly, I had to defend Sarah.

One of my assistant pastors set up the video camera in my upstairs study. After praying again, we started recording. I asked God to help me say only what He wanted me to say. I made my case in a passionate and heartfelt way.

As I leaned toward the camera that Friday morning, I felt God's peace flood my soul.

The truth is paramount. Sometimes the truth hurts, but it must be told. One thing is certain. I did exactly what God told me to do, and I did it exactly how He told me to do it.

I sent Sarah and her husband the video to review. She called me back weeping and was so grateful that I would be willing to do that for her. She didn't know it, but I was doing this for all of us.

The truth had to be told. It was evident to me that if people were going to get anything resembling the truth, they were not going to get it from the church in Santa Clara. All that was coming out of there was Fake News. I could not stand by and let it go unchallenged. I knew the truth, so it was up to me to be the one to tell it.

I sent the video to each of my deacons to review. They endorsed it completely. That was all I needed. I had the support of the victim I was trying to help. I had the support of my church leaders. I had the leadership of the Spirit. I was fully prepared for the waves that I knew this video would create.

I prayed again. Then I uploaded the video. It was Friday, May 18.

18

Tidal Wave

"The floods have lifted up, O LORD, the floods have lifted up their voice; the floods lift up their waves."
Psalms 93:3

* * *

I expected feedback. I was not ready for the amount of it. To make sure the video was seen by those that needed to see it, we put it on YouTube and Facebook. We boosted it with some key words in order to reach the specific demographic to whom I felt it pertained.

I received a few critical emails for boosting the video. I didn't understand their logic. If I didn't want anyone to see the video, why bother to make it in the first place?

My communication with the leadership at North Valley earlier in the week had been clear – if you don't handle this, I will. They didn't, so I did.

The victim didn't like how they handled it. I didn't like how they handled it. The feelings were mutual. I'm sure they didn't like how *I* handled it. At least I was kind enough to give them first option on dealing with it. It wasn't my fault that they opted for the good-ole-boys IFB spin cycle.

We boosted the video on Facebook to a specifically targeted audience. I asked God to help it make a difference. The scandal that had just fallen into my lap was not an isolated case. I knew there were others.

The ensuing effort to cover it up and minimize it was also not an isolated attempt. Remember, I am a fifth-generation independent Baptist preacher. I have been in a host of churches in the last forty-six years. I knew that this would hit a nerve with God's people. I knew that I was kicking over an ant bed, so to speak. But it had to be done.

The amount of views climbed to upwards of 75,000 within just a few days. My inbox was slammed with emails. My phone started ringing and did not stop for weeks. Nine months later, I am still receiving phone calls. I got hundreds of text messages. The response was overwhelming.
Believe it or not, I received very few negative responses.

The stories that hit my inbox were heartbreaking. I got letters from mothers all over America whose children had been abused inside their church. I got emails from church members who had witnessed unimaginable sexual crimes and cover-ups. I got letters from people who had reported crimes and been kicked out of the church for doing so. I got everything from one-sentence notes of encouragement and support, to long, detailed stories of personal pain and hurt.

My whole world came to a screeching halt. For days, all I did was answer emails, text messages and phone calls. People from all over the world reached out to me. Missionaries on foreign fields made contact. Pastors and their wives from all over the United States took the time to write or call to thank me for taking a stand.

It became abundantly clear to me after the video went out that the silent majority had been silenced for way too long. People saw me as a person they could come to with their stories and finally be heard. They looked at me as a person who would take the time to listen, and not turn away.

The requests poured in for me to do more – to say more – to bring more attention to this national epidemic of sexual abuse and cover-ups in our churches. I never in my wildest imagination anticipated the reaction that video would cause.

Fourteen days after Sarah had gone public with her accusations, she received a personal phone call from Dr. Jack Trieber. She had asked me for his phone number, and I had given it to her. She reached out to him asking if she could speak with him. He called her back in a conference call with several others in the room.

I will not divulge the details of the call, but suffice it to say that Sarah was grateful. Once that phone call had been facilitated, I felt that the video had served its purpose. I pulled it down off of YouTube and Facebook. I did not feel it was necessary to continue to beat a dead horse. The word was out. The truth had been told. I caught a lot of flak for taking it down. A lot of people thought I had been intimidated or threatened. That was not the case. Some thought I was having second thoughts. That was not true either. I put it up because I felt that is what I needed to do, and I took it down for the same reason.

Little did I know that the tidal wave was about to grow into a tsunami.

19

Tsunami

*"I sink in deep mire, where there is no standing:
I am come into deep waters, where the floods overflow me."*
Psalms 69:2

* * *

The number of victims continued to grow. A woman named Donna Hudson reached out to me in a heartbreaking email. Her email told of going to Cameron Giovanelli for marital counseling and the sordid affair that developed. She had seen Sarah's Facebook post and felt it was time for her to tell her own story. Her name was Donna Peters back when all of these activities allegedly occurred.

Her email was long and detailed. She was dealing with an enormous amount of shame and hurt. I immediately reached out to her and after a couple of failed attempts, I finally got her to agree to meet with me and my wife.

Donna brought her best friend with her to the meeting with us. She and Donna had shared all their secrets with each other. Donna had told her friend about her pastor's texts and romantic attention. Her friend confirmed that she had been aware of the details of the affair both before, during and after. She verified everything that Donna told us that day.

Her story was pitiful. She and her husband had been married by Pastor Giovanelli. Their children were enrolled in the school and they attended the services at Calvary Baptist Church. Several months after her wedding, Donna alleged that she and her pastor exchanged cellphone numbers during marital counseling.

He counseled her and her husband together a time or two, then he spoke with her alone five or six times, according to her recollection. Their text messages started as words of encouragement and Bible verses. It slowly turned into inappropriate comments and erotic conversation.

Giovanelli's wife had taken a group of women up to the Sword of the Lord Conference at a church in New Jersey. Donna did not recall the name of the conference, but remembered that the women were all together somewhere for a few days in another state. She said that she and Giovanelli had texted each other inappropriately the entire time, including late into the night.

Their texting resulted in his invitation to meet her at a local pumpkin farm. He brought his children and she brought hers. They pretended to accidently meet and spent a long time together while their children played. She recalled him going into the store and buying her some things.

The next week, one thing led to another and eventually it resulted in a rendezvous at the pastor's house. It was then that she alleged that she and Giovanelli had sexual relations. Donna remembered immediately calling her friend and telling her what just happened. Her friend confirmed that conversation.

I began to cross-examine Donna about the timeline. My wife and I asked every sort of question we could think of to double-check her story. She described the inside of the Giovanelli's home and confirmed the timeline. My staff and I checked the church calendar from 2010 and the timeline fit with the ladies' trip to New Jersey.

The wife of one of my deacons recalled a time when Giovanelli specifically told her to let him know when Donna was on the property. She recalled him saying that he did not want to take a chance of running into her because of how she dressed. Imagine that.

My wife and I sat heartbroken as we listened to this woman who had gone to her pastor for counsel on how to be a better wife, only to be seduced and victimized by his charisma and charm. In a time of extreme vulnerability, she became the prey. The shepherd was a wolf.

She said that Giovanelli started pulling away from her after their sexual rendezvous at the parsonage. She thought there was another woman taking him away from her. My wife and I looked at each other in shame. He was married, having an affair with a woman in the church, and she thought there was ANOTHER woman. She said that he told her what they had done was not right, and that he had gotten right with the Lord. He told her that the two of them would have to take their affair to their grave. He never texted or interacted with her again.

She said their adulterous affair abruptly ended with the pastor preaching a series on the marriage. She expressed to me and my wife that she sat there in disbelief as she listened to a man she had been having an affair with for months preach about being a faithful and loving husband.

She left the church and never returned. She took her children out of the school. She later got a divorce and is now remarried. She was just more collateral damage -- another broken and ruined life thrown to the curb. Another mangled lamb devoured and spit out by the ravening wolves.

I called Giovanelli and told him that another woman had come forward alleging an affair. He asked me if she was a minor. That seemed to be his only concern. I cannot tell you how much that bothered me. I hung up the phone after that conversation and I have never spoken to him again.

After the meeting in my office, Donna called my wife and told her some things that she had not felt comfortable talking about in front of me. She gave my wife a lot of very specific details; things she would never have mentioned with me in the room.

My wife asked her if Cameron Giovanelli's wife were to call her and ask for specifics, would she be willing to talk to her? Donna told my wife that she would do anything she could if it would help Sarah Jackson get justice.

Donna later told her story in several national publications. Her pain from the entire ordeal is still ongoing. She will never get over what happened to her. Our church is doing everything within our power to try to help her heal.

I am grateful for Donna's permission to share her painful story.

Sophia Lee, a reporter from World Magazine, contacted me after seeing my video. She had questions. I was hesitant at first. Just how far was I willing to go to help the victims who had come to me? How committed was I to their cause? Was I prepared to see this through? Was I willing to walk through whatever door the Lord opened up in front of me? She was working on a story that far exceeded my church and this situation. I felt I had no choice but to answer her questions.

The September 15 edition of World Magazine featured a story entitled "We Too." The magazine covered a variety of church scandals involving sexual abuse and cover-ups, including the one that we encountered at our church. The article went on for ten pages and included direct quotes, a photo of Giovanelli, among others, and dates. I was amazed at the willingness of the victims to share their story. Their courage was unbelievable.

Not long after that article came out in World Magazine, I got a call from a reporter with the Dallas-Fort Worth Star-Telegram. Sarah Smith was doing an in-depth investigative report on sexual abuse in independent Baptist churches. It started when she covered an incident in Mesquite, Texas in February of 2018. A couple of bus ministry workers had been arrested and charged with multiple counts of sexual assault on a child. Though he knew about it, the pastor had failed to notify the authorities for over two weeks and was arrested for it.

As she covered that story, she started seeing a pattern. People were commenting on their Facebook posts about how they knew this preacher or this church that had similar things happen. She started following the trail of bread crumbs and made a startling discovery. Even though these churches were "independent," they all seemed to somehow be connected. Either by relatives or Bible college affiliations; there was an undeniable interwoven network of associations.

After eight months of investigation, her findings were published in the Star-Telegram on Sunday, December 9, 2018.

Prior to publishing her four-part series of articles entitled "Spirit of Fear," she called me several times to discuss my past abuses that I referred to in my video, as well as the current storm we had just weathered. She was polite and professional. She never gave me the impression that she "had it out" for independent Baptists. She simply started pulling on a thread and discovered that it was attached to something big.

The four-part series of articles was published in a large number of newspapers across the country. It was featured in newspapers in California, Miami, Raleigh, Kansas City, Tennessee, and Michigan to name a few. It was also covered by Baptist News Today and Christianity Today. Several big websites picked up the story. It was featured on DrudgeReport.com for a couple of days. It was covered on CBC and on Huffington Post's website, along with many other news sites and religious blogs. The article quoted me directly by name and told of our scandal. The whole world now knew.

It was interesting to me how many leaders in our fundamental ranks finally felt compelled to speak up. It seemed that everybody was writing an article or posting an opinion on the subject. What stood out to me was the number of pastors, Bible college presidents, leaders and evangelists who contacted me after my video went viral. They were in full support of my effort to curb the tide. They were all for it. They admired my stand and my courage. They extended their hand in fellowship and gratitude.

I couldn't help but wish some of them would have used their platform to publicly support what I was trying to do. We need more people who are willing to risk everything for the sake of truth and right. Imagine what would happen if every Christian in America did that.

20

Aftermath

*"Open thy mouth, judge righteously,
and plead the cause of the poor and needy."*
Proverbs 31: 9

* * *

It was only a few days after North Valley's official statement that I learned where Cameron Giovanelli was. Instead of hopping on a plane to Baltimore to confront his accusers and to try and clear his name, he was busy with job interviews. Instead of coming to the church he pastored for eleven years, and striving to retain his reputation, he was preoccupied with salvaging his career.

It seems that Dr. Greg Neal, pastor of Immanuel Baptist Church in Jacksonville, Florida, couldn't resist such a highly talented man who had suddenly hit the market at a massive discount.

I never cease to be amazed at the "bargain hunters" in the ministry. After being exiled from North Valley and GSBC, Giovanelli's options were extremely limited. He could have gotten an honest job to provide for his family, but that would have been too honorable.

As soon as I heard that Giovanelli was going to Greg Neal's church, I flipped. The backstory on this new development made this almost impossible to believe.

My last trip to North Valley's Pastor's Conference, Greg Neal approached me at my book table and we struck up a conversation. I had never met him, but we had a lot in common. We both grew up in the ministry. We enjoyed writing. There were a lot of similarities in the way we thought about the ministry. We stood around and talked for a long time.

After he left, Cameron Giovanelli walked up. I asked him if he knew anything about Greg Neal. He looked at me strange and said that he did. I asked him if he was a good man. He warned me to be careful of him because he had skeletons in his closet.

I was surprised. He certainly had seemed like a nice guy. I was disappointed to hear that. I asked Giovanelli, "What skeletons?"

He wouldn't tell me. Instead, he told me to do an internet search of Greg Neal and I would see it for myself.

So I did.

It seems that back in 2011, a video surfaced that was made in 2001. The news articles I read accused Greg Neal of voyeurism. He was accused of hiding a video camera in his office and recording young women changing clothes.

The video was discovered in a box of videos of basketball game footage.

I read the articles and no official charges were made. The State's Attorney's office believed they had a solid case, but the statute of limitations had expired. Their church went bankrupt and had to move across town. They changed the name from Berean Baptist Church to Immanuel Baptist Church. He insisted he was innocent, and the church, or what was left of it, stood with him.

I was extremely disappointed at what I learned. I avoided Greg Neal for the rest of the conference. I did not know what to say.

A few weeks later, Greg asked me to contribute an article to his new magazine. I told him that I would pray about it. I called Cameron. I asked him what he thought about it. He begged me not to do it. He promised me if I even as much as wrote for Greg Neal's magazine, it would hurt my reputation and my testimony. I was sobered by his insistence.

Not too long after that, Greg Neal informed me that he was going to be traveling in our area, and wanted to know if he could come by and promote his new book, "Satan's Toolbox." He had sent me a copy after meeting him at the conference in California. It was a very well-written book and dealt with the attacks of Satan against the Christian and the men of God. It was evident that the book was birthed in his heart as a result of the scandal and the fallout that had ensued in his own life.

At first, I told him he could come by, but the more I thought about it, the possibility that he could be guilty of the charges started eating at me. I wrote him a long email and told him that I was struggling with what I heard about him, and that I changed my mind and I didn't want him to come to my church.

He responded graciously. I asked him if I could call him and hear his story. He agreed.

I picked up the phone and called Greg Neal. I told him that several people had advised me not to have anything to do with him. I told him that several of my preacher friends had told me not to even write for his magazine and that their manner was so persuasive I felt compelled to believe them. However, I wanted to hear his side of the story. I told him that I felt it was only fair to hear both sides when an accusation was made.

He agreed and told me his story. By the time he had finished defending himself, I was relieved. He said that it was a group of people in the church that wanted to destroy him, his dad, Dr. Tom Neal, and their church.

I remembered seeing the articles in the newspaper with people standing in front of the church protesting with posters. They were calling the church a cult and all sorts of things. It looked very sketchy.

Hearing him tell it made sense to me. He swore he was innocent, and that he had taken two lie detector tests and passed them. He said his wife believed him. His church believed him. They had made him the senior pastor after his dad retired. There seemed to be a lot of unanswered questions. It was just a big mess.

After speaking with him, I felt better. He had a kind and meek demeanor. He didn't sound guilty. He didn't act guilty. I was just glad he didn't get angry at me for asking him if it was true. His attitude made me feel he was OK.

I later agreed to submit an article for his magazine. Not too long after that, Dr. Tom Neal called me. He had been following me on Twitter and was impressed with my stand. He asked if I would be willing to come preach in October for their big Conference. My schedule was open that week, so I told him I would.

I have never met Tom Neal. I would not have known him if he had walked in the door. But he liked me and wanted me to come preach, so I told him I would do my best to make it. He was glad and thanked me for agreeing to come.

I will never forget his statement to me on the phone. "Brother Shiflett, you are a maverick. I like that about you."

I remember being amused. I've been called that for twenty five years. So I put the date for the October conference down on my calendar.

After I launched my video, I sent both Tom Neal and Greg Neal a text message with the link to it. I told them that if after seeing my video, they were uncomfortable having me in their meeting in October, I would understand. I graciously offered to disinvite myself if they felt that was necessary. Neither of them responded to me. I tried again a few days later, but still no answer. I finally sent them a text message telling them that I would just not come to the meeting. I was kind and professional. They would not respond to me. I have decided to include a few screenshots of some of the conversation that took place because things have a tendency to be exaggerated or misrepresented at times.

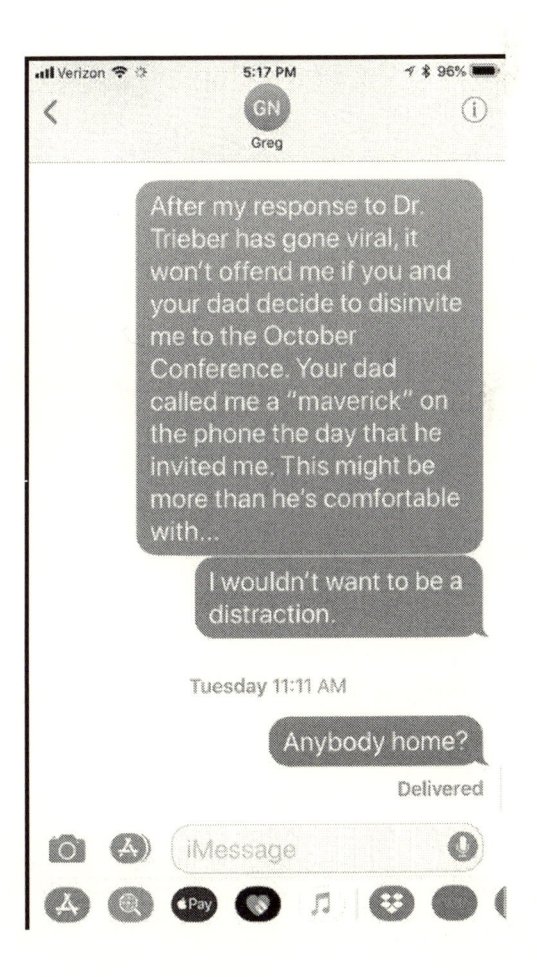

> After my response to Dr. Trieber has gone viral, it won't offend me if you and your dad decide to disinvite me to the October Conference. Your dad called me a "maverick" on the phone the day that he invited me. This might be more than he's comfortable with...
>
> I wouldn't want to be a distraction.

Tuesday 11:11 AM

> Anybody home?
> Delivered

> I have reached out to both you and your son in regards to the meeting in October you had asked me to preach in. Neither of you have responded. It might be possible that neither of you got my text message.
>
> After seeing Bob Gray Sr.'s response to my position, and since I know he will be at your conference, I respectfully decline the invitation.
>
> Thank you for the invite.
>
> Pastor Stacey Shiflett

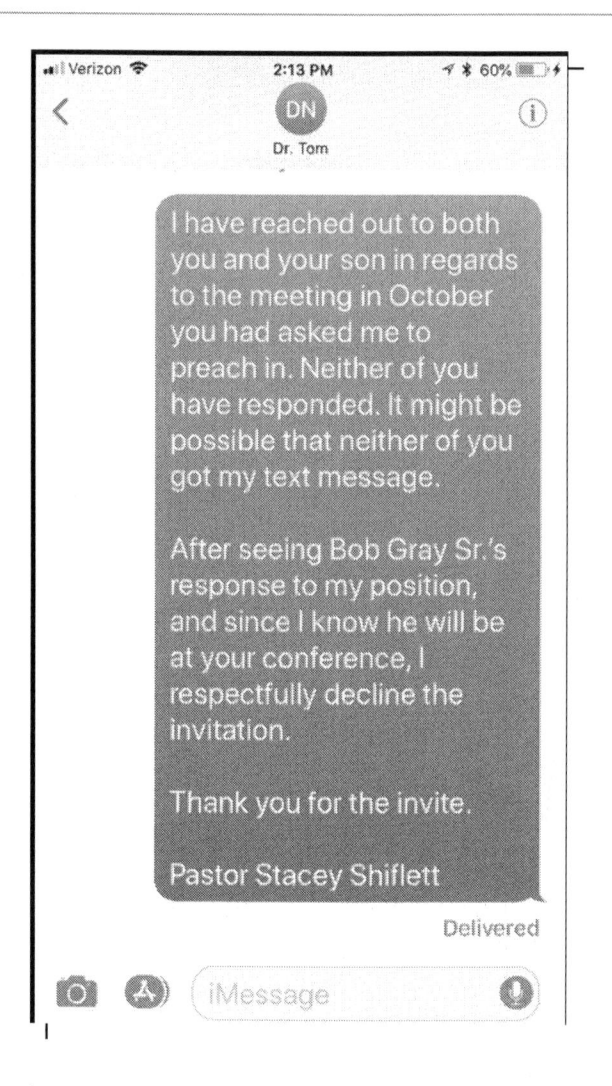

    Imagine my shock at learning that the Giovanelli's were being moved by professional movers from Santa Clara, California all the way to Jacksonville, Florida. Cameron was moving to the church where he believed the pastor had skeletons in his closet. He had advised me not to even write an article for their magazine; now he was moving his family there? How was that possible?

I picked up the phone again. This time I needed answers. Greg wouldn't answer the phone. I texted him and his dad on May 21, 22, 28 and June 2. They would not text back. This went on for two weeks. I finally sent them both a text that I knew they could not ignore.

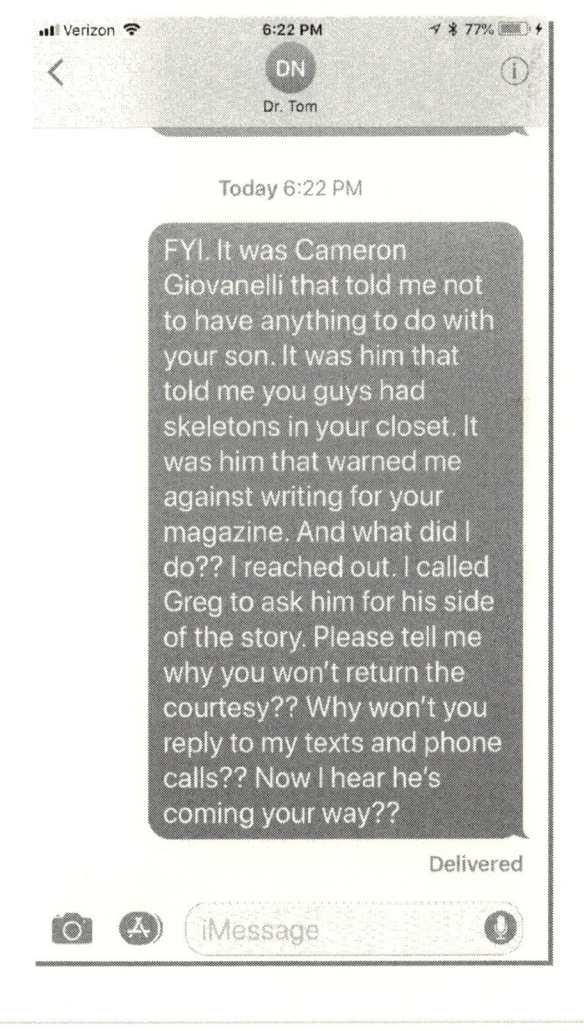

> FYI. It was Cameron Giovanelli that told me not to have anything to do with your son. It was him that told me you guys had skeletons in your closet. It was him that warned me against writing for your magazine. And what did I do?? I reached out. I called Greg to ask him for his side of the story. Please tell me why you won't return the courtesy?? Why won't you reply to my texts and phone calls?? Now I hear he's coming your way??

Tom Neal never responded to my text or answered my phone call. He had called and asked me to come preach for him, but did not have the decency to even respond to me. I had graciously offered to disinvite myself. A simple "OK" would have been nice. I got nothing.

After multiple text messages trying to get Greg Neal to respond to me, he finally agreed. He called me on June 5 and we talked for almost an hour.

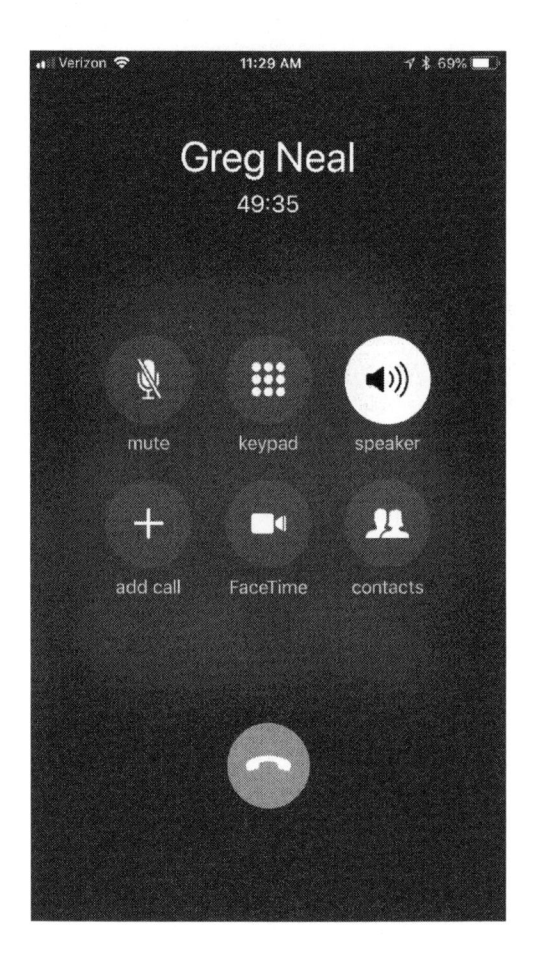

I told him everything. I told him what all had gone on and the incredible amount of corroborating evidence I had gathered. The comment that he made multiple times throughout the conversation was "Let me play devil's advocate" (this coming from the man that wrote the book, "Satan's Toolbox"). The irony was not lost on me.

I was astounded. I was blown away that, after calling him and asking to hear his side of the story when Cameron had told me something bad about him, that he would not do the same. He had no interest in the facts. He'd already told his church that God had led him to move the Giovanelli's to Immanuel Baptist Church. He made it seem to me on the phone that since his wife and Cameron's wife were close friends, and Cameron's wife was the one that wanted to move to their church, that he felt obligated to help them. I'm sure Cameron Giovanelli's talents and skill set had absolutely nothing to do with it.

Nothing I said to him mattered. Greg Neal's kingdom in Jacksonville needed a man with Giovanelli's abilities. Apparently Cameron's charisma and bubbly personality were just too good to pass up. The wheels were literally in motion. The professional movers were already headed to Florida. The Giovanelli family stopped by Disney Land in Anaheim, California on their way to Jacksonville. My daughter bumped into them at the *It's A Small World* attraction. You cannot make this stuff up!

Not a single person from Jacksonville called me to find out if any of the allegations could possibly be true. Not one man in that church with daughters called me or Sarah Jackson to ask a single question. I couldn't believe it. Not one woman from that ministry called to ask what evidence I had. Bringing a man into the church that was under investigation for being an alleged pedophile was obviously no big deal.

After all that had just transpired, Cameron was back in the ministry. Immediately. He and his wife posted a short video July 4th on Greg Neal's brand new YouTube channel. Cameron Giovanelli maintained his innocence in one short sentence, and then changed the subject. He then talked about how good God was to them, and how excited they were to be at Immanuel. His poor wife stood beside him looking like she wanted to be someplace else. It was the most pitiful thing I have ever seen.

The outrage that ensued on social media was off the charts. The response was so brutal that Greg Neal took the video down almost as fast as he put it up. That was the day I put my original response video back up on my YouTube channel.

Cameron Giovanelli is now the assistant pastor of Immanuel Baptist Church. He is the director of Berean Publications. He has a podcast. He has his own website. He's calling every preacher he can think of, and rebuilding his network of friends and associates. He's back on social media. He's traveling around the country preaching and singing for preachers and churches.

I promised Sarah Jackson that Cameron Giovanelli would be finished. He isn't.

I promised her that his alleged sexual abuse against her would not be forgotten. It has.

I assured her that it would not be swept under the rug. It was.

I promised her that Cameron Giovanelli would never have the opportunity to do to anybody else what she said he did to her. Now he does.

Sarah, I am so sorry.

21

Calling Out the Hypocrisy

"The words of a wise man's mouth are gracious; but the lips of a fool will swallow up himself. The beginning of the words of his mouth is foolishness: and the end of his talk is mischievous madness."
Ecclesiastes 10:12, 13

* * *

We stand in our pulpits and warn our people of the dangers of hypocrisy and deceit. We encourage our people to live a life of honesty, godly morals and character. Then when the church is faced with a scandal, the backtracking and flip-flopping that occurs many times is beyond belief.

The only way our churches will be able to restore our credibility is when we get back to conducting the business of the church with integrity. To hear men of God stand in their pulpits, look out over their congregations and make statements that are blatantly false and misleading is reprehensible. The blogs and posts of evangelists and preachers that came to the defense of the accused were so full of inconsistencies that one doesn't even know start to refute it. The blatant misrepresentation and the double-speak is unfathomable.

What is equally disturbing is that nobody ever seems to call these men out on any of this stuff! They can write the most distorted, unintelligible gibberish and nobody says a word. Verses are taken out of context to prop up some of the most unbiblical and ridiculous philosophies. It doesn't seem to matter. These guys maintain their following. They keep on preaching meetings, keep on getting invited to the conferences and continue selling their books.

I shake my head in disbelief. How in the world do they manage to retain any semblance of credibility? Why don't more people speak up and point out their unbiblical philosophies?

I cannot remain silent anymore. I'm calling them on it. I can no longer sit back and let this gross mishandling of the precious Word of God go virtually unchallenged. I would prefer for men with a larger platform and louder voice than I to say something. It doesn't look to me like that is going to happen anytime soon. The hypocrisy and inconsistency of these positions must be exposed. The time for tiptoeing through the tulips has come to an end.

Four days after my video was uploaded, a friend of mine wrote a nine-point rebuke and put it on his website. At the time, Dr. Allen Domelle was both an evangelist as well as the president of Texas Independent Baptist Seminary in

Longview, Texas. He is now pastoring a church in Oklahoma City. He publishes a morning devotional on his website, OldPathsJournal.com, and sends it out each day in an email to those that subscribe to it.

Many of my people are subscribers to his devotionals. He has preached in our church for many years. I have had him in several times since I came in 2014. He would usually preach all day on the Sunday before Thanksgiving. We would fly him in from Texas on Saturday and enjoyed great fellowship together during his visit. We became friends over the year.

It would be safe to say that Allen Domelle and I would probably agree on most subjects. We have a lot in common. My only gripe with him was the fact that he is a big Alabama fan. Being a Georgia Bulldog fan all my life, I hate Alabama. We ribbed each other every year during the championship games with text messages and funny memes.

The day I posted my video, I sent him the YouTube link via text message. Later on that Friday evening, he called me. He asked me what was going on. I shared a little bit with him about what was occurring in our church and how committed I was to this terrible sin not being swept under the rug. I asked for prayer and he promised to pray for us.

He and I chatted for a while and we hung up. Not once during our phone conversation did he give me any indication that he disagreed with how I handled things. Not once did he say anything to lead me to believe that he had a problem with my video response or anything that I had said.

So you can imagine my surprise on that following Tuesday, May 22, when some of my church members sent me a link to his article. As of this writing, it can still be found here: *https://oldpathsjournal.com/publish-it-not/*.

I have saved copies and filed them in the event it ever gets removed from the site. The title of the article is "Publish It Not."

He never once mentioned my name. He didn't have to. Everybody who knew me or had seen my video and then read his article knew exactly who he was talking about.

The article began with an immediate blanket statement about false accusations. He said, *"Sadly, much of the accusations that have been thrown at people are nothing more than conjecture, lies, and attempts to bring down someone that those who accuse don't like."*

Accusing me for trying to "bring down someone that I didn't like" was absolutely ludicrous. Cameron Giovanelli and I had a great friendship that had developed over the four years that I was here. When these accusations surfaced, I was devastated.

But let's not muddy the talking points with petty things like facts. The case being made was that this was all about personal vendettas, politics, back-stabbing preachers and their dishonorable tactics. The conversation is just getting started, and the accused is already portrayed as the victim. The accuser is the villain, and the accused is the hero.

That is the standard defense of a fallen preacher. His friends rally around him with righteous outrage over the "attempts to bring down" their comrade. They reach way back in their archives and dust off the old talking points. They resort to repeating the same worn-out rhetoric that has been used over and over again. It went downhill from there.

Notice the quick assertion right off the bat that the allegations and the current ongoing criminal investigation by the detectives of Baltimore are *"nothing more than conjecture and lies."* Forget that he never once called and asked for the corroborating evidence that I have. Never mind the fact that he never spoke with the victim, or my staff members or deacons that believed her story was credible. No. It is much easier to just state as fact that the allegations are nothing more than conjectures and lies.

What exactly is "conjecture?"

CONJECTURE, *noun*

Literally, a casting or throwing together of possible or probable events; or a casting of the mind to something future, or something past but unknown; a guess, formed on a supposed possibility or probability of a fact, or on slight evidence; preponderance of opinion without proof; surmise. We speak of future or unknown things by conjecture and of probable or unfounded conjectures.

(Source: *Webster's 1828 Dictionary online edition)*

The word "conjecture" does not apply in this situation. My video was not the result of a person *"throwing together possible or probable events"* or something *"unknown; a guess formed on a supposed possibility..."* No. This word does not accurately describe the situation. Just because a person WANTS an allegation to be "conjecture" and just because they never made any effort to VERIFY the allegations, doesn't qualify it as "conjecture."

The next paragraph took the reader straight to the martyr argument. He said, *"The same has happened in the Christian world since the days of Christ. It was the accusations thrown at Jesus that led the majority of people to have Him killed and Barabbas spared."*

Since Jesus Christ was falsely accused and ultimately crucified because of those accusations, then pretty much any Christian that is accused is experiencing that same anti-Christian sentiment. Someone needs to inform the dear evangelist that Jesus wasn't accused of sexually exploiting a sixteen-year-old girl in his office for over a year.

It sickens me to see someone compare accusations of pedophilia to the crucifixion of our Lord and Savior Jesus Christ.

To openly and shamelessly compare the confrontation of alleged sexual abuse to the sufferings of Christ is borderline blasphemy. God help us!

The reference to 2 Samuel 1:20 from whence the title of the article was taken was then used to set the table. *"Tell it not in Gath, publish it not in the streets of Askelon; lest the daughters of the Philistines rejoice, lest the daughters of the uncircumcised triumph."* The very next sentence then declares that having presented this verse – the verse about King Saul's shameful death and David not wanting the heathen nations to know about it – that we will now learn how to handle accusations against a believer.

Now I have read that passage forward and backward a number of times. It is beyond me how anybody, much less a Bible college president and a career evangelist, could possibly apply these verses to this situation. How is David not wanting the heathen to hear about King Saul's death in any way, shape or form applicable to exposing child molesters in the church? These two situations are so far removed from commonality that it is ridiculous!

The article proceeded to argue a number of points. The first point was that just because there has been an accusation that does not mean it is true. I agree wholeheartedly. I will deal with the unfortunate reality of false accusations in a later chapter. However, just because an accusation has been made doesn't meant it is false, either.

The statistics are clear: less than 8 percent of accusations of sexual misconduct are proven to be false or retracted. That means that over 90 percent of them are true. So statistically, we do not have the right to assume that ALL accusations are false. That is a scientific impossibility. And just because you happen to personally know, or be friends with the accused does not make it *not* true.

The second point he made was that *"just because you can, that does not mean that you should."* In other words, the accused pedophiles and their associates can do and say whatever they want, but the rest of us should just sit down and shut up.

They can write articles and post blogs and email out morning devotionals, but we have to remain quiet. They can educate all of us on what to do, and what to think and how to respond or not respond, but we must keep our opinions to ourselves.

"Just because we can doesn't mean that we should." They can write their books and preach their messages and push their agendas, but God forbid anyone that disagrees with them exercise their liberties and rights to do the same.

They can use their social media platforms to criticize and lambaste and expose preachers they don't like, but the rest of us are not permitted to do that. Because they said so. That is not how it is done. We are just a bunch of ignorant peons and our opinions and thoughts and feelings and investigations do not matter.

They can use their platforms to defend their friends, but we can't use our platforms to defend the victims. They can preach and lecture and expound on the tragedy of hurting their preacher friend, but we cannot say anything about the tragedy of hurting children and victims.

The rules have changed. The rule used to be "Just because you can does not mean that you should." I like this one better: *"Just because you said I can't, doesn't mean I can't!"*

If they can make their point on social media, then I can too. If they can use all their available resources to run roughshod over the church and the people of God that insist on truth and transparency, then we will use all of our available resources to point out their blatant hypocrisies.

Their years of self-serving inconsistencies and double standards have contributed greatly to the diminished credibility of Baptist preachers.

What is good for the goose is good for the gander! I have just as much of a right to rebuke them as they have to rebuke me.

The third point in this article was quite blunt. "It is none of our business." That was the shocking conclusion of this nationally renowned evangelist. In case you did not read that correctly, I will repeat talking point number three. Domelle said, "It is none of our business."

Really? Is he really saying that a man accused of molesting a teenage girl in his office for her entire senior year of high school and who went on to become the president of a Bible college where he was surrounded by beautiful, young, innocent women all day, every day, is none of our business?

Keep in mind, my twenty-one-year-old daughter was there. Don't forget that half a dozen of the young people in my church were there. Yet it was none of my business?

They were enrolled in Giovanelli's classes. They walked the same hallways and classrooms with him. He preached in chapel and led the singing in the church services. They were in and out of his home for meals and times of fellowship. But it was none of my business?

Domelle then referenced Philippians 4:8 *"Finally, brethren, whatsoever things are true, whatsoever things are honest, whatsoever things are just, whatsoever things are pure, whatsoever things are lovely, whatsoever things are of good report; if there be any virtue, and if there be any praise, think on these things."* He went on to explain that if it is not a "good report" then it is none of our business.

Wow! Can you possibly butcher the Scripture any worse?

Was Paul in violation of his own admonition when he warned Timothy in 2 Timothy 4:14 by saying, *"Alexander the coppersmith did me much evil: the Lord reward him according to his works: Of whom be thou ware also; for he hath greatly withstood our words."*

According to our dear evangelist friend, how could that possibly be any of Timothy's business? I mean, it definitely wasn't a "good report." In fact, it was a bad report. Just because Alexander had done evil to Paul, did that give Paul the right to warn Timothy to beware of him? Was the Apostle Paul guilty of "sowing discord among the brethren?" Too bad Paul was not aware of the "publish it not" passage.

And Domelle himself was the president of Texas Independent Baptist Seminary when he wrote this! Imagine sending your daughter to a Bible college where the president does not think that exposing pedophiles and warning people of their wicked behavior is anybody's business! That's scary!

The fourth point he attempted to make was another atrocious misrepresentation of a glorious Bible doctrine. It was titled, "It Is A Local Church Matter." Let me say, I love the doctrine of the Church. I preach on this subject often. I've written extensively about the church and studied the doctrine for years. I believe in the authority of the local church from the top of my head to the soles of my feet.

The word "church" is used 115 times in the King James Bible. In 114 of these passages, the Greek word "*ekklesia*" is used. Of the 115 New Testament references to the church, 111 of these refer to Christ's local assembly. I believe strongly in the local church and her God-given right to deal with problems.

I just have one question that was never clarified in this article. Pray tell me - WHICH local church was supposed to deal with these accusations? The local church that the alleged crime happened in? Or the local church he was a member of when the accusation surfaced? Or the local church he landed in after the scandal broke? Which local church is supposed to perform church discipline?

There was no mention of the fact that biblical church discipline was totally ignored through this whole process. But it is a local church matter.

OK. Let me follow this shell game we are playing now. Our local church in Baltimore, Maryland informed Giovanelli's local church in Santa Clara, California of his alleged behavior. They shipped him off to another local church in Jacksonville, Florida.

So let me ask the question again. <u>Which</u> local church is responsible to implement Biblical church discipline?

Let's throw another dynamic in the mix. North Valley Baptist Church is a local church that also happens to have a Bible college. They invite all the other local churches in America of like faith to send their kids to Golden State Baptist College. Then they ask these local churches to send them money each month to help train the next generation of Christian leaders.

So we do. We send them our students. We send them our monthly support. We support their conferences. We fellowship and interact and enjoy the ministry together. We buy boxes of their publications and stock our church bookstores with them. *(I know we did!)*

Then a scandal breaks out. Their College president is accused of being a child molester. And what do their friends do? They pull out the "local church" card. They are a local church and it is a local church matter.

In other words, "Send us your young people. Send us your money. Have our tour groups come sing in your church. Have our traveling preachers preach in your pulpit. Let us set up our display tables in the back of the church. Let us sell our singing CDs, books, and recruit all the high schoolers in your church. Put our tour group up in a hotel and provide us with meals. And please give us a love offering to cover our expenses. But if you happen to hear that a possible child molester is running our ministry, mind your own business! This is a local church matter."

Do you see the insanity in this philosophy? Pardon me for pressing the matter, but a church that stocks its pews with another pastor's church members voluntarily waives a certain degree of independence. At the very least, there is the expectation of transparency and communication.

Did GSBC communicate to their monthly financial supporters what was going on? Did North Valley attempt in any way to allay the fears and anxieties of the pastors and church members that made their college possible? Of course not.

We continued to support GSBC for a couple of months after the scandal broke. We did not receive a single letter, or any attempt to explain what was happening, or what had occurred at the college. Apparently, it was a local church matter. Just keep sending your money and mind your own business.

As an example of accountability, my family and I were missionaries to South Africa from 2000 - 2006. We went all over the Southeast sharing our burden for the African people. In less than a year, God in His goodness allowed us to raise 100 percent of our financial support through the help of many wonderful churches. Those pastors graciously allowed us to come in and present our burden.

We were given the opportunity to preach, sing, show our slides, and minister to those precious churches. In turn, most of the churches we visited partnered with us to make it possible for us to go to the field. We labored in Bloemfontein, South Africa for 5 ½ years with the money and prayers of those churches making that possible.

Understand this important fact. I started and was pastoring a local church. As a church planter, it was my goal to see that church become self-supporting and then leave to go start another church. But while I was there, I was the pastor. Our church plant was an established, biblical local church. I was accountable to that church.

But wait. I also had a sending church in Harlem, Georgia. We were members of *that* church, so therefore, I was accountable to *that* local church. I sent my tithes and monthly mission's offering to my home church in Georgia.

But that's not all. I had over a hundred local churches paying my salary. I was accountable to them as well. I gave them detailed reports of my activity. I sent out newsletters every two months giving updates of our ministry. I had a website with dozens of pages of photos and news items.

Those churches that supported me deserved that accountability and interaction. I owed it to them.

But a Bible college in the USA, that is supported by hundreds of local churches and whose classrooms are full of other pastors' kids and church members, wants to pull out the "local church" card when something happens that affects me and my church members? I don't think so!

What happened at that college was *not* just a "local church matter." It *was* my business. It was all of our business! It was the business of every church that supported that ministry. It was the business of every parent who had a child enrolled there. It was the business of every pastor who had one of his church members attending that college. It was everybody's business. Yet the level of transparency and the amount of communication was zero.

Needless to say, our church voted unanimously to discontinue our monthly support of GSBC. I will not send a dime to a ministry that will not even take a phone call from one of its supporting pastors. I cannot support a ministry that asks me for money, but has no concept of transparency and basic communication.

Local church matter? Not hardly.

The fifth point in this article reminded us that Jesus' example was not to destroy, but to save. I honestly have no idea what this had to do with the situation. The only destroying that I was aware of had occurred in the pastor's office with a teenage girl. According to her account, her life, her innocence, her purity, her heart and mind were destroyed. Her family was destroyed. The guilt and shame she lived with for the past twelve years was about as destructive as it gets. So I am not sure how supporting an abuse victim could ever be construed as destroying anything or anybody.

I am fully aware that Jesus came to save. But he didn't just come to save pedophiles. He came to save little children. He came to save hurting and broken people. The victim and her family was one of my highest priorities. It was my desire to see her saved if she wasn't. I wanted to see her family reached for Christ. Our church prayed for her family to be salvaged. We prayed for our church's testimony in the community to be saved; to see my ability to minister at this church saved.

The only thing I was guilty of destroying was the false image of moral leadership that had been portrayed to so many people for so many years. We simply must stop talking all the time about saving the pedophiles, and start focusing on saving their victims!

Point number six was as bizarre as anything I had read up to this point. The point was simply, "What About Restoration?"

He began by asking us, *"Whatever happened to the mindset of trying to restore the fallen?"* When I read that, I was as confused as a woodpecker in a rock quarry. Restore the fallen? Who is the fallen? Up to this point, everything was conjectures, lies and false accusations. For this entire article, we have been led to believe that the only person who has done anything wrong is the one making the accusations.

Now you're asking me to restore the fallen? So are we to understand now that the accused is actually guilty? Is that what we are supposed to gather from this point? Are you confirming that the accused is what he is accused of being -- a child molester? I'm trying to follow the hairpin U-turns in this article. Can you restore someone who is innocent?

As you continue reading the article it becomes clear that the preacher that is accused of being a child molester is now considered the "fallen." Just a few paragraphs before, he was being falsely accused. Like Jesus. He was suffering. Like Jesus. He was being "crucified" because people were trying to destroy him. Like Jesus. Now, he's a fallen preacher. And we should restore him. Just like that.

There was not a single word about restoring the broken, little girl who is now a broken wife and mother. There was no mention of restoring the credibility of the office that has been defiled and desecrated. There was no admonition to restore the church full of broken hearts and discouraged people. It was all about restoring the fallen preacher. Forgive and forget. And if you don't have that mindset, you are not of God, but of Satan. That is what he said.

For too long, churches have made the restoration of fallen leaders more of a priority than the restoration of the victims. My mindset toward the fallen when it is a sexual predator or pedophile is exactly the same as the mindset of the Lord Jesus Christ. *"And whosoever shall offend one of these little ones that believe in me, it is better for him that a millstone were hanged about his neck, and he were cast into the sea."* (Mark 9:42)

Do I believe that sex offenders can be forgiven? Yes.

Do I believe that the blood of Jesus was shed to save pedophiles from hell? Absolutely.

Do I believe that a pastor who has molested children should be restored to the pulpit? A thousand times NO!

Any church that allows a man with that sin in his past to be on staff, to preach, to pastor, to lead in that church should have its doors welded shut. Any ministry that puts men like that in front of their people as a spiritual example is repulsive to me. And we wonder why there is no revival in America!

Any church member who knowingly attends a church with credibly accused sex offenders running the show should have their heads examined. Any pastor who would bring a man on staff knowing that man is currently under investigation for gross and illegal sexual misconduct with a child does not understand the Scriptural basis for being a shepherd.

The eighth point in this grossly, unbiblical Bible devotional was that people like me are hindering the harvest. People like us who speak out against sexual abuse in the church, and the covering up of those sins, are keeping people from getting saved.

The old and worn-out argument has always been that if the lost in our community hear about sexual abuse in our churches, then they will die in their sins and go to hell. I want to clarify that. If the lost in our communities hear about sexual abuse in the church, and _watch the church cover it up and blame the victim_, THEN those lost people will probably die and go to hell.

The average person has enough sense to know bad things will happen sometimes. As terrible as sexual abuse in the church is, most people can cope with that reality. What people _cannot_ handle is watching the very people who preach hell and damnation to those on the outside of the church, turn a blind eye to illegal and immoral activity that goes on inside the church.

The unsaved and unchurched cannot get their head wrapped around a man being allowed to keep preaching after fondling and molesting little kids. I can't blame them. I can't fathom it either. I cannot imagine listening to a preacher while thinking about his sick behavior the whole time. People see that horrible injustice and they get out of church and never go back.

It is not because of the sexual abuse itself -- which is horrible in and of itself, but because of how it is mishandled and covered up. That is what is hindering the harvest!

When I posted my video, I anticipated a lot of feedback. What I did not expect was to hear from as many unchurched and disenfranchised church members as I did. My phone and email exploded with people who wanted to tell me if they had a pastor who stood like I did and handled it like I did, they would still be in church.

I had people all over our community reach out to thank me. It was one of the most humbling experiences of my life. Getting phone calls and text messages from unsaved and unchurched people is not something that happens to me every day. Many of them had been hurt in a church somewhere in the past and had simply never returned. They had given up hope that anybody would ever buck the system and call a spade a spade. I do not know how many times I heard the comment, "If I ever decide to go back to church, I'm going to go to that Calvary Baptist Church in Dundalk!"

We had more visitors in the weeks following that video than ever. Former members came back to express their gratitude. Unsaved families visited our church as a result of that video. It proved the exact opposite of Domelle's (and so many others') way of thinking.

Cover-ups and spin will not work anymore. It never worked. We are tired of the super-spiritual virtue signaling. Souls will only be won when we stop hiding and protecting wolves in our churches. The harvest will be reaped when we stop covering up sin in our church and in our pulpits.

I need to point out another seriously flawed attitude. Just because a person is a "soulwinner" doesn't mean he is above reproof. The attitude has been that a person has committed the unpardonable sin if he criticizes or rebukes a church or preacher that is involved in soulwinning.

I want to be the first one to say this. <u>Being a soulwinner is not your get-out-of-jail-free card!</u> These men hide behind their tract racks, visitation programs and bus ministries. They act like because they are trying to win the lost, they are somehow exempt from rebuke.

Excuse me, but the children's ministry worker who is bringing kids on the bus each week, only to find out one of the men in the church is molesting them might have something to say about that! The faithful soulwinners in the church who bring families in to discover that one of their children is being victimized inside the church might beg to differ!

The ninth and final point of Allen Domelle's article pointed to the long-term negative effect exposing pedophiles in the church would have on the weak and the innocent. There was no mention of the long-term effect that sexually abusing the weak and the innocent might have. There was not a whisper of outrage over the lifetime of hurt and pain that being fondled in your Sunday school class, or molested during youth camp, might have on a child. No.

The worst thing you can do, according to this preacher, is to openly "spread dirt" and reveal to the world that the church is not perfect. Evidently, it is our responsibility to maintain the image that the "man of God" is above reproach and incapable of doing wrong. It is the church's duty to help prop up the preacher's facade of infallibility. Apparently, being real and genuine and honest with the lost people in our communities when a preacher falls into sin will send them all to hell, along with their children.

His closing statement was the icing on the cake. *"My desire for this article is not to attack anyone, but to warn of the dangers of going public and getting involved in accusations. You may ask, "Bro. Domelle, who do you think is telling the truth?" My answer is; it is none of my business. Whether the accused or the accuser is right is not my area..."*

Because it was none of his business, he sat down at his computer. He wrote a 2,000 word article about the situation without doing any legitimate research. He chose to title his nine-point rebuke disguised as a devotional, "Publish It Not." Then he PUBLISHED it. Because it was none of his business.

The reason I feel compelled to devote such a large portion of this book refuting these points is because it is these very unbiblical philosophies that have contributed to the deplorable state we find ourselves in today.

I reached out to him with a text message after reading his article, but he never responded. I actually tried to make light of it. I was not angry with him. I still am not angry with him. He's just wrong.

He has never called or spoken to me again.

Wolves Among Lambs

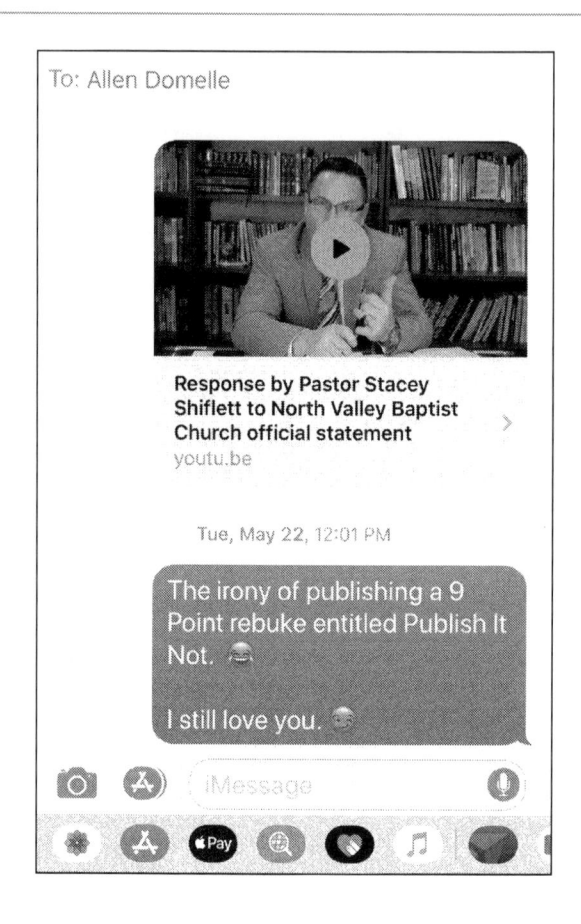

> To: Allen Domelle
>
> Response by Pastor Stacey Shiflett to North Valley Baptist Church official statement
> youtu.be
>
> Tue, May 22, 12:01 PM
>
> The irony of publishing a 9 Point rebuke entitled Publish It Not. 😂
>
> I still love you. 😊

He has, however, continued to have Giovanelli into his church. He has continued to share the pulpit with him at different places. He still preaches at Greg Neal's church. He continues to allow Berean Baptist Publications, of which Cameron Giovanelli is now the director, to publish all of his books. But it is not his business to pick sides. Remember that. Don't misunderstand. To try and decide which one - the accused or the accuser, is right, is "not his area."

But he *did* pick sides. He made that abundantly clear in his article. My congregation and I were expendable. The preacher who was accused of child molestation made the team.

One thing that really bothered me more than anything is what I discovered only recently. I remember every year when Domelle would preach for us, he would somehow always manage to mention in his message that his dad was in prison. I never asked him what his dad had done or why he was in prison. I felt it too personal of a question to ask, so I didn't. It didn't seem important to me at the time.

Imagine my shock just a few days ago when I heard that Allen Domelle's father was in prison for multiple counts of child molestation. I could not believe it.

A quick internet search yielded multiple pages with the sordid news reports.

Here is just one example:

Pastor Admits Molesting 2 Girls

By George B. Sanchez
Monterey County Herald [Salinas CA]
January 20, 2006
http://www.montereyherald.com/mld/montereyherald/news/13670305.htm

A Salinas pastor accused of sexually molesting his adopted daughter and a handicapped girl pleaded guilty less than two months after authorities began investigating him.

Donald Domelle, 65, pastor of the Baptist Temple of Salinas, admitted to two felony counts of lewd conduct with a child and agreed to a minimum of 15 years in prison Thursday in a remarkably swift case that kept one young woman and a teenager from recounting in court their stories of repeated sexual abuse at the pastor's hands.

"(Domelle) has accepted responsibility from the beginning," said defense attorney John Coniglio. The pastor was arrested at his church Dec. 21 after Sheriff's investigators looked into allegations that he sexually molested a 16-year-old girl that prosecutors described as "educationally challenged." Initially, Domelle denied the allegations, said prosecutor Gary Thelander, but during a two and a half hour interview with sheriff's deputies he admitted to having sex with the first known victim. At the conclusion of the interview, Thelander said, Domelle asked to write a letter of apology to his victims. "He ultimately was the source of the second victim," Thelander said.

Seven days later, investigators contacted Domelle's 25-year-old adopted daughter, who was living in Northern California with her biological father. That is when authorities confirmed there was a second victim, Thelander said.

The daughter came under Domelle's custody when she was 3 years old and was adopted six years later. Between the ages of 10 and 19, Thelander said, Domelle repeatedly had sex with her. "She never told law enforcement. She told people in the community and nobody believed her," Thelander said. "(Domelle and his wife) then sent her off to Christian school in Texas."

With bail set at $1.5 million, Domelle was facing more than 50 criminal charges. He signed a plea agreement Thursday morning, hours before his case was to be heard.

Source:
http://www.bishopaccountability.org/news2006/01_02/2006_01_20_Sanchez_PastorAdmits.htm

Source: The Californian - (Salinas, California) 03 Mar 2006, Friday • Page 2

I would never in a million years want to appear that I blame Allen Domelle for any of this. He is in *no way* responsible for the actions of another person, including his father. I would never, ever want to exploit what occurred in his family. I imagine he is very embarrassed by all of this. I guess he is. I would be.

But for some reason, he reminded our church every time he preached that his dad was in prison. He somehow managed to work it into his messages, every single year. But finding this out about his dad, I am more confused now than ever; almost to the state of complete bewilderment.

I just have one question. Can someone please explain to me how that my friend, Allen Domelle would choose to stand with Cameron Giovanelli, considering what he has been accused of? He watched his own father, who was a Baptist pastor, plead guilty to crimes of sexual abuse against his own children and children in his church -- yet, for some unknown reason, he chose to take sides with an accused pedophile against me and my church.

He never one time spoke with Sarah Jackson. He never spoke with my deacons. He never asked for a single shred of evidence. He never considered the possibility that my church and I might be right in our findings. He never considered the possibility that Cameron might actually have done what Sarah and others have accused him of.

He cared absolutely nothing about the alleged victims. He cared nothing about a church full of people where he had preached for years. Hundreds of people that were hurting from the discovery of their former pastor's alleged criminal activity. He just chose to accuse everybody of making false accusations. In doing so, he made his stand with the accused.

In spite of me having pages and pages of evidence of highly inappropriate conduct, he chose rather to go straight to his computer and portray us all as false accusers trying to destroy a good man. In Domelle's mind, my violation of the all-supreme "publish it not" protocol was the unpardonable sin. But possibly being a pedophile is still covered under the rules of "restoration."

How can anybody explain this madness?

Jesus put it like this. Matthew 23:24, *"Ye blind guides, which strain at a gnat, and swallow a camel."*

How is it that my eighteen-minute video warranted a 2,000-word article filled with sharp rebukes, but somehow Cameron Giovanelli who was accused of <u>months</u> of illegal sexual misconduct with a minor got a free pass? It only took Domelle FOUR DAYS to arrive at a verdict of "guilty" when it came to <u>my</u> conduct. But when it came to allegations of sexual abuse, with multiple victims all saying the same thing, the jury is still out. Almost a year later.

Is it any wonder that victims remain silent?

Is it any wonder why pastors are afraid to go on record for believing victims and seeking justice?

Is it any wonder that many of our churches are safe havens for sexual offenders, when the "champions for truth and right" seek to annihilate anyone that dares expose them?

One newspaper article that I read about Donald Domelle's trial stated that in spite of his admission of guilt, even though he was facing over 50 charges, and even with his multiple apologies to the victims, many in the courtroom *insisted that he was innocent*. I cannot begin to describe just how bad this bothers me. Something is terribly, terribly wrong with this scenario.

Apparently, my transgression crossed the threshold of "restoration." Not a single one of the men who publicly rebuked me have tried to "restore" me for my horrible sin of posting a video – Dr. Allen Domelle, Dr. Bob Gray, Sr., Dr. Tom Neal, none of them. Not a single one has taken the time, or made any effort, to try and "restore" me if they think what I did was so unscriptural and so wrong. Apparently, I was not worth "restoring."

They waxed eloquent with their condescending analysis of a situation they knew virtually nothing about. They published their strong disapproval of a pastor on the internet while rebuking me for publishing my disapproval of a pastor on the same platform. While virtue-signaling about the biblical command to "restore the fallen," they simultaneously ground their heels into me along with everything and everybody I represent.

And trust me when I say that I represent a multitude of people. These men and their cronies have ground their heels into the thousands of victims and church members and good pastors across this nation that are sick of watching perverts protected and moved from one church to another with no condemnation.

These men and men like them, grind the heels of their polished wingtips into anybody that threatens to expose their blatant inconsistencies. They grind their heels into anybody who has the guts to stand up to their cyber-bullying and cowardly backhanded tactics. They grind their heels into anybody who dares call them out for their unbiblical and idiotic methods of dealing with sex offenders in the church. While talking about Jesus coming to save rather than destroy, they seek to destroy both the victims of alleged sexual abuse and anybody that defends them. What a bunch of hypocrites!

People like that have been grinding their heels into me since I was a teenager. I'm pretty much used to it by now. However, thousands of church members across America have grown weary of it. It's time somebody called out this crowd for their inconsistency and hypocrisy.

It did not surprise me, that to my knowledge, not a single preacher felt the need to publicly call Allen Domelle out on his ludicrous mishandling of Scripture. If they did, they did it privately. I've got a feeling that nobody did. As of this writing, his grossly unscriptural article is still on his website for all to see.

22

IFB Paradigms and Paradoxes

"A time to rend, and a time to sew;
a time to keep silence, and a time to speak;"
Ecclesiastes 3:7

* * *

The time has come for me to speak up.

I have been in the independent, fundamental Baptist movement my entire life. I was born into it. For five generations, we have been independent Baptist. Unlike a host of pastors, I have no plans to abandon the independent Baptist name. Instead of alienating myself from the problems, I want to do everything within my power to change them.

I will always be a Baptist in my conviction. I will always believe in the fundamentals of the faith. I will always be independent of any controlling denominational head or office.

Though I was born into the independent Baptist system of beliefs, I am one today because of conviction. I am not an independent Baptist because my parents were or because my heroes were. I am not an independent Baptist because I lack the courage to walk away. I am an independent Baptist. I believe the problem with our movement is not the doctrines we adhere to, but the unbiblical philosophies, cult-like atmosphere and narcissistic leaders in our movement that have gone virtually unchallenged.

Don't get me wrong. Some of the most wonderful people in the world identify with the IFB crowd. Some of the godliest, most compassionate and spiritual men I have ever had the privilege to meet are IFB preachers. Their passion for God, their family, their church, and for souls is unsurpassed. Their families are godly, precious people with a pursuit of holiness that is admirable and refreshing.

I could spend forever writing of the courageous men and women who serve the Lord and attend independent Baptist churches.

The majority of my friends are independent Baptist. They are all either independent Baptist pastors, evangelists, missionaries or church members.

The Critics

What really bothers me is the only real critics of the IFB movement are usually former IFB people. To conclude from this book that I have turned on the independent Baptists would be wrong. Make no mistake. I dislike what the IFB label has become, especially as described by bitter, former IFB members. They lump all IFB into the same basket. They criticize both our shortcomings and our sound doctrine and somehow make them sound inseparable.

Our passion for souls is mocked. Our desire to promote holiness is belittled. Our separation and standards for clean living are made fun of relentlessly. Somehow to these bitter and angry people, there is a connection between not going to the movies and molesting children. They connect dots that do not connect. They hate everything about the IFB crowd, thereby negating any credible complaint they may have.

In their mind, trying to promote holiness in general is somehow a path to sexual abuse. To them, believing in biblical, pastoral authority is to blame for sexual abuse in the church. Teaching Christians to dress modestly is still biblical. That belief is not what makes evil men want to do terrible things to little children.

Most of the critics of the IFB movement were either part of a cult or they were terribly mistreated in some way. Many of them were just plain rebels, and have a problem with God, the Bible, authority and religion as a whole. That crowd is entitled to their opinion, but they are not really going to fix the problems within our Baptist churches. They will often only make our churches more resolved to keep making the same mistakes over and over again.

Making fun of us for the doctrines that are true and biblical will get them nowhere. They want to discredit everything we believe because there are some bad apples in the bunch. They tell their stories of how they were hurt or when they were done wrong, hoping to justify their bitterness. Bitterness is wrong, regardless of what happened. Crude and carnal people pointing out the problems with independent Baptists is counterproductive in my opinion. There are less and less people today who want to talk about the problems with our movement while choosing to live in open sin and ungodliness.

If people want to criticize us, it would be much more effective if they were not living their lives in direct violation of Scripture. Rubbing their sin in the faces of Christians is not an effective strategy. They can gripe, but nobody is listening.

A large percentage of our critics do great disservice to themselves without realizing the irony of their position. When they walk away from our Bible-believing Baptist churches and join liberal, non-denominational churches, pretending to be more spiritual for doing so, they invalidate every one of their arguments.

Would they lead us to believe there is no sin occurring in those churches, either? They may be liberated from the dress codes and emphasis on modesty, but does that excuse their blindness to the immorality among their own ministry leaders?

I get weary with people criticizing the elements of the independent Baptists that has nothing to do with sexual abuse, while trying to make it part of the problem. Is our effort to encourage a distinction between the sexes the real cause for kids becoming victims of sexual abuse? Is our desire to promote modesty, and encourage biblical purity the real cause? Making any kind of correlation between the two is ridiculous. Holding to a standard of personal holiness and trying to keep worldliness out of the church is not a prerequisite to abuse. That is just crazy!

Are there pedophiles in some of our Baptist churches? Obviously! From all indications, there are lots of them! And it sickens me. But to act like this is a Baptist problem or the result of Baptist beliefs and Baptist interpretation of Scripture would is ridiculous. Pedophiles can be anywhere. They are in every kind of church under the sun.

Are there hypocrites in our Baptist churches? Of course there are! That's what this whole book is about. But there are hypocrites in *every* church, regardless of their doctrine. Putting on a front and pretending to be something you aren't is not a distinctly Baptist characteristic. Hypocrisy is everywhere.

What bothers me are the ex-IFB critics who criticize the shortcomings of Baptist churches, but won't criticize the shortcomings of their new crowd. That blaring inconsistency is not lost on those of us who have stayed put and are trying to address our shortcomings from within. We are not the only ones with problems.

The difference in me and these former Baptists critics is I am trying to address and change what is wrong *from the inside*. I'm not going to throw the baby out with the bathwater.

It bothers me when people make harsh and hateful remarks about the IFB churches simply because we still believe things they do not believe. If you don't agree with what we believe, go to church somewhere else. We don't mind.

The Mormons don't believe in drinking coffee. That doesn't bother me. I'll just drink my coffee and keep going to the Baptist church.

The Muslims make their women wear hajibs. I think that is strange, but I don't fuss at them about it. If that's what they want to wear, fine. I don't care.

If the Amish communities want to plow with horses and live without electricity, more power to them *(pun intended!)*.

But let the Baptists preach the Bible the way we see it. Making fun of us will not stop us. Mocking our efforts to win souls will not stop us. Many of us have embraced our position as "…a chosen generation, a royal priesthood, an holy nation, a peculiar people; that ye should shew forth the praises of him who hath called you out of darkness into his marvellous light:" (1 Peter 2:9)

Laughing and making fun of our strict interpretation of the Scripture may cause some of our members to change their mind, but many of us will keep right on believing what we believe.

The Complaints

Let's talk about the *legitimate complaints* that people have against us. If our practices are inconsistent with what we say we believe, we deserve to be criticized!

"Having a good conscience; that, whereas they speak evil of you, as of evildoers, they may be ashamed that falsely accuse your good conversation in Christ. For it is better, if the will of God be so, that ye suffer for well doing, than for evil doing." (1 Peter 3:16)

We should be blamed for the trend of following personalities rather than principles. We have allowed that to hurt our testimony in many cases.

I was Baptist-born and Baptist-bred, and when I die I'll be a Baptist dead! It is because of my love for "my crowd" that I feel that I am the one to point out our issues. A little leaven leaveneth the whole lump. Re-packaging it won't fix the problem. Covering it up will only make matters worse. Defending it only causes us to lose more credibility.

We have some major issues. The sexual abuse and covering up of it is just one small tip of the iceberg. The problems that surround this issue are multi-faceted. It will take one of our own to address the problem and hopefully be heard.

I will be the first to admit that I am not the *only* person qualified to write about this. But I will also claim without hesitation that I am *just as* qualified as anybody else to write about it.

I have always identified with the IFB crowd, and I will probably always be labeled as IFB, in spite of my increased distaste for the label. I am a New Testament, Bible-believing Baptist. I like that term much better. Call me what you want to, I am not your every-day, run-of-the-mill Baptist preacher. I have a unique perspective on things.

I am genuinely ashamed of the amount of nonsense and many of the preachers within the IFB "movement." I detest being lumped in with some of these guys.

I will defend our biblical practices until the day I die.

I will also protest our unbiblical practices until I die.

I am ignorant about a whole lot of things, but not about Baptists. I grew up in the home of a Baptist pastor. My wife did as well. I've been in the ministry my entire life. At an early age I realized that I was a stick-in-the-mud. I have always been a non-conformist. I think for myself. I do what God called me to do without fear or favor. I was never a rebel. I'm still not a rebel.

As a young preacher, though, I was not cult bait. I respected my elders, but I did not worship them. I followed them as they followed Christ. That is what we are commanded of God to do. Somehow, the biblical admonition to submit to the pastor and honoring the pastor evolved over time to the pastor becoming the pope.

How anybody could sit under an individual who fails to understand his own accountability to the church is beyond me. Even the pastor is subject to the authority of the local church.

Wolves Among Lambs

As a young preacher, I saw other young preachers try to emulate and worship some big-named preacher and it turned my stomach. Men became larger than life. They became drunk with power. They became god-like to their people, and in our movement, they were celebrities. They could do no wrong. We have this problem still today.

It was the followers of these men who ultimately created the monsters they became. Preachers would say things like, "Let your people know that you have feet of clay, but never let them see your feet." You see, that would destroy the "mystique" they've created around themselves. The holy aura they've cultivated of being "God's man" would be jeopardized.

Cult leaders are created by their cult-bait followers. All it would take is a group of Spirit-filled men, armed with the Word of God and some backbone, to put a stop to this nonsense. They sit in the pew like dumb sheep and say nothing. In doing so, they become part of the problem.

Their cult leader becomes more and more supreme in the church, until the whole place is built on him and his personality. Their sin and hypocrisy goes unchecked.

Paul confronted Peter in Galatians 2:11, 14. "But when Peter was come to Antioch, I _withstood him to the face_, because he was to be blamed… when I saw that they walked not uprightly according to the truth of the gospel, I said unto Peter _before them all_…"

Peter was older than Paul. He had been in the ministry longer than Paul. He had walked with Christ for three and a half years. He preached at Pentecost and three thousand souls were saved. That did not stop Paul from confronting him. He didn't care who he was.

Why don't we see more God-called preachers doing that anymore? Many have, and I thank God for every one of them. I've watched some of my preacher friends grab the tiger by the tail and it was a sight to behold. They uncovered scandals and sin. When they tried to deal with it, they ended up on the short end of the stick.

There are many men of God, and Christians, who have stood up for what was right and spoke truth to authority. But there needs to be a lot more of that taking place, and it would cut down on a lot of this unscriptural power-wielding we see going on in our ranks.

Romans 12:3 says, "For I say, through the grace given unto me, to every man that is among you, not to think of himself more highly than he ought to think; but to think soberly, according as God hath dealt to every man the measure of faith."

When nobody else would say anything, it seems I was always the one who would. I have been on somebody's hit list for much of my ministry. It makes them very nervous when they cannot shove you into their mold.

They have always been suspicious of me because I did not go to any of their Bible colleges. I graduated from my small, local church Bible institute. That makes me an "outsider," I guess.

I've watched men talk like they wanted to have me preach for them, but they don't. They promised to have me come in, but they never do. They keep me at arm's length because they cannot own me. I will not wear their brand.

My loyalty is to Christ and the Word of God. I am not going to give my loyalty to a college or a preacher or a ministry that supersedes my loyalty to God.

I've been labeled a maverick, a loose cannon. I have no alma mater to dictate my positions. I do not have a camp or group that I identify with. I refuse to be controlled by the big names and their attempt to influence me. I am not intimidated by them or impressed by them.

It would be nice to be able to respect and be nice to people without kissing their ring. If that is not possible, then I can't be respectful and nice. I won't kiss anybody's ring. I will not promote men, ministries or Bible colleges. I promote the Lord Jesus Christ and His precious Word.

Colossians 1:18 reminds us, "And he is the head of the body, the church: who is the beginning, the firstborn from the dead; that *in all things he might have the preeminence*."

I try to surround myself with preacher friends who can and will disagree with me. I love a friend who will call me and tell me he thinks I'm wrong. That doesn't bother me.

Only an insecure little man would be unable to have people in his circle tell him he's wrong. Some of my closest preacher friends never went to Bible college. And they can preach circles around half of these guys with honorary doctorates.

I am not a "yes man" and I do not surround myself with "yes men." I have zero respect for a "yes man." I also have no respect for a rebel. It is important to find the biblical balance.

The Bible says in 1 Timothy 5:1, "Rebuke not an elder, but intreat him as a father; and the younger men as brethren." The problem with some in our movement is that if a member of the church gets up the courage to intreat his pastor, he gets run off. Beware of a pastor with a "my way or the highway" mentality.

I thank God for the precious men of God who have influenced my life. I owe so much to so many preachers and pastors. They have been used of God in ways they could never imagine. Their example of faithfulness and integrity has been an inspiration to me.

Having said that, I have no respect at all for a preacher who puts on blinders or a muzzle because he is worried about what the "brethren" will say. We profess to be "independent," but our network of friends and allies is so tight and intertwined that there's not nearly as much independence as we would lead people to believe.

Fear of the brethren has choked the life out of so many preachers. Pastors are limited in their options because of the preachers in their "fellowship." Evangelists won't take a stand many times because they will lose meetings if they do. Missionaries have to stay quiet if they want to receive support and get to the mission field. Mission board directors won't take a stand because they are trying to help their missionaries get support.

The muzzles on preachers come in all shapes and sizes. They see things, but they can't say anything. They know things, but they can't tell anyone. They hear things, but they never look into it. They do not want to make waves. The price to pay is too great. They remind me of the three monkeys. See no evil. Hear no evil. Speak no evil.

I ask, "Why won't you say something?" The answers are all over the spectrum.

"My friend goes to that church."

"My kid is married to that pastor's kid."

"My staff member came from that college."

"My staff member has family on staff at that church."

"I have a family in my church with family members that go to that church."

"That preacher, who always preaches for me, also preaches for that guy."

The list of intertwining scenarios is endless. We are "independent" but we are joined at the hip with so many other "independent" Baptist churches until it is ridiculous.

I marvel at the amount of peer pressure among IFB pastors and churches. The peer pressure among Baptist preachers is far worse than the peer pressure that we preach about to our teenagers. The pressure to keep quiet at some point becomes suffocating.

We have been quiet too long. We have no problem calling out everybody else and their issues. But when it comes to saying something about our own hypocrisy, it pretty much amounts to treason. Let me be clear. It is not the ones who speak out that give us a bad name. It is the sin we remain silent about that is killing our testimony.

The blatant inconsistencies in our movement are appalling. What is equally appalling is how few men ever point it out. It's not the elephant in the room; it's a whole herd of them that need to be exposed.

Any church that will rail against the homosexuals and the legalization of marijuana, and then tolerate pedophiles in its ministry ought to be put out of business

Any pastor who pretends to hate sin, while covering it up on his own staff, should be run out of town on a rail.

A church that would perform church discipline on a teenager for fornication, but give a contract extension to a staff member who fools around with teenagers, has forfeited its right to exist.

We cannot expect to have any credibility while holding such a double standard. If we are going to salvage our youth, and retain our young preachers, we must confront and address the insanity masquerading as "the way it should be done."

"Woe unto you, scribes and Pharisees, hypocrites! for ye pay tithe of mint and anise and cummin, and have omitted the weightier matters of the law, judgment, mercy, and faith: these ought ye to have done, and not to leave the other undone." (Matthew 23:23)

The blacklisting and ostracizing that takes place when you do speak out will remain with you for life in many cases. The exciting conference that you once looked forward to attending turns into a minefield, so you stop attending. The church that once held you in high esteem now makes it clear that you are no longer welcome. The preachers you once had into your church are no longer willing to come. The places where you were once invited to preach no longer ask you come.

The churches, revival meetings, conferences and events where you can go without bumping into somebody you've offended starts to dwindle. You finally get to the place where your sphere of influence has been reduced pretty much to your own local church. You may have a lot of private cheerleaders, but if you expect them to stick their neck out for you, forget it. It's too risky. People much prefer the polished, diplomatic, anemic statements from the "experts" than the plain and honest truth. Isaiah 30:9, 10 says, "That this is a rebellious people, lying children, children that will not hear the law of the LORD: Which say to the seers, See not; and to the prophets, Prophesy not unto us right things, speak unto us smooth things, prophesy deceits:"

Politics in the IFB movement is alive and well. "Get on board with us and our agenda, or go away."

The IFB crowd loves it when Rush Limbaugh and Sean Hannity expose the hypocrisy of the liberals. They rejoice to see Tucker Carlson rip liberals to shreds on his Fox News television program. They love it when President Trump pledges to "drain the swamp." They clap with fervor when he stands up to the establishment, saying what everybody else is thinking, but nobody else has the guts to say.

But let one of our own do that, and it's a totally different story. Try and point out the crazy, unbiblical philosophies that have remained unaddressed for the past forty years and see what happens. Jesus would look at many in our ranks today with this response; "O generation of vipers, how can ye, being evil, speak good things?" (Matthew 12:34)

As bad as I hate to admit it, some of the meanest, most hateful, cold-hearted, demon-possessed people you would ever want to meet go to an independent, fundamental Baptist church. They would just as soon cut your throat as look at you. There is not a drunkard, a drug-dealer, a prostitute or a liquor store owner anywhere in the world that has done more to try and destroy me than other independent Baptist preachers. Not even close!

"Woe unto you, scribes and Pharisees, hypocrites! for ye make clean the outside of the cup and of the platter, but within they are full of extortion and excess." (Matthew 23:25)

The Cronyism

I speak for a lot of good Baptist preachers and church members when I say that we will no longer capitulate to the mob bosses of our "movement." I learned at an early age that some (not all, obviously) Baptist pastors, evangelists and leaders operate in a manner much like the mafia. Their tactics are so underhanded that it can leave their church members broken and scarred for life.

Their attitude and actions reflect a genuine belief that they are God's "Untouchables." Their favorite passage of Scripture is Psalms 105:15. "Saying, Touch not mine anointed, and do my prophets no harm." They teach it to the children, and they quote it from the pulpit. Often.

Many of these guys pull out that verse like a dirty cop flashing his badge when he's breaking the law. That verse is their license to do what they want, say what they want, treat people any way they want, and there is nothing you can do or say about it.

I could write a separate book just on the IFB mafia I have encountered in my ministry. These guys are as cold-blooded, crooked, and corrupt as Al Capone ever was. The difference is, Capone didn't call himself a "man of God" while he systematically and deliberately destroyed people's lives.

These ministry kingpins surround themselves with subordinates who jump when they say to jump. They always have a few fixers in their circle who will do their dirty work for them. They manipulate and coordinate the utter destruction of other people while pretending to know nothing about it. They insulate themselves so they can maintain a certain plausible deniability. They work behind the scenes planning, scheming, undermining, and doing whatever is necessary to protect their turf and their kingdom.

The backroom discussions, while without the cigar smoke and machine guns, are no less corrupt and destructive. They gather around the tables at restaurants after church, and sow discord and gossip about other preachers and ministries. They organize their schedules so they can attend wherever will provide them the greatest amount of exposure.

Every decision they make is made on the basis of how it will help them move further up the food chain. They will butter up one preacher friend, and then, take the same knife and slit the throat of another.

These IFB "Untouchables" will not tolerate anyone who challenges their decisions, their actions, and their unbiblical preaching. They will not tolerate anyone questioning their ministry philosophy and wisdom. They will fight, maim and cripple in defense of their friends, if it is to their advantage. But they will remain silent and detached when a young preacher or pastor is getting his guts ripped out, especially if there is nothing in it for them.

I learned long ago that for these "Untouchables," the bottom line is money and power. If it doesn't get you one or both of those things, it's not important. Money and power. Take those two away and everything would change tomorrow.

Needless to say, many of us have seen the ugly underbelly of many IFB ministries. My inbox is full of emails from pastors and church members all across America who have seen it. Our young people have seen it. The moms and dads in the pews have seen it. And we are sick of it.
Stuff like this is why we have severely damaged our testimony in the world. Even though these men make up a small minority of IFB preachers, for some reason they seem to dominate the movement. It is high time that the men of God who are honest, and genuine and aware of what is going on help to lead our people away from the cult leaders and self-appointed gurus.

The only way to stop these "untouchables" is to stop supporting their meetings, buying their how-to books and ministry manuals. We need to stop justifying their crimes and misdemeanors against the church of the living God. We must stop bowing at their altars and tiptoeing around their blatant disregard for Christ's example. Their power was given to them by their blind and silent followers.

The smaller churches and hundreds of unknown pastors need to turn to the Lord and His word for guidance; not the big, "successful" ministries. The politics have to end. The unquestioned loyalty for men who will stand in their pulpits, and mislead their people must end.

Accountability, transparency and integrity must be restored in those places where it is lacking.

Jesus called out the religious leaders of his day in Matthew 23. The entire chapter was Jesus teaching his disciples about the hypocrisy of the spiritual leaders, the elite, and the establishment of His day.

I am confident if Christ were here today, He would be turning over a lot of tables. He called the religious leaders of His day snakes, vipers, whited-sepulchers full of dead men's bones, blind guides, fools and hypocrites! Don't tell me it is not Christ-like to call out the hypocrisy in my own crowd. Jesus did it. Many times! The Apostle Paul did also.

"And no marvel; for Satan himself is transformed into an angel of light. Therefore it is no great thing if his ministers also be transformed as the ministers of righteousness; whose end shall be according to their works." (2 Corinthians 11:14, 15)

The people of God deserve men of principle as their leaders. Our children must have churches that stand on the precepts of God's Word without fear or favor. Our communities will only be reached for Christ when the church's credibility is restored. I am resolved to do everything in my power to bring about change. The church of the living God must repent and turn back to biblical principles if we want to see revival. We must get away from man-worship, and get back to pleasing the Lord in all we do.

Don't worry. Nothing I've ever experienced has soured me on the wonderful and priceless blessings of the local church! We are too close to the Rapture to quit now. Jesus is coming soon, and I want Him to find me faithful. With God's help, we must keep our eyes on the infallible Jesus and not on fallible men. They will let you down, but He never will.

As the songwriter, Bill Henry once said, "I've never been disappointed in Jesus! Doubt has never crossed my mind, for in Him no fault I find. I've been discouraged with some family, forsaken by some friends. But I've never been disappointed in Him." AMEN!

~ SECTION TWO ~
Restoring Our Credibility

* * *

PART FOUR
Responding Biblically

* * *

23

A Clear Position on Sexual Abuse

"A double minded man is unstable in all his ways."
James 1:8

* * *

Abuse of any kind is tragic. There are multiple forms of abuse. Some people are abused physically. Sadly, other people are abused psychologically or emotionally. One thing I believe we can all agree on is abuse of a sexual nature is one of the most traumatic things that can occur in a person's life.

If a church's first response to allegations of sexual abuse or assault is anything other than concern for the victim, something is very wrong. Regardless if the victim is a child or an adult, male or female, the effects of this kind of mistreatment carry life-long repercussions.

It is absolutely essential that, as Christians, we have a clearly defined position on the terrible nature of sexual abuse. Abuse of any kind is horrible, no doubt. However, sexual abuse has a unique way of inflicting deep, psychological scars unlike any other.

A church or pastor who treats sexual abuse like it is just any other sin or transgression is sending a terrible message to their people. God's perspective on sexual abuse, and crimes of a sexual nature, is unmistakably harsh. The church must have a unified voice. It should be clear, biblical and reiterated often to insure that the people have no doubts about the stance of the church on this subject.

Two Responses

One of the first accounts we find in the Bible of a sexual crime is found in Genesis 9:22-14. Noah and his family had recently survived the worldwide flood. The Bible tells us that Noah began to be a husbandman and planted a vineyard. He drank of the wine and became drunk. Some have speculated that the new atmosphere, and the changes in the weather patterns may have caused grape juice to ferment faster than it did before the Flood. I have no idea. Whether Noah's drunkenness was deliberate or accidental, he got drunk nevertheless.

As a result of his inebriated state, he was in his tent unclothed. Verse 22 says that Ham, the son of Noah saw the nakedness of his father, and told his two brethren without. Shem and Japheth, Noah's other sons took a garment and laid it on their shoulders. Then they walked in backward and covered the nakedness of their father. The

Bible says that their faces were turned backward and they saw not their father's nakedness.

When Noah awoke from his drunken sleep, he knew what his younger son had done unto him. His anger at the deed resulted in him cursing Ham. He said in verse 25, "Cursed be Canaan; a servant of servants shall he be unto his brethren."

Without reading too much into that story, it seems abundantly clear that what occurred in this passage was more involved than it appears on the surface. The Bible is clear that Noah *"knew what his younger son <u>had done unto him</u>."* It appears that whatever happened, it was a deed of some sort. I do not believe it was just an innocent glance into the tent. I do not believe he walked into his father's tent and accidentally saw him lying there unclothed. The text leads us to believe that his actions were dishonorable in some way.

Regardless of the exact details, there were two stark contrasts in his sons' reaction to Noah's condition. Ham's was, at the very least, passive, possibly even immoral. Noah's other two sons, Shem and Japheth, responded with integrity and compassion. In spite of the fact that Noah was drunk as well as naked, they approached him in his state of vulnerability with extreme carefulness and propriety.

As a direct result of these two responses to Noah's situation, Ham was cursed and the other two sons were blessed. We are reminded that our response to sexual sin matters to God!

God's Guidelines for Sex

God's parameters for sexual activity is clear. God created human beings to desire sexual fulfillment. However, it should only be between one man and one woman within the confines of holy matrimony. Anything else is forbidden. "Marriage is honourable in all, and the bed undefiled: but whoremongers and adulterers God will judge." (Hebrews 13:4)

God addresses the issues of sexual sins many times throughout Scripture. Passages dealing with God's position on fornication, adultery, harlotry, homosexuality and sexual abuse are clearly laid out in His Word. Multiple passages of Scripture clearly teach the dangers of immoral sexual behavior. Contrary to social trends, God's Word never changes.

Paul the Apostle referred to the sin of premarital sex (fornication) as the only sin that is committed against one's own body. "Flee fornication. Every sin that a man doeth is without the body; but he that committeth fornication <u>sinneth against his own body</u>." (1 Corinthians 6:18)

The sin of extramarital sex will produce a reproach that can never be wiped away. "But whoso committeth adultery with a woman lacketh understanding: he that doeth it destroyeth his own soul. A wound and dishonour shall he get; and <u>his reproach shall not be wiped away</u>." (Proverbs 6:32, 33) The blood of Jesus can and will cleanse us from all sin, but the dishonor and reproach in a person's life cannot be eliminated after committing the sin of adultery.

The sin of homosexuality is described in strong language in the book of Romans. "For this cause God gave them up unto vile affections: for even their women did change the natural use into that which is against nature: And likewise also the men, leaving the natural use of the woman, burned in their lust one toward another; men with men working that which is unseemly, and receiving in themselves that recompence of their error which was meet." (Romans 1:26, 27)

The act of consensual fornication is a sin against one's own body. The sin of consensual adultery brings a reproach that cannot be wiped away. Homosexuality is "against nature," "unseemly" and an "error" that is so vile that God gives these people "over to a reprobate mind."

If illicit sexual activity between consenting adults is condemned in the scripture with this much fervor, imagine God's feelings toward these acts committed with people *against their will*?

If God turns men over to a reprobate mind for consensual homosexuality, what does He do with men that do these things to little boys?

If a man cheating on his wife with another woman brings a reproach that cannot be wiped away, imagine the wound, the dishonor, and the reproach of cheating on his wife with a little girl?

If God's Word teaches that a man guilty of adultery is marked for life, why are churches so quick to restore them to the pulpit? If the dishonor and reproach cannot be wiped away, why are so many men still in the ministry that have committed adultery? How can a man be accused of sexual molestation and pedophilia, and people's first impulse is to restore them?

I'll tell you why. They have an unbiblical position on the seriousness of sexual abuse involving minors. Plain and simple. Protecting their church's reputation trumps protecting their children.

Why does the fact a person's crimes are no longer chargeable because they have passed the statute of limitations alleviate the church of responsibility? Why would a church employ a man that the state believes committed sexual crimes? If they have a case, but cannot prosecute, is that man free to re-enter the ministry? Of course not!

If the sin of adultery has a lifetime stain and reproach, how much more would sexual crimes be a lifetime of reproach? How can a man of God meet the biblical guidelines to be "blameless," and have pedophilia and adultery in his background? Just because there may not be legal grounds to prosecute shouldn't minimize the seriousness of the crime.

The church should demand a much higher standard for those in leadership. Unfortunately, the local businesses in our communities have higher hiring standards than some of our churches. Some churches, these days, will hire anything and anybody it seems.

A Sex-soaked Society

Our society, as a whole, has forsaken God's precepts for normal sexual activity. People's normal inhibitions have been under assault for generations. As a result, sexual perversions have manifested themselves in a variety of ways.

The sexual nature of television commercials are simply unbelievable. The sexualization of nearly everything is the norm these days. Cars are sexy. Trucks are sexy. Food is sexy. I recently saw an Applebee's commercial showing succulent ribs and chicken being cooked on a grill to the tune of Marvin Gaye's "Let's Get It On." Seriously?

The headlines are a constant barrage of subjects of immoral nature. Porn actresses, such as Stormy Daniels, receive wall-to-wall coverage. Her image dominates the websites and magazines. Who would have ever dreamed of a time when, not only a porn star would attain national celebrity status, but her lawyer would as well? The minds of society are constantly being turned to the subject of sex and immorality.

Movies and television programs have glorified illicit, sexual activity for years. The general desensitization of people's attitude toward sexual sin is complete.

Pregnancy outside of marriage no longer has a stigma attached to it. People live together before marriage without any hesitation or shame. Pornography is now available everywhere, including multiple social media platforms.

DID YOU KNOW?

An estimated 28,258 people every second, mostly men (72%) but also women (28%) view pornography. Every 39 minutes a new pornographic video is being created in the United States.
https://www.focusonthefamily.com/marriage/divorce-and-infidelity/pornography-and-virtual-infidelity/virtual-infidelity-and-marriage

When surveyed, 53% of men who attended Promise Keepers said they viewed pornography that week. More than 45% of Christians admit that pornography is a major problem in their home. An anonymous survey conducted recently by Pastors.com reported that 54% of pastors admitted viewing porn within the last year. In an online newsletter, 34% of female readers of Today's Christian Woman admitted to intentionally accessing Internet porn.
https://www.focusonthefamily.com/marriage/divorce-and-infidelity/pornography-and-virtual-infidelity/virtual-infidelity-and-marriage

Twenty-one percent of Christian men and 2% of Christian women say they think they might be "addicted" to pornography or aren't sure if they are (compared to 10% of non-Christian men and 4% of non-Christian women). *2014 Pornography Survey and Statistics. Proven Men Ministries. http://www.provenmen.org/2014pornsurvey/ (accessed Dec. 29, 2015).*

Twenty-eight percent of Christian men and 11% of Christian women say they were first exposed to pornography before the age of twelve (compared to 23% of non-Christian men and 24% of non-Christian women). *2014 Pornography Survey and Statistics. Proven Men Ministries. http://www.provenmen.org/2014pornsurvey/ (accessed Dec. 29, 2015).*

Here are just a few statistics on the incredibly far-reaching impact that pornography is having on our society. Source: *https://fightthenewdrug.org*

1. Porn sites receive more regular traffic than Netflix, Amazon, & Twitter combined each month. *(HuffPost)*

2. Thirty-five percent of all internet downloads are porn-related. *(WebRoot)*

3. The most common female role stated in porn titles is that of women in their 20's portraying teenagers. *(Jon Millward)*

4. Recorded child sexual exploitation (known as "child porn") is one of the fastest-growing online businesses. *(IWF)*

5. 624,000+ child porn traders have been discovered online in the U.S. *(Innocent Justice)*

6. Between 2005 and 2009, child porn was hosted on servers located in all 50 states. *(Association of Sites Advocating Child Protection)*

7. Porn is a global, estimated $97 billion industry, with about $12 billion of that coming from the U.S. *(NBC News)*

CHECK OUT THESE SOBERING STATISTICS:

Per the International Labor Organization, there may be as many as 24.9 million victims of forced labor across the world. Of these, 4.8 million were in forced sexual exploitation. *THE WHITE HOUSE, Office of the Press Secretary (April 11, 2018) whitehouse.gov*

Over 99% of trafficked individuals trapped in forced sexual exploitation are women. *THE WHITE HOUSE, Office of the Press Secretary (April 11, 2018) whitehouse.gov*

Over 21% of those trafficked for sex are children. *THE WHITE HOUSE, Office of the Press Secretary (April 11, 2018)whitehouse.gov*

In 2017, DHS's Immigration and Customs Enforcement Homeland Security Investigations (ICE/HSI) initiated 833 human trafficking cases, resulting in 1,602 arrests and 578 convictions, and identified 518 victims of human trafficking. *THE WHITE HOUSE, Office of the Press Secretary (April 11, 2018) whitehouse.gov*

Since 2007, the National Human Trafficking Hotline has received reports of 22,191 sex trafficking cases in the United States. *THE WHITE HOUSE, Office of the Press Secretary (April 11, 2018) whitehouse.gov*

Of the nearly 25,000 runaway children reports to the National Center for Missing & Exploited Children, one in seven were likely victims of child sex trafficking. *THE WHITE HOUSE, Office of the Press Secretary (April 11, 2018) whitehouse.gov*

The underground sex economy is a multimillion dollar industry. A 2014 Urban Institute study estimated the combined worth of the underground sex economy in Atlanta, Dallas, Denver, Kansas City, Miami, Seattle, San Diego and Washington, D.C. to be between $39.9 and $290 million. *THE WHITE HOUSE, Office of the Press Secretary (April 11, 2018) whitehouse.gov*

Reports of suspected child sex trafficking jumped 846 percent between 2010 and 2015, according to the National Center for Missing and Exploited Children. *THE WHITE HOUSE, Office of the Press Secretary (April 11, 2018) whitehouse.gov*

Human trafficking is the fastest-growing organized crime activity in the United States, making almost $32 billion a year for traffickers, while destroying the lives of tens of thousands of innocent children. Nearly 70% of these transactions now take place online. *THE WHITE HOUSE, Office of the Press Secretary (April 11, 2018) whitehouse.gov*

According to "The Global Coalition To End Human Trafficking Now" there are 10 million child prostitutes worldwide. *(The Global Coalition To End Human Trafficking Now)*

One in 6 endangered runaways reported to NCMEC in 2014 were likely sex trafficking victims. National Center for Missing and Exploited Children. (2015) *Child Sex Trafficking.* [Accessed 29th December 2015] http://www.missingkids.com/1in6

The United Nations estimates that out of the more than 1.8 million children who are exploited as part of the illicit commercial sex market each year, approximately 100,000 American children are the victims of trafficking. *(June 6, 2014); The Internet Pornography Pandemic: The Largest Unregulated Social Experiment in History, Donna Rice Hughes, etc.*
http://enough.org/objects/christian-apologetics-journal-spring2014.pdf

It is estimated that 100,000 children in the U.S. are in danger of sexual slavery. The average age of entry into the sex trade is 14 years old. *"Child Sex Trafficking At-a-Glance." Polaris*
Project (2011).
http://www.traffickingresourcecenter.org/sites/default/files/ Child Sex Trafficking AAG.pdf

Source: *https://enough.org/stats-sex-trafficking*

Why is it that the politicians and advocate groups of our country are outpacing the church of the living God in their protection of our children? Why are pastors so slow to act?

Why are churches so hesitant to take a bold and decisive stand?

Most churches today will not even address immorality in the church, including among the leaders. It seems that every few weeks you read of a pastor that is getting a divorce and marrying another woman in the church. People have grown accustomed to either the scripted denials or the emotional apologies. Either way, in most cases, life goes on.

I remember when the huge scandal occurred in the suburbs of Atlanta concerning Bishop Eddie Long. Five young men came out in 2010 accusing him of sexual abuse. He denied it, settled out of court for an undisclosed amount of money and kept on pastoring his congregation of 25,000 people. He never admitted any wrongdoing, and the church still honors his memory today. Long died of cancer in 2017.

Source: *https://www.nytimes.com/2017/01/17/us/bishop-eddie-l-long-accused-of-sexual-misconduct-dies-at-63.html*

What Jesus Said About Sexual Abuse

One of the greatest perversions of sexual activity is the exploitation of children and teenagers. This kind of sexual activity receives far greater condemnation than other types of sexual sins. In regards to the hurting of children, Jesus did not mince words.

In Matthew 18, Jesus took a child and placed him in the midst of the disciples. Then He said, "But whoso shall offend one of these little ones which believe in me, it were better for him that a millstone were hanged about his neck, and that he were drowned in the depth of the sea."

The word "offend" here is the Greek word "*skandalizo*" which is where we get our word "scandal." These words of Christ refer to something much deeper than hurting a child's feelings. He was talking about a scandal. The word carries with it the meaning *"to put a stumbling block or impediment in the way, upon which another may trip and fall, metaph. to offend; to entice to sin; to cause a person to begin to distrust and desert one whom he ought to trust and obey."*

Quite frankly, this text is addressing this issue of luring and enticing a child to sin. It is referring to any act that causes them to distrust someone they should respect and obey. Clearly, sexual abuse fits this description perfectly.

Jesus' recommendation for anyone that would "offend" one of these little ones would be for something worse to happen them than tying a millstone around their neck and casting them into the sea. In fact, Jesus said that was too good for them.

How many of our churches and ministries share the same sentiment as Jesus Christ when it comes to this subject? How many pastors boldly declare that shared opinion from their pulpits? How safe do our children and young people feel when it comes to the issue of sexual abuse?

What I want to reiterate is just how crucial it is for our churches to land on the right side of this issue. Sexual abuse is real, and it is serious. Any pastor, church or ministry that takes a passive stance on this subject is in desperate need of a wake-up call. Any church that would downplay allegations of sexual abuse of any kind forfeits its moral high ground. Period. Any ministry that minimizes both the victim's right to speak out as well as the demand for justice loses all credibility as far as I am concerned.

I want to point out the Bible's clear emphasis on the proper perspective when it comes to the treatment of the flock of God. The little lambs in our church deserve our utmost love and protection. In fact, it should be one of our greatest priorities. Too many churches promote a host of good things, but fail to properly protect the children and teenagers in the church. This has to change!

Notice the emphasis that Jesus Christ placed on the importance of little children. "And he sat down, and called the twelve, and saith unto them, If any man desire to be first, the same shall be last of all, and servant of all. And he took a child, and set him in the midst of them: and when he had taken him in his arms, he said unto them, Whosoever shall receive one of such children in my name, receiveth me: and whosoever shall receive me, receiveth not me, but him that sent me." (Mark 9:35-37)

Jesus equated our reception of a child to our reception of Christ and of God Himself. Jesus said in another place that the children were the greatest in His kingdom. (Matthew 18:1, 2)

The disciples of Jesus were rebuked soundly for their failure to properly understand the importance of babies and children. "And they brought young children to him, that he should touch them: and his disciples rebuked those that brought them. But when Jesus saw it, he was much displeased, and said unto them, Suffer the little children to come unto me, and forbid them not: for of such is the kingdom of God. Verily I say unto you, Whosoever shall not receive the kingdom of God as a little child, he shall not enter therein. And he took them up in his arms, put his hands upon them, and blessed them." (Mark 10:13-16)

The word *"forbid"* in verse 14 is a powerful word. In the Greek it is the word *"koluo"* meaning *to hinder, prevent forbid; to withhold a thing from anyone; to deny or refuse one a thing.*

I believe with all my heart this goes beyond simply forbidding them to come to Jesus. This means withholding or refusing them basic human respect. If a child is violated, and nobody listens, they are forbidding or denying that child the justice they deserve. If they are denied the protection they deserve, as a helpless and vulnerable child, that is a travesty. When churches protect the wolves, and leave the broken and hurting lambs without recourse, injustice of the worst magnitude is the result.

Too many people today do not realize just how condescending they are toward the youth. By failing to protect them, they dishonor them. By refusing to hear their cries for justice when they have been violated, we dishonor them. When we will not defend them, we dismiss them as insignificant.

When they tell us they have been hurt or abused, do we hush them up, or do we listen? Do we warn them to keep quiet, or do we seek to learn the facts? When a young woman says that someone in the church has done something wrong to her, does anybody care? When a young man says he's been targeted, is there anyone in the church that will hear what he has to say and help discover the truth?

24

Reality Check

"Which say to the seers, See not; and to the prophets, Prophesy not unto us right things, speak unto us smooth things, prophesy deceits:"
Isaiah 30:10

* * *

I had to come to grips with a devastating reality. Most people in the church do not want to know what is going on. They simply do not want to know if the allegations are true. They do not want to hear the stories. They do not want to believe that we have a problem of sexual abuse and cover-ups in our churches.

One of the most disturbing revelations of recent months is the fact that we have a serious problem in our churches. I have always had a nagging feeling that it was bad, but I now realize it's beyond anything I could have ever imagined. What we are seeing reported in the news is not isolated incidents. This stuff is happening everywhere, all the time.

This book would be three inches thick if I shared the stories that I have firsthand information about, or have been made aware of.

If you don't believe me, then I challenge you to go public with a video stating that you believe victims. People you've never heard of will look you up just to tell their story. Until they find someone that will listen to them, they have no motivation *whatsoever* to speak out.

I will not spend time in this book delving into other people's stories. I have been contacted by a large number of people who have shared their stories with me.

I am not an investigative reporter. I do not plan to take the time to investigate every story, track down every lead, listen to every allegation and confront every perpetrator. I have read several books in the last few months that list an enormous amount of scandals involving pedophilia, child molestation, and sexual abuse spanning a period of over forty years. The research in those books was tedious. It has been well documented that we have had an epidemic of child molestation and pedophilia in many of our churches. I have personally interviewed more victims and heard more stories than I ever thought possible.

Trust me when I say that it is so deep in many churches that we will never know the full extent. It is an ugly, demonic monster that is hidden just under the surface. Only eternity will reveal how many people have been hurt, victimized, abused, raped, fondled or molested in our best and most spiritual churches.

Sorting through the rubble has been one of the most despicable things I have ever had to do. And I was a victim. The things that happened to me pale in comparison when you dig down beneath the surface of some of these churches and ministries. Yet people refuse to believe it.

The atrocities of the late Dr. Bob Gray of Jacksonville, Florida are beyond comprehension. I have spoken with some of his victims and family members. What that man did for over forty years while pastoring Trinity Baptist Church is inconceivable.

I've read the transcripts of his interviews with the detectives. Books that I have read, giving detailed accounts of his many years of molesting, sodomizing and raping little boys and girls will make you sick to your stomach. His victims possibly number in the hundreds. He molested at least three of his own daughters.

I am personal friends with a man who was married to one of Bob Gray's daughters for a number of years. He told me that while they were married, she informed him of the ongoing sexual abuse she had received from her famous preacher dad. When Bob Gray was confronted by his son-in-law at a family event, he admitted it.

Another of Gray's victims, Ann Wagner, has written her story in a book entitled, *"Hope for the Hurting."* After seeing my video, she contacted me. In our phone conversation, she thanked me for taking such a public stand against sexual abuse in the church.

Her story is heartbreaking. She described in her book the grooming process that began when she was just a six-year-old girl. Her pastor, Dr. Bob Gray, showered her with love and attention and ice cream and treats and kisses. She would sit on his lap. He would hold her hand as they walked.

The relationship that seemed so innocent at the time culminated in criminal abuse. She was violated by her pastor in his office several times as a sixth-grader.

Ann Wagner was twenty-one years old, and married, before she told what had happened to her. In her book, she deals with the pain of dealing with secret abuse and betrayed trust.

What was also grossly disturbing about this story were the firewalls and protections in place for the man that perpetrated the crimes. He had built a fortress around himself; both literally and figuratively -- from his customized, sound-proof office to the layers of loyal staff, spineless deacons and blind church members. He was free to molest and grope and rape children for decades.

How else can you describe the brazen audacity to summon little girls to your office over the school loudspeakers during school hours? What secretary could be so oblivious as to never question a senior pastor of a mega-church taking little boys and girls into his private, soundproof office for extended periods of time without another adult or their parent in the room? How disconnected from reality would a staff member have to be to go along with that?

The dark secrets that have seeped out of that place over the years baffle the mind. The atrocities that took place behind those sand-filled, concrete block walls are crimes of the lowest and filthiest degree. The stories that abound of that man and his sexually deviant behavior are too numerous to list.

According to author Tim Gilmore, that the number of sworn depositions alleging child abuse by the victims of Bob Gray exceed four hundred pages. (Source: *Devil In The Baptist Church: Bob Gray's Unholy Trinity, 2016 - page 273*)

Many people today still believe he was innocent because he died before going to trial. Somehow, people are able to rationalize that over four hundred pages of sworn depositions by dozens of victims are all false allegations. I struggle to comprehend the irrational loyalty!

It is overwhelming at times how many people in our churches have experienced a traumatic experience of a sexual abuse nature and they have never been able to tell anyone or deal with it. I am sure that for every one person who is upset by my comments and my position, there are dozens of moms who thank God for someone who will speak up and go against the grain.

In the video I posted on my YouTube channel, I made the point that covering up scandals of epic proportions has become the "M.O." in fundamentalism. Several people took issue with that blanket statement. I realize that not every pastor and not every church is guilty of this. I would say that most are not. Many have handled these very disgraceful situations with wisdom and biblical leadership.

But the sad fact is there is still an epidemic of covering up sexual abuse. I say *epidemic* because the word means *(of a disease) affecting many persons at the same time, and spreading from person to person in a locality where the disease is not prevalent.*

As I said in the video, we let these perverts go without facing their sin, and permit them to go down the road to another church and do it all over again. An epidemic happens when an infected person leaves and goes to an uninfected place and spreads the disease.

Our failure to stop these abusers and hold them accountable has enabled them to go into new churches, new schools, new Bible colleges, and new ministries and do the same thing there that they did in the last church. THIS HAS TO STOP!

Again, I want to recognize the many churches and pastors that handle these horrible sins correctly and biblically. Not every church is guilty of cover-ups. Not every pastor is a pedophile. Not by a long shot! Thank God for those that fight the good fight and hold the blood-stained banner of the Lord up high. But in spite of this great multitude of godly leaders, the epidemic is still ongoing.

I have heard well-meaning men make comments about how small the percentages are of these cases happening. They are dead wrong in that assessment.

1. Only a small percentage of actual abuse becomes public

Statistics state that only one out of ten cases of sexual abuse are reported to law enforcement. Another staggering statistic is that the average child molester will offend 117 times before being caught. And fewer than 3 percent of offenders are caught!

According to the FBI:
- The FBI estimates each child has almost a 25 percent chance of being molested, with a sex offender living 'in every square mile of the United States.'
- They also believe approximately 1 in 10 men have molested children, with only a 3 percent chance of being caught for their crimes.

According to Ken Wooden:
- Male offenders who abused girls had an average of 52 victims each
- Men who molested boys had an astonishing average of 150 victims each

- Only 3 percent of these crimes had ever been detected.
- Forty-nine percent of offenders of victims under age 6 were family members
- Forty-two percent of offenders of victims ages 7-11 were family members
- Twenty-four percent of offenders of victims ages 12-17 were family members

(Source: *www.childluresprevention.com*)

According to the Family Watchdog:
- One of 5 girls and 1 of 6 boys will be molested before their 18th birthday.
- Ninety percent of all sexual assaults against children are committed by someone whom the victim knew.
- The typical sexual predator will assault 117 times before being caught.
- The re-arrest rate for convicted child molesters is 52 percent.

(Source: *www.familywatchdog.us*)

    The scary fact is we have no way of knowing just how bad it really is. These statistics prove one thing very clearly. We are a long way from getting out in front of this.

    Now I know these statistics are not "church" statistics. But let's be real; wherever there are people, there is abuse.

Just because it didn't make the headlines doesn't mean it didn't happen. Just because you didn't hear about it doesn't mean it didn't happen. Just because it didn't happen to you, or one of your family members doesn't mean it didn't happen. It just means that the perp got away with it.

To deny that sexual abuse happens a lot more than we realize is simply sticking your head in the sand.

2. We need to re-define the definition of "sexual abuse."

Sexual abuse far exceeds the molesting of children. Any person who is in power has an unfair advantage over others when it comes to pressuring them for sexual favors or activity.

A pastor who has a consensual adulterous affair with an adult woman in his church can many times be guilty of sexual harassment or assault. I know of hurting, vulnerable women who have sought marriage counseling from their pastor only to be seduced and get involved with him. Though they were not underage, or though there may not be a clear-cut crime committed, that is sexual assault and harassment nonetheless.

In the situation that I experienced with James Kelley, that was without a doubt sexual assault. Though he never touched me, it was sexual assault. Though I never gave in to his demands, it was sexual assault. Though no clear crime was committed (that I am aware of), let me be clear – that man sexually hurt me! The discomfort, the trauma, the stress, the dilemma, the conflict that he inflicted on me for six months was without a doubt a form of sexual assault.

One well-known evangelist, Dr. Bob Gray, Sr. of Texas, felt it necessary to challenge this fact after seeing my video. He not only attempted to discredit my story, but he insisted that it did not even qualify as abuse. After he saw my video, he posted on his website a scathing rebuke of me – not of the alleged child molester that I referred to, but of *me*.

He never bothered to call me or contact me in any way. Instead, he hid behind his computer screen and lobbed hollow mockeries and insults. As programmed by his mentors, he also managed to work in the worn-out, inapplicable 2 Samuel 1:20 *"publish it not"* reference.

I can't help but wonder if these men are capable of independent thought. They parrot the same arguments and talking points used and misused for the past forty years. Every time a scandal is uncovered that involves one of their friends, they dust off the same old narratives and shove them down everybody's throats. They didn't work back then, and they still do not work today.

I'm also a little leery of a man who quotes the late Dr. Jack Hyles more than the Word of God when trying to make his point. Anyway, I must have really gotten under his skin.

Twenty-one times in his article he referred to me as "disturbing."

In an article titled, "Judge, Jury and Executioner," posted on his website May 21, 2018, he ridiculed the idea that I had ever been abused at all.

He said, and I quote, *"I was disturbed at the bitterness I detected from what he claimed happened to him in the past. I did not need to know those things either and once again, it was one man's unsubstantiated accusations."*

Unsubstantiated accusations? How would he know? He never asked me.

He went on to say, *"I was disturbed because of the portrayal of himself as a victim. I fear we often misunderstand what victims really are. He calls himself a victim because he was propositioned. Am I a victim every time I am enticed to sin? It appears to me that he has claimed victimhood as his defense for attacking another."*

To equate what happened to me over a six-month period as "being enticed to sin" is ludicrous. I wasn't enticed to sin. I was recruited, targeted, groomed, hounded, badgered, ridiculed, pressured and propositioned in a hotel room BY MY PASTOR. If that is not sexual assault and harassment, I don't know what is! Gray simply ignored the first time I was abused. He was too busy denigrating my "portrayal of myself as a victim" to even listen to what I said in the video. This is standard operating procedures for these men. They immediately attack the victim, smear their credibility, insult and harass before even listening to anything they have to say.

Any person in a position of power who uses that power to intimidate and manipulate someone under them is guilty of abuse – plain and simple. We must redefine the meaning of the phrase "abuse" to include all of the tactics and behavior that lead up to the actual crime.

1. When a person in power makes unwanted advances on someone under him, *that is abuse*.

2. When a person in power makes sexual innuendos to those under his authority, *that is sexual abuse*.

3. When a person in power shows unwanted attention, grooms, pampers with gifts, touches, hints, flirts, manipulates events or has an agenda to break down the resistance of a person under him, *that is abuse*.

After not responding to any of my phone calls or text messages in May, Dr. Tom Neal of Jacksonville, Florida went to a lot of trouble to ridicule my personal experiences as legitimate sexual abuse. He created a website named after himself for the sole purpose of attacking me. I say that because his website was launched in July of 2018, and as of this writing, it still only has two articles on it; both of them are directed at me. One even has my picture at the top of the page.

He posted a 3,400-word article that was so bizarre that, at the time, I decided not to respond. I thought about it, but he caught so much flak for it that I just decided to let it go. He eventually had to disable the comments option on the bottom of the webpage because of the non-stop outrage. The extent of his "investigation" was to sit down with Cameron Giovanelli and ask him "some hard questions."

Upon hearing his denials, he then moved to phase two of his "investigation." He went online and scoured Sarah Jackson's social media accounts in order to discredit and slander her. The fact that she is involved in some things he doesn't believe is right was all he needed to convince him that she was a liar. What has that got to do with what allegedly happened to her twelve years ago when she was a sixteen year old girl in the church?

Tom Neal went to great lengths to discredit Sarah as well as her husband. He used words like "Potiphar's wife," "godless," "unsavory" and "narcissistic" in his attack. Funny though, that even in his 3,400-word diatribe, he never got around to explaining why the "man of God" Giovanelli was privately texting intimate messages to this "godless woman" right up until the day he got caught! Somehow that little detail fell through the cracks.

He wrote that I had "obviously been bullied." He went on to say, *"I don't know how and I don't know when but it is obvious he has been bullied. A trained counselor who watched his video and read his writings said he immediately detected the signs of a man who had been bullied or even abused in his past."*

I was amused at the intelligent deductions of this so-called "trained counselor." I very clearly stated in my video that one of my reasons for speaking out was because I had been sexually abused on two separate occasions. I explained that it was partially due to those experiences that I was compelled to make the video. I felt that having heard Sarah's story firsthand, and having interviewed all the people involved, I had no choice but to stress the credibility of the allegations.

Anybody who watched the video knows that I had been abused in my past. I said as much; several times. It didn't take a "trained counselor" to figure that out!

I could write a couple of chapters pointing out the multiple fallacies in Neal's exposé but I won't.

His endless veneration of all things Hyles, along with his repeated threats to fight me if I did not leave his friends alone, were so ridiculous that I do not think too many people even took him seriously. I know I didn't. Here's a man that concludes that I have been bullied, and his first response is to bully me some more. That's real godly wisdom and experience!

He accused me of attacking and criticizing Dr. Jack Hyles. He said that I was not even worthy to tie Jack Hyles' shoes. I never met Jack Hyles. I have never been to Hammond, Indiana. I never visited the church where he pastored. I have also never attacked or criticized him. However, he has had zero influence on me and my ministry.

If only half of the good things I have heard about Jack Hyles is true, he was next in line to the Godhead. On the other hand, if only half of the bad things I've heard about him is true, he should have died in prison.

Most people in the IFB circles either loved him or hated Jack Hyles. There's not much middle ground. So since I never met him, and I have no idea what all is true and what all is false, I just don't say anything. I'll let those that knew him best write their opinions of him.

I will say this though. It is sickening how many men there are who appear to be trying to outdo each other in their worship of Jack Hyles. Someone needs to inform these dear brethren that he is no longer with us and they can stop kissing his ring now. Their obsession with him is embarrassing.

It does make me wonder, though. If these older, more "seasoned" men would be so bold as to publicly mock and make light of an accusation of sexual abuse coming from me, a forty-six-year-old man, what would they say to an accusation coming from a child?

If they would go to such great lengths to try and discredit a man who could defend himself, how would they treat a helpless, scared teen girl who came to them with her story?

If I -- a father of five, with twenty-five years of ministry experience, was treated with so much disdain when telling my story, what chance would a young woman that few people know have of being taken seriously?

If the fact that both of my abusers admitting their guilt doesn't exempt me from their scathing and condescending rebuke, what would?

My accounts of personal abuse are backed up with court records, guilty pleas, prison sentences and a room full of witnesses to verify them. Clearly, if that is not enough to "substantiate" my story, what child in their right mind would turn to these people for help if they were victimized?

The answer seems abundantly clear to me. Pity the person that dare brings an allegation of sexual abuse to one of these guys. They wouldn't stand a snowball's chance in the Sahara of getting justice from that crowd.

Here is my point: mocking someone's experiences is the wrong response. Making light of their story is not the right way to go about helping them. Minimizing the seriousness of their abuse story is not helping the multitudes who are hurting.

We need a cultural revolution in the way we think about abuse. As long as people that come forward are subjected to ridicule and mockery, they will never be free to tell their stories.

If we take the incidents of child molestation, underage abuse and all the ungodly crimes committed against a child or a minor, and add the cases of adultery within the church involving the pastor or the leadership, the number grows exponentially.

On the surface, many of these stories just look like a case of immorality. We hear cases where the pastor ran off with his secretary or the piano player. We will never know how many of those relationships started out unwanted and uncomfortable for the woman.

Over time, an experienced abuser will not only break the resistance of his target, but he can create a relationship that "feels" legitimate and real. Even though they know it is wrong, they are convinced that they are special and they are loved. Those feelings, those strong emotions, are cultivated in secret over time by a man who is nothing but an abuser.

We have all heard of the "Stockholm Syndrome." The dictionary defines this as, *"an emotional attachment to a captor formed by a hostage as a result of continuous stress, dependence, and a need to cooperate for survival."* (Source: *dictionary.com*)

A person who has been kidnapped can develop Stockholm Syndrome in an effort to cope with an uncontrollable situation. There are children who were kidnapped and abused for years that experienced this phenomena. They developed an emotional relationship with their abusers simply in order to survive. They can even get to the place where they can go out in public with their captor and make no attempt to escape or call for help.

Their situation, as bad and as unnatural as it is, seems perfectly normal to them. They can even get to the place where they feel pity for their captors and sympathize with them.

I believe with all my heart that many of the cases where pastors or church leaders fall into sin with women in the church involve something akin to Stockholm Syndrome. These women are overwhelmed with the fact their pastor, priest, or ministry leader would want to be with them. Many of them feel they are in love with their abuser, making it even more difficult to break the emotional ties that have been created.

I would never suggest that ALL of the cases of immorality in the ministry fall into this category. We all know of many cases where the exact opposite occurred. There are many times when the woman targeted the man and sinful behavior occurred. Unfortunately, I can speak from experience that not all the women in the church are chaste, godly and spiritual. There are plenty of Jezebels out there!

What I am saying is the statistics are not going to reflect the many cases where it appears on the surface to be a consensual adulterous affair, but in reality was the result of long-term pressure and intimidation. Once a woman is unfaithful to her husband and chooses to be with the church leader who seduced her, it is not easy for her to come clean about how it started. To do so would make her look weak and vulnerable. The only thing she can do many times is to make the best of it and pretend that what they have is real and special.

Many times, these affairs destroy homes, ruin marriages and split churches. Many times, they do not even last. The "love" they thought they shared was not a godly love. The blessings of God were definitely not there. The whole relationship was built on sin, control, lies, deceit, and wicked lusts. A powerful, persuasive man seduced, groomed and broke down a woman until she was in so far she could not see a way out.

Once they have crossed a certain line, whether it be an inappropriate text message, an intimate voicemail, a subtle caress, an unexpected kiss or something else, the trap is sprung. The leverage then turns to blackmail. For that woman to leave that situation and confide in her husband, or for that teenager to go tell his or her parents, would require an enormous amount of courage. Only eternity will reveal how much this has occurred.

The percentage of churches affected by both sexual crimes and sexual scandals is astounding. There are more churches than we realize that have a story in its past of some sort of sexual abuse and in many cases, a cover-up.

God is a merciful and longsuffering God. In many situations when the sin is confronted, confessed and forsaken, He will have mercy. He will still be able to bless and work in that church. But only after the sin has been dealt with. "He that covereth his sins shall not prosper: but whoso confesseth and forsaketh them shall have mercy." (Proverbs 28:13)

3. You would have to have a personal relationship with every single ministry to know the full extent.

Even with my extensive network of pastor friends, church members, Bible colleges, etc., my firsthand interaction with just the independent Baptist churches is miniscule. I looked through my phone just a few months ago and realized that I have the cell phone number of over a dozen Baptist Bible college presidents. I am acquainted to some extent with probably another dozen. Yet I have NO IDEA what goes on in most churches because I am not there. I do not know the pastor. I am not at all affiliated or associated with those churches, and there are thousands of them.

For me to say the number of cases is small would be sheer madness. If the number of cases that exist in the churches that I know about are any indication, then trust me – WE HAVE AN EPIDEMIC! And again, I'm just talking about the independent Baptist crowd. I do not even want to think about what is going on with the other denominations and religions.

Sexual abuse is happening. There is no question about that. But that's only half of it. The other half is the extreme measures that churches go to in order to cover it up. The problem with the whole cover-up culture is that it severely distorts the actual numbers.

For example, I am told that there are roughly 6,000 independent Baptist churches. I have no idea how realistic that number is. I cannot find anyone that actually knows. The Star-Telegram newspaper reporter found 412 reports of sexual abuse in 187 of these churches. That number may include some cases that were recanted or refuted, so let's take that into consideration. That's more than 2 victims per church where it was occurring. Regardless of the exact numbers, the claim is that only about 3 percent of IFB churches are affected by abuse.

There is no way these percentages can be true. According to the National Sexual Violence Resource Center, the statistics tell us that only 12 percent of actual abuse crimes are even reported! When you factor in the culture of suppressing victims, coupled with the unbiblical and unreasonable protection of the perpetrators, that percentage of ACTUAL reports has to be a lot lower than 12 percent.

Do you realize what that means? It means that if the 412 cases that have been reported are less than 10 percent of actual cases, this problem could very well be affecting THOUSANDS of our churches. How can we deny how bad it is? Statistics are telling us the opposite. The numbers do not lie!

Our IFB circles have cultivated a culture of covering up sins and crimes that should not be hidden from the public. The covering up of abuse only enables more abuse. When pedophiles and perverts are allowed to operate under anonymity, then that is the ultimate win-win for them.

On February 10, 2019, the Houston Chronicle released a series of articles entitled "Abuse of Faith." The article reveals that over the span of twenty years, more than 700 victims of sexual abuse were discovered in Southern Baptist churches. Many of the abusers served predominantly in the state of Texas. Since 1998, approximately 380 Southern Baptist church leaders and volunteers have faced allegations of sexual misconduct. The article goes on to say that *"about 220 offenders have been convicted or took plea deals, and dozens of cases are pending. They were pastors. Ministers. Youth pastors. Sunday school teachers. Deacons. Church volunteers."*

Source:

https://www.houstonchronicle.com/news/investigations/article/Southern-Baptist-sexual-abuse-spreads-as-leaders-13588038.php

    The article described the findings by the authors, Robert Downen, Lise Olsen, and John Tedesco, and their team. Seven hundred victims were uncovered in just six months of research. This is just Southern Baptist churches! And people still deny we have an epidemic of sexual abuse in our churches?

    We will not be able to change the behavior of the pedophiles; not apart from a supernatural work of God in their hearts. We cannot change the unnatural lusts that motivate them and move them to deeds of criminal and devastatingly hurtful activity. We will not be able to thwart this epidemic by simply focusing on the perpetrators. There are some ways though we can limit them and their despicable conduct.

It will be different from what we've seen in the past, but I guarantee that it will be more effective. Though no system is 100 percent foolproof, I believe that the implementation of these simple policies will force the perverts and the pedophiles into retreat. My prayer is that these safety measures will put the wolves on the run.

25

The Real Problem

"Most men will proclaim every one his own goodness:
but a faithful man who can find?"
Proverbs 20:6

* * *

Much of the blame for the abuse and cover-ups in our churches lies squarely in the laps of the leadership. Dr. Lee Roberson once said, "Everything rises and falls on leadership."

The people in the church look to their leaders to keep them safe, establish safety policies and handle matters with integrity and wisdom. The biblical guidelines of church leadership have been questioned, even challenged. Many of the #MeToo proponents and feminist call it a "patriarchal system." In their mind, because a church is led by men, that is the root of the problem.

The problem is not the fact that men are in charge; the problem is the KIND of men that are in charge. The answer is not to rewrite the Scripture and strip leadership roles in the church away from men just because they are men. The answer is to get back to biblical guidelines for leadership.

There are many today who want to rewrite the biblical qualifications for church leadership. In their opinion, it is too archaic as it stands in Scripture. It is not politically correct. It is not "woke" enough for the 21st-century believer.

Ironically, neither are many other Bible truths. It is not hard to find those who want to explain away fundamental doctrines like the virgin birth of Christ, the bodily resurrection, the substitutionary death, and the literal return of Christ, just to name a few. Many in the religious realm will argue the validity of the Genesis account of Creation. They will debate the Flood and the age of the earth along with many of the biblical miracles and narratives.

I will not debate those people. I know my position on this subject is controversial, but so is my position on many other Bible doctrines.

There are multiple passages that make it clear that the order for church leadership has always been Spirit-filled men of God who have the Divine call of God upon their lives to lead God's people. The passages that lay out the qualifications of the New Testament office of bishop and deacon are crystal clear. *(See I Timothy 3:1-7; Titus 1:5-9; I Timothy 3:10-13; I Timothy 2:11-15)*

As Bible believers, we should strive to adhere to the Bible's qualifications for the bishop (pastor) and the deacon.

The Word of God is unchanging and is the Final Authority for all matters of faith and practice. We should not allow social trends, political climates, ecclesiastical philosophies or the unpopularity of a biblical principle to dictate our position.

I believe the Bible. Plain and simple. The Bible gives detailed qualifications for the bishop and for the deacon. Each one very clearly indicates that these positions in the church are to be held by qualified men. When a church is led by a God-called, holy, upright man with the anointing of the Holy Spirit, the sheep will be safe.

When a church is led by a man POSING as a man of God, but who is actually a wolf in sheep's clothing, the flock is in danger. Matthew 7:15 says, "Beware of false prophets, which come to you in sheep's clothing, but inwardly they are ravening wolves." I pity the church whose membership lacks the discernment to know the difference!

The problem with this epidemic of sexual abuse in the church is not that the leaders are men. The problem is that many leaders are biblically *unqualified* men. In some cases, we have the fox guarding the henhouse. The people in leadership are exploiting the people under their watch-care.

God has some extremely harsh words for this group. "His watchmen are blind: they are all ignorant, they are all dumb dogs, they cannot bark; sleeping, lying down, loving to slumber. Yea, they are greedy dogs which can never have enough, and they are shepherds that cannot understand: they all look to their own way, every one for his gain, from his quarter." (Isaiah 56:10, 11)

There were a couple of brothers in the Old Testament who were priests. They were so wicked in their greed and immorality that God referred to them this way: "Now the sons of Eli were sons of Belial; they knew not the LORD." (1 Samuel 2:12)

The passage goes on to describe their selfish disregard for the offerings. The law permitted the priests to take a small portion of the offerings for their food. But the sons of Eli, Hophni and Phinehas, would insist on the people giving them a portion of their meat before it was offered. They even threatened to take it by force if they did not comply with their demands.

This type of bullying leadership was so wicked that the Bible said in verse 17, "Wherefore the sin of the young men was very great before the LORD: for men abhorred the offering of the LORD."

It is no small wonder that these greedy priests that threatened and stole from the people were also extremely immoral. The Bible describes the depths of their depravity in verse 22. "Now Eli was very old, and heard all that his sons did unto all Israel; and how they lay with the women that assembled at the door of the tabernacle of the congregation."

It has been my observation that two things seem to go hand in hand: financial improprieties and sexual improprieties. Show me a leader who leads by selfish force, and I will show you a leader who has money problems or morality problems – or both. I've yet to see a ministry built around a personality that doesn't stray from Biblical principles. The church is to be built on Jesus Christ; not on a man and his charismatic personality.

Nowhere in the Bible does a leader in the church have the right to be a dictator. The pastor is commanded to rule (Hebrews 13:7, 17), but not to lord over God's heritage (I Peter 5:2, 3). He is commanded to be an example to the flock. The pastor is called an under-shepherd. His role is to lead the flock; not beat the flock. He is to feed them, love them, preach to them, teach them, warn them and protect them.

Too many church leaders today have taken more upon them than God intended. They are accountable to no one. They do not answer to their church for their actions. They do not submit themselves to the Word of God. They are their own authority, above rebuke and correction.

Their sense of entitlement has blinded them to their God-ordained boundaries. They feel they are immune to the biblical principles of local church accountability. The lines between right and wrong become blurred and they consider themselves the final judge.

The Apostle Paul warned the believers of this kind of men. In fact, Paul was very clear on the limitations of biblical leadership, even as an Apostle of Jesus Christ.

"Brethren, be followers together of me, and mark them which walk so as ye have us for an ensample. (For many walk, of whom I have told you often, and now tell you even weeping, that they are the enemies of the cross of Christ: Whose end is destruction, whose God is their belly, and whose glory is in their shame, who mind earthly things.)" (Philippians 3:17-19)

Paul spent much of his time warning the New Testament churches of fakes, frauds, phonies, false prophets and false teachers who would try and destroy them. There have always been liars and thieves who hide their evil intentions under their ministerial robes. That is nothing new.

The problem is that many church members do not have enough biblical knowledge to discern one when they see it. They sit for years under a man who has no right to be in that position.

The other problem is many people lack the courage to confront these false teachers. These wolves are simply allowed to do whatever they want, ruin as many people as they want, pad their pockets, and answer to no one until they become more and more powerful. Rumors swirl with little or no effort to confirm them. People who make accusations are belittled and dismissed.

Any hint of impropriety by the leadership is obliterated without hesitation. A church that permits a wolf to inhabit the flock is just as guilty as the wolf in my opinion. Pity the child or teenager who has to grow up attending a church with such spineless, weak "Christians."

26

When Allegations Surface

"And have no fellowship with the unfruitful works of darkness, but rather reprove them. For it is a shame even to speak of those things which are done of them in secret. But all things that are reproved are made manifest by the light: for whatsoever doth make manifest is light."
Ephesians 5:11-13

* * *

There are very few things more devastating than allegations of sexual abuse. There is not a church or a ministry that does not dread the mere mention of the possibility.

Of all the things that can go wrong in a ministry, the surfacing of sexual abuse or sexual immorality is one of the most devastating. When the allegations occur, the fallout begins immediately and can last for the remainder of that ministry's existence.

The very nature of the allegations create an interest that is unsurpassed. People's ears perk up at the very mention of the topic. Gossip runs rampant. The stories can take on a life of their own.

It is vitally important to the church or ministry to have a plan in place to address this situation. No one is ever really prepared for it, no matter how much they think they are. These incidents happen unannounced, and are completely unexpected. The people involved, the names that surface, the details, the crimes and the pain is always far more of a shock than you can prepare yourself for.

There are a few key things to remember when, and if, this tragic occurrence comes knocking on your door.

1. A time of crisis is when leaders need to step up and lead.

A leader cannot become a weathervane, turning and pivoting with the wind. A leader must have a moral compass that is unwavering.

In the next section, we will discuss what to do if the person being accused is the senior pastor or ministry leader. If the accused is the pastor or the person at the top, then the leaders under him need to assume their role of leadership with a steady courage. It is not the time to second-guess one's position or right to act.

The people in the church have a structure of leadership that is in place for the purpose of leading. If the leaders balk, faint, run, hesitate or fold under pressure, they are essentially worthless to the church. Jesus was clear about the difference between a shepherd and a hireling.

John 10
- *11 I am the good shepherd: the good shepherd giveth his life for the sheep.*
- *12 But he that is an hireling, and not the shepherd, whose own the sheep are not, seeth the wolf coming, and leaveth the sheep, and fleeth: and the wolf catcheth them, and scattereth the sheep.*
- *13 The hireling fleeth, because he is an hireling, and careth not for the sheep.*

When trouble comes, when the wolves show up, a true leader will stay and fight. A hireling will pack up and run. Leaders must be prepared to take on the challenges of enormous magnitude when allegations of sexual abuse surface. The ride will be rough. Without decisive, bold leadership, the ride will be even rougher.

People have zero respect for a pastor or a deacon who abandons his post during a time when the church needs him the most. A leader who does not have the stomach for problems should not be in a leadership position.

So many times when a church enters into a storm of a sexual abuse nature, those who should stay and hold the church together are the very ones who start the mass exodus. If a church is worth attending during the good times, it is worth fighting for when the wolves show up!

One thing I have learned in my ministry is that sheep are skittish. When problems arise, their first reaction many times is to stampede. They will run in any direction, as long as it is away from the problem. The church needs leaders with clear heads and the ability to rationalize and pray and lead effectively during a crisis.

I have also learned that people will always gravitate to the coolest head in the room. Falling apart is counterproductive. Calling meetings without real answers and real solutions is foolish. Getting everyone's feedback and taking polls is not leadership.

Kicking into "damage control mode" before you even learn what happened is also very unwise. The people in the church have grown weary with the idea of bringing in outsiders to spin and manipulate the narrative. It is the leaders in the church who people know and trust that need to take charge of the situation and do their job – LEAD!

2. If the accusation is against the pastor.

If it is the senior pastor who is accused, the church has not only the right, but the obligation to handle the situation.

The pastor is unable to effectively lead a church through a scandal if he is the target of the accusations. The authorities should be immediately called and asked to lead the investigation. The church should not be taking the responsibility to handle the investigation internally. This is where cover-ups can occur.

Any pastor that is truly innocent will gladly and quickly relinquish allowing the authorities and deacons to handle the investigation. He will not only vehemently deny his innocence, but he will cooperate fully with both the church and the authorities. He will not do anything to cover his tracks. He will submit to the church.

The Bible is clear; the authority of the pastor exists only as long as he remains submitted to the authority of the local church. The pastor who is accused should work with the church to prove his innocence, and to establish an unmistakable pattern of transparency and accountability.

Too many times the pastor resorts to mob-like tactics to clear his name. A true man of God will not strong-arm his church in a time of crisis. He will not call deacons' meetings and tell them how to investigate him or what to say. He will submit to any questions, interrogations, investigations or attempts of the church to address the issue. He will do more than just repeat that he did not do it. He will do everything in his power to refute the accusations.

If the accuser is a minor, the child should not be required to face the accuser. However, if this is an adult, the pastor should be willing to meet with those who make the allegations. He should be given the opportunity to face his accusers and to clear his name. Any man who is accused and refuses to meet with his accusers is greatly impairing his attempt to claim innocence.

I seriously doubt the innocence of a man that makes no effort to clear his name. I have imagined myself in that position on many occasions, wondering what I would do. I would do anything and everything possible to prove my innocence.

I would subject myself to a public lie detector test. Invite the whole church. Invite my accusers. I would become an open book with full transparency and accountability. They would have full liberty to do whatever they felt was necessary. That is the only way to settle the hearts and minds of the people.

If the accusations are false, that will come out. Going on the offense against the church and against the leaders is no way to clear your name. Attacking and smearing the accusers is not an effective strategy. Give the pastor an opportunity to make his case, clear his name and retain his integrity.

If the evidence that is presented is clear, the pastor should resign immediately.

If a pastor will not step down, he should be removed from leadership according to the church's by-laws and constitution. This will require Spirit-filled and dedicated leadership in the church. The Bible is clear in 1 Corinthians 14:40, "Let all things be done decently and in order."

The need for the leaders in the church to confront the pastor is essential. Many church members have been taught to never question authority. That is unbiblical on a number of levels. If a pastor is accused, there is a biblical way to handle it.

"Against an elder receive not an accusation, but before two or three witnesses. Them that sin rebuke before all, that others also may fear." (I Timothy 5:19, 20)

Beware of any pastor that loves to quote verse 19 but never includes verse 20. An elder (pastor) should be approached with respect and with the benefit of the doubt.

The Bible is clear that before an elder is confronted, there should be an effort to establish credibility to the accusations. This is where many church leaders fail miserably.

Let me be clear. If a child or a parent comes to the church with accusations against the current pastor, the authorities should be notified immediately. Let the police begin their investigation as soon as possible. Let the authorities help determine whether the accusations are legitimate. In the meantime, asking questions and conducting your own internal review can help expedite the process.

It is a mistake to simply hand it off to the authorities and not attempt to discover the truth if you are able. Listening to the victim and establishing timelines, witnesses, etc. is a common sense response.

If an adult brings forward accusations from many years ago, notifying the authorities is still recommended, even though they feel the statute of limitations has expired. There is almost always multiple victims. Even though a victim brings out an old allegation, the investigation could lead to uncovering recent abuses that are still within the time frame to prosecute.

It may be impossible to find two or three witnesses if a child says the pastor fondled or molested them when they were alone. There will be little or no physical evidence. There will be no way for the church leaders to verify if the accusations are true.

Let the police do their job. They have ways of getting to the bottom of accusations. Cooperate fully with them. Do not create a buffer between law enforcement and the accused. Let the process work.

We can no longer dismiss an accusation of criminal activity simply because there are not two or three witnesses. It has been my experience that once the allegations become public, more victims will surface. There is rarely just one victim. Sexual predators have multiple victims.

Sometimes you will only find the two or three witnesses after the first witness is treated correctly. Most victims think they are the only one, which is why most crimes go unreported.

Remember this staggering and heartbreaking statistic; only 3 percent of sexual molestation incidents against minors are detected. That means that 97 percent of sexual abuse crimes go unreported.

Sometimes all it takes to open the floodgates of other victims is for the first victim's allegation to be taken seriously.

To find two or three witnesses, you have to ask questions! You will have to move out of your security zone and put forth effort to corroborate the accusations. The witnesses do not always come forward immediately. Many times they do not realize they are witnesses, or they do not realize that there are more. It has been my experience that many people hesitate to "pile on" a person that has been accused, not realizing the biblical precedent for multiple witnesses.

If you know something, you are obligated to say something. Many church members simply want to remain neutral. That is not an option. It should be every church member's desire to see a swift and biblical resolution to a matter of this nature.

If you know something that would help confirm, or discredit the allegations, you need to speak up. You should not keep important and credible information to yourself when something this important is on the line. Get involved, and do your part.

Take your evidence, or your observations, to the leaders. They need help establishing the facts. Many times, what we dismiss as something odd or a "red flag" can actually be very crucial to establishing a pattern of behavior. It is when you put together all the pieces that the puzzle becomes clear.

3. Establish a clear priority to find the truth

There is nothing more unsettling than a pastor or group of church leaders who drag their feet in pursuit of the truth. The truth is out there, you just have to look for it.

One reason many churches or ministries implode during a crisis of a sexual abuse nature is simply because many times, the number one priority is to conceal the facts rather than to reveal them.

Laymen in the church are sick of being told from the pulpit that "the truth" is paramount only to see "the truth" buried when allegations surface. I do not know which is worse: to assume the people can't handle the truth, or to think they won't know the difference! Either one of these assumptions is an insult to the congregation.

For too long the people in the pews have been disrespected with a combination of inaction and incompetence. Those two, coupled with deception and cover-ups, are a perfect recipe for disaster. If an allegation of sexual abuse arises in the church, do not compound the sin by attempting to mask the truth. Attempting to hide the true nature of the sin from the church will create more questions and distrust.

Most people appreciate an honest attempt to get to the bottom of a situation. What they cannot handle is their leaders spending more time ducking and diving than actually attempting to discover the truth.

3. Protecting the church means protecting the people.

Usually when an action is taken to "protect the church," what that means is not what it sounds like. That is actually code language for "protect the assets" or "protect the mortgage" or "protect the credit" of the church. What many ministries fail to remember is that PEOPLE are the church.

Protecting the church should mean protecting the hearts and the trust of the people; not the buildings. Because of high debt, the offerings become many church's number one priority. Protecting the church means doing nothing to hurt the finances of the church. They can't focus on the broken hearts because their actions are dictated by their bills. The leaders cannot and will not get to the bottom of an allegation because they are distracted by the bottom line.

The bottom line is money. To many pastors and church leaders, protecting the church means doing whatever you have to do to limit the financial hit that will inevitably occur. In other words, feed the people whatever line of baloney sounds most feasible and pass the offering plate.

The church deserves to know what happened and that justice and judgment will follow. I believe most people can handle the pain of a betrayal when it is a sexual offender who has been accused. What they can't handle is the lengths many churches will go to in their attempt to mask, hide, cover, blur and misdirect. That is adding insult to injury.

Furthermore, protecting the church means protecting the victims. If someone has mustered enough courage to speak up about an alleged abuse, that person deserves to be loved and protected until the story proves to be a false accusation.

So many times I have seen a church throw the victims and their families under the bus in their efforts to "protect the church." Excuse me, but that little girl IS the church. That little boy IS the church. That young woman or that teenage boy IS the church.

Protecting the church means you must protect and love the people *in* the church!

27

False Accusations

"Thou shalt not bear false witness against thy neighbour."
Exodus 20:16

* * *

There are times when false accusations are made against a person. For a multitude of reasons, some people make the unimaginable decision to accuse a person of sexual abuse when there is absolutely no truth to it. The reasons for doing this range from blackmail to just downright meanness.

The thought of being falsely accused of something as horrible as a sexual crime or a sin of a sexual nature causes me to tremble. In this #MeToo era, we have already seen many examples of women who craved the spotlight to the extent they would tell stories without any factual basis at all.

Any person that would take advantage of our society's heightened sensitivity to abuse by spreading lies and false accusations should be called out. There are far too many real victims for us to waste our time with fabrications. Thousands of people are hurting from genuine abuse, only to be obscured by a few people's attempt to steal the limelight.

Once a person's reputation has been smeared with accusations of this nature, it is almost impossible to ever regain that good name. I cannot imagine the pain, frustration and anger that a person who has been falsely accused must feel. In one day, a lifetime of integrity and good character can be destroyed. With one false accusation, a person's entire life can be changed forever.

Along with the rest of America, I watched the U.S. Senate confirmation hearings for Judge Brett Kavanaugh with extreme interest. Having just gone through this ordeal in our church, I devoured every morsel of information that was made available.

When Dr. Christine Blasey Ford, came forward with her accusations against Judge Kavanaugh, I held my breath. What a nightmare! I was excited about Judge Kavanaugh's nomination to the U.S. Supreme Court, but this development was a real buzzkill. I hoped and prayed it was not true, but experience had taught me that anything is possible these days.

As I listened and observed, I noted several key things that posed a serious threat to Dr. Ford's credibility:

1. Her strong anti-conservative animus
2. Her inability to remember key details

3. Every one of her named "witnesses" denied it ever happened.
4. She went to Senator Feinstein instead of law enforcement.
5. She didn't want her identity to be revealed.
6. The timing of the delayed leak from Senator Feinstein's office
7. The inconsistencies about her fear of flying
8. The lie about her credentials as a licensed psychologist
9. The timeline of her adding another front door to her residence

...and the list goes on and on.

I listened intently to her testimony on Capitol Hill. Then I watched Brett Kavanaugh with his wife sitting behind him. What I saw and heard and the debacle that ensued turned my stomach.

The scores of colleagues and associates who vouched for his character made a powerful argument, along with the half dozen FBI background checks that he had already passed. Then there were more allegations popping up all over the place. I honestly lost count. They were disjointed and salacious.

The media was salivating over the news, but one by one the allegations were either withdrawn or proven impossible or untrue. Nothing panned out. They threw everything they could think of up against the wall, hoping something would stick. Nothing did.

When Senator Susan Collins from Maine stood on the Senate floor and gave her passionate speech, it was over. The Senate voted to confirm Judge Kavanaugh. I realized that no matter how conflicted people are in these situations, they usually go with the presumption of innocence. It is called "due process." I am a firm believer in the presumption of innocence.

It doesn't take a professional investigator to realize that Dr. Ford had no corroboration at all. None. I was listening for anything that would add credibility to her allegations, and there simply was nothing. Her own lawyer administered a lie detector test, and the public never saw it. The more she spoke, the worse she sounded. As Judge Clarence Thomas once said, when falsely accused by Anita Hill, what we were witnessing looked like nothing more than a "high-tech lynching."

False accusations are a nightmare. Statistics tell us that the prevalence of false reporting is low — between 2 and 10 percent. For example, a study of eight U.S. communities, which included 2,059 cases of sexual assault, found a 7.1 percent rate of false reports. A study of 136 sexual assault cases in Boston found a 5.9 percent rate of false reports. Researchers studied 812 reports of sexual assault from 2000-2003 and found a 2.1 percent rate of false reports.

Source: *2018 National Sexual Violence Resource Center website, https://www.nsvrc.org/statistics*

Do false accusations ever happen to pastors and church leaders? Absolutely!

Should our first response to an allegation be to deny it just because the accused says he is innocent? No.

Do we believe a person is innocent until proven guilty? Yes.

We do not have the option of assuming it COULDN'T happen. When we do that, we are left with the conclusion that it DIDN'T happen. It is statistically impossible for every allegation to be false. A large percentage of them prove to be true. Too many times, allegations are dismissed outright without any apparent interest in the truth.

We must not enter into an investigation with a bias influenced by our own personal agendas. The only agenda that any church should have when dealing with an accusation of sexual abuse is FINDING THE TRUTH. Plain and simple. We cannot take sides before the facts are presented.

As preachers, we are always emphasizing the importance of the truth. The Bible says that the truth shall make you free, yet many times preachers are painfully and willfully negligent in discovering the truth because they are in a state of denial. His preacher friends say he's innocent, so that is the end of it.

It makes no sense to think that a man who will molest a child will not lie about it. A sexual predator by his very nature operates in lies, deceit and manipulation. He will not only maintain his innocence, but also make it extremely believable. Yet many times the extent of a church's or a pastor's investigation into an allegation is to simply ask the accused if he did it. When he says no, that is all they need to hear. Because they do not want to believe it, they don't.

How foolish! How unfair for the victim! The same man who can convince a sixteen-year-old girl that he's in love with her can just as easily convince his colleagues that he would never do anything like that.

28

Analysis versus Paralysis

"And David said to Saul, Let no man's heart fail because of him; thy servant will go and fight with this Philistine."
1 Samuel 17:32

* * *

One of the most frustrating things to witness during allegations of sexual abuse is the snail's pace many churches resort to in order to "handle things right." They are so afraid of doing the wrong thing that in many cases, they do nothing.

Part of it is understandable. Dealing with a sexual scandal of a criminal nature is not your everyday ministry activity. The learning curve is straight up if you've never dealt with it before. The myriad of emotions, scenarios and possible outcomes can be almost paralyzing.

The ramifications of a scandal in a person's church are huge. The testimony of the church is at stake. The community that you have been trying to reach will now associate your church with things that are dark, illegal and frightening.

It would be easy to take only evasive action, to kick into a defensive posture and try to put a protective bubble around your church. The place that you love, the people you worship and serve God with, the church that you and your family have devoted their life to is under attack.

Closing the shutters and crawling under the table is not an option. You cannot afford the luxury of hunkering down in your proverbial storm cellar until the skies clear. The wolf is loose in your church, and someone has to deal with him.

I totally understand the need to call your legal representatives and get advice. I completely agree that the legal liabilities in these situations can be astronomical, depending on the allegations. I am very much aware of the biblical basis for wise counsel. In fact, to not get counsel during a crisis of this magnitude would be foolish. Proverbs 11:14 says, "Where no counsel is, the people fall: but in the multitude of counsellors there is safety."

What we have to avoid is the over-analysis of a situation that will not only portray an appearance of indecisiveness to your people, but can drag into a failed opportunity to maximize your effectiveness to bring resolution to the crisis. Because covering up sin has many times been the norm, it is absolutely imperative that a church not do anything dubious. They cannot make it look like they are trying to hide what happened, or working behind the scenes to protect the accused.

One of the reasons people have lost faith in the church is because its leaders always seem to "cook the books" when something goes wrong. They pull in their lawyers and issue formal "statements" that are as phony as a three-dollar bill. Their reasons are always the same. They are trying to "protect" the church.

In the meantime, the victim is left trembling and weeping in the back room, the pedophile is concocting a cover story, the church is not getting straight answers, and the cycle continues. While the leadership wrings their hands, the days drag into weeks and nothing is done.

People lose heart. The church loses credibility and its leaders lose the trust of the people. The victim or victims lose all hope of justice being done.

The sex offender is the only one who wins in these situations. While everyone else is losing, he is gaining. He gains time to plan an exit strategy and build his network of lies and deceit. He gains the opportunity to gather sympathy for being accused. He gains time to get on the phone and gather his cronies around him to build a firewall of protection against the horrible lies that are being spread about him.

Never mind that the people that swear on a stack of Bibles that he could have never done anything wrong live five states away and have never spent more than a few hours at the time with the accused. Somehow, because they are in the same line of work and they "know" each other that is all that is necessary to shoot down any accusations.

While the church wrestles with what move to make next, the sexual predator takes advantage of the downtime to plan his next move and his next church. I have seen it all too many times. Analysis can produce paralysis.

There comes a time when you have to suppress the urge to analyze and simply mobilize. The thing that needs to be done first is so obvious that is seems almost juvenile to have to mention it. Yet here we go.

Investigation versus Intimidation

The church needs to spend more time finding out the facts than trying to silence the accuser. Proverbs 25:2 says, *"It is the glory of God to conceal a thing: but the honour of kings is to search out a matter."*

When allegations surface, what the church needs more than anything is answers. Someone needs to fill in the blanks. The avalanche of questions following a public accusation of a sexual abuse or allegation of misconduct is overwhelming.

There is only one way that the church is going to get through this nightmare. SOMEBODY HAS TO ASK SOME QUESTIONS – not just any questions, but the *right* questions.

It absolutely blows my mind at the sudden aversion to the truth during these types of situations. The fact that nobody is trying to find out the truth makes me think they know the allegations are true and they are afraid of finding out something that will confirm it. It makes absolutely no sense to me to not ask questions!

Obviously, if a crime has been committed (allegedly), then the law must be notified. Whether a phone call is placed to the local police department or child protective services office, the authorities must be informed. Plain and simple. If they show up and conclude there was no crime, nothing is lost. You have done your due diligence and will not be liable for covering up or failing to report a crime.

If a child has been molested or assaulted, the child's parents should also be encouraged to report the crime with the full support of the church. Trying to keep a parent from calling the police when their child or teenager has been victimized is not only foolish, but it is illegal in most cases.

In the case of accusations by or concerning a minor victim, if the accusations presented are very uncertain or immediately questionable in terms of their credibility, it makes sense to conduct a preliminary internal investigation before reporting to law enforcement for the sole purpose of determining if reasonable grounds exist to believe that the minor has been molested or abused. If reasonable grounds do exist, the matter must be reported.

I look back over the horrible day in May when I was first told about Sarah Jackson and her allegations against the former pastor here at our church. I started asking questions. I needed to find out what happened.

It should go without saying, but so many times the first step is completely skipped. Talk to the victim. It is not rocket science. You do not need to be a licensed police interrogator to pick up the phone and ask some basic questions.

If the accuser is local, do your best to arrange a meeting. Allow them the opportunity to bring whoever they want to bring so they will be comfortable. If you can't meet in person, arrange a phone call; a conference call with multiple witnesses is preferable.

No matter how you go about it, one thing is clear. Somebody has to start asking some questions, and fast.

It is strange to me that many times the church and the leaders talk to everybody except the ones who know what happened. Why is it so many times the alleged victims are never invited to sit down and give their account of abuse?

Why do the victims find themselves repeatedly trying to facilitate a meeting with the church or the leadership? It should be the other way around!

Once the church is aware of an event of the sexual abuse nature, its leaders should immediately contact the victim to find out what happened. The problem I have seen over and over in our churches is the leaders launch an all-out Intimidation rather than an Investigation. The people who know are ignored. The facts are suppressed. The story is squelched. The allegations are denied unanimously before anybody has even spoken with the victim.

What happened to loving and valuing the truth?
What happened to the pursuit of the truth?

I was appalled in May of 2018 at the number of people who used their bully pulpits and social media platforms to wholeheartedly declare with all authority that the accusations were false. The problem was, not a single one of them had the foggiest idea what actually had happened.

The church in California refused for nearly forty-eight hours to accept the resignation of its college president, instead urging him privately to defend his good name. They refused to believe the accusations were true, and threw their full support behind the perpetrator of alleged pedophilia.

The shocking fact is that they never once contacted the victim to hear firsthand what the accusations were. It was abundantly clear to me that *they did not want to know*. Her initial post on Facebook was very ambiguous. The idea of sexual abuse against a minor was clear, but the details were not included in her post.

Instead of picking up the phone and placing a call to her for clarification, the church leaders in California kicked into damage control mode. There was not a single expression of concern for this woman and what she had been dealing with for the past twelve years. There was not an ounce of Christian love and compassion for her plight.

Not a single person in leadership at that church or Bible College called her, or me, or anyone in my church *for days*. It took them from Friday until Wednesday to initiate any communication at all with me. It took a total of fourteen days to get them to talk with Sarah on the phone – and that was only after she sent messages begging them to call her. She had asked me for the pastor's cell number, and I gave it to her.

I got lambasted for giving this "wicked woman" the phone number of a man of God. I was at fault for giving this "Potiphar's wife" the phone number of a pastor. I was criticized for how I went about trying to facilitate what would be the FIRST contact that the church had with the woman who had made the public accusations. It still blows my mind that I had to do anything. If the tables were turned, you can believe things would have been handled much differently!

I would have flown to Baltimore personally with my college president and met with the church, the deacons, the pastor, and the accuser. We would have had a "come-to-Jesus" meeting until the truth was established.

How hard would it have been for that pastor to bring a couple of deacons into his office and place a conference call with Sarah and simply ask her what happened? That's the least he could have done. It would have taken just a few minutes of communication for the story to be told by the victim herself. When that happens, then you can claim to be conducting an "investigation." By talking to the person who says it happened, you are now beginning to fill in the blanks.

I am fully confident of this fact. If Pastor Trieber had called Sarah Jackson when the story broke, he would have been able to detect in her voice the sincerity, the hurt, the shame and the resolve that we did when my deacons and I spoke with her.

I do not want to place too much emphasis on following your "gut," but there's something to be said for the deep, nagging awareness that what someone is saying is credible. Law enforcement, detectives, and the FBI, all follow leads and pursue certain people by following their instincts. When a person is lying, you can tell it many times. When a person is making something up, it just doesn't sound right.

But when a person is pouring out her heart and soul, and opening up herself in a time and fashion where she is most vulnerable, you can tell just by asking questions and listening to her if her story is credible.

No one ever said that everything Sarah alleged was true. In fact, I said there was no way I could ever know if everything she said was true. Only Sarah Jackson, Cameron Giovanelli and God really know what happened. But one thing I did know, and I said as much, repeatedly. I said after talking with her and her husband, my deacons and I were unanimous in our agreement that her story was credible.

What does that word mean exactly?

CREDIBLE, adjective [Latin]

1. That may be believed; worthy of credit. A thing is credible when it is known to be possible, or when it involves no contradiction or absurdity; it is more credible when it is known to come within the ordinary laws or operations of nature. With regard to the Divine Being and his operations, every thing is credible which is consistent with his perfections, and supported by evidence or unimpeachable testimony, for his power is unlimited. With regard to human affairs, we do not apply the word to things barely possible, but to things which come within the usual course of human conduct, and the general rules of evidence.

2. Worthy of belief; having a claim to credit; applied to persons. A credible person is one of known veracity and integrity, or whose veracity may be fairly deduced from circumstances. We believe the history of Aristides and Themistocles, on the authority of credible historians.

(Source: *Webster's 1828 Dictionary online edition*)

We believed Sarah's story to be "credible." We discovered *"no contradiction or absurdity."* We did not conclude that her story was "credible" because it was *"barely possible."* We drew the conclusion that it was "credible" because it came within the *"usual course of human conduct and the general rules of evidence."*

How did we arrive at the conclusion as a church that her story was "credible?" Simple. WE TALKED TO HER. We asked her a number of questions, and her answers provided us with an account of events that was believable.

When Pastor Trieber and his lawyer and his office manager called me on that Wednesday, I made it clear to them that I felt they had waited entirely too long to contact me.

He informed me that he couldn't call me without his lawyer present. He had to wait until his lawyer flew in and was a witness to the conversation. I was obviously aggravated with them for days of stonewalling. In spite of that, I refrained from informing them of the technology available today that makes it possible to conduct a conference call from multiple locations. It apparently never occurred to anyone in his office to bring up that option!

He could have at least sent me a text message or an email letting me know he was planning to call me as soon as he could. He could have let me know that as one of their supporting churches, they were praying for us during this difficult time. He could have reached out with anything, from anybody. Instead, he had to wait until his lawyer flew in and was in the room to speak to me.

The reason for the delay was simple. They were worried about getting sued. They were fearful that somehow, someway, they would be legally and financially liable for an alleged event that took place nearly three thousand miles away in another church over a decade ago. Really? How is that even possible? But the trend has always been to spend more time intimidating than investigating.

It was interesting to me that they didn't advise me to have MY lawyer present for the phone call. After all, the alleged crimes had occurred at MY church, in MY Christian school, in MY office, in MY house. Why wasn't I told that maybe I should have MY lawyer as a witness to the phone call?

It seemed to me that they were not concerned about me, or my church, or the victim. From all indications, they had no real desire to truly know what happened. I believe the only reason he called me was I told them through my legal liaison that I was getting the feeling there was a cover-up brewing and I would not stand for it. After repeated requests for a phone call was denied, I warned them that if they tried to sweep these allegations under the rug that I would "go nuclear." Those were my exact words. It was only then that they made any effort to talk to me.

Looking back now, I feel that their primary objective when they called me was to pacify and disarm me. They never had any plans of investigating the allegations. To this day they still haven't, as far as I know. They were preoccupied with minimizing the fallout and protecting their kingdom. That was all. I gave them the opportunity to control the narrative, and they failed miserably. So I did what I said I would do. I went nuclear.

When we get to the place in our churches where we are not afraid of the truth, or those that try to prevent us from telling the truth, then, and only then, will we be taking a huge step in the right direction. As long as we shield our people and ourselves from the facts, we will continue to mishandle and botch these situations.

People's lives are at stake. The reputation of the church is at stake. The justice of a possible pedophile's criminal activity is at stake.

At some point, you have to stop talking about it and praying about it and *do something*. Somebody must start asking questions.

29

Open Door Policy Re-examined

"For I know this, that after my departing shall grievous wolves enter in among you, not sparing the flock."
Acts 20:29

* * *

We must create an environment in our churches where sexual predators are simply not welcome. As pastors and church leaders, we absolutely have to shut the doors of our churches to those with known sexual crimes and predatory tendencies.

I know this may seem radical. In fact, I want to clearly state that this has not always been my position. My attitude toward the seriousness of this has evolved over the past four or five years.

In the past, I could have, and should have, taken a much stronger stand in this area. By the grace of God I will continue to grow and increase in wisdom in all areas of ministry, not just this one. I am so grateful to the Lord that as far as I know, I have been spared from seeing my leniency in this area result in anyone becoming a victim.

My policy on this issue began to evolve years ago, not just as a result of our recent scandal. In fact, I preached a message at Calvary Baptist Church in November of 2017 entitled, "Hanged and Drowned" taken from Luke 17:2. During the course of the message, I stated my position clearly. I dealt with the subject of sexual abuse of children and shared a little portion of my past sexual abuse with my church. This was six months BEFORE the scandal involving the former pastor broke. That message is still available on our church's YouTube channel.

I'm confident that this chapter will be controversial. Some will even declare it unbiblical and un-Christlike. I'm prepared for that. I will stand before God for my current position on this subject. Please allow me to make my case.

1. Jesus took an extremely harsh stance with people who hurt children.

Jesus said in Matthew 18:6, "But whoso shall offend one of these little ones which believe in me, it were better for him that a millstone were hanged about his neck, and that he were drowned in the depth of the sea." We have looked at this verse already in a previous chapter, but I want to expound on it further for a moment.

We many times hear pastors and church leaders talking about how we should welcome the sinners and receive those with sexual deviations into our church. Jesus didn't say anything about receiving the pedophiles. Jesus clearly told us to receive the little children. To receive the sexual deviants that currently are in unrepented sin so they can come in and prey on our children is the EXACT OPPOSITE of what this verse is teaching.

Jesus did not say that one who offends or scandalizes a little child should have a millstone hanged about his neck and drowned. No. He said it would be BETTER for him if that is what happened to him. Jesus was teaching us that any person who scandalizes a child would be better off if he were hanged and drowned.

That doesn't sound like a pastor with open arms to me! That definitely doesn't look like a group of church elders and leaders opening the doors to people that have a history of abusing children and bringing them into the church so they can do it again. Absolutely not!

Now if you are one of those super-spiritual people that is appalled at the idea of keeping certain people out of the church, you just might be part of the problem. If you feel that a sex offender has just as much right to come in and sit down in the church as the children do, you are part of the reason we have this epidemic in the first place! Certain people have NO PLACE inside the church. I can prove it with multiple passages of Scripture.

2. Wolves do not belong with sheep.

Matthew 7:15 *Beware of false prophets, which come to you in sheep's clothing, but inwardly they are ravening wolves.*

Granted, Jesus was warning the people about the dangers of men coming into the flock and preaching false doctrine. But let me make a point. If we are not supposed to let "wolves" into the flock to teach or preach something that does not line up with Bible, how much more should we reject men who want to come in and molest our children?

Notice the warnings of the Apostle Paul as he was about to depart from the church at Ephesus. He gathered the leaders of the church together and in no uncertain terms reminded them of their OBLIGATION to protect the sheep. "Take heed therefore unto yourselves, and to all the flock, over the which the Holy Ghost hath made you overseers, to feed the church of God, which he hath purchased with his own blood." (Acts 20:28-31)

This was a strong warning to TAKE HEED – meaning *to observe, notice, be on the lookout; be on the alert.* He reminded them that the position they held as leaders was a position God put them in to be OVERSEERS.

OVERSEER is the Greek word episkopos. It means *an overseer; a man charged with the duty of seeing that things to be done by others are done rightly, any curator, guardian or superintendent; the superintendent, elder, pastor, or overseer of a Christian church; the NT uses the term bishop, overseers, pastors, elders, and presbyters interchangeably* (Source: *Strong's Concordance*)

The role of the pastor is to GUARD. There is no question in my mind that the pastor and the leadership should make it a high priority to guard our children and our people from those who would turn them into victims! "For I know this, that after my departing shall grievous wolves enter in among you, not sparing the flock." (Acts 20:29)

Once again we see the comparison of a flock of sheep and the wolves. He used the word "grievous" to describe these wolves. The word "**grievous**" means: *heavy, violent, cruel, unsparing.* In other words, we should protect the flock of God from those who are violent, cruel and unsparing. If that doesn't describe a pedophile, I do not know what does! But the Apostle Paul is not just warning about the wolves that will creep in from the outside.

He warns of the ones that are already inside the church. "Also of your own selves shall men arise, speaking perverse things, to draw away disciples after them." (Acts 20:30) From these verses we conclude that from within the congregation, men will rise up, and with perverse lips and perverse words, they will draw and seduce people and followers after themselves.

How many times have we seen that happen? Sunday school teachers, deacons, pastors, bus workers, children's ministry workers rise up and with perverted hearts and perverted hands and perverted words seduce and pull people into their traps.

Paul was so passionate about the overseer's duty to protect the flock of God that he warned everyone night and day for three years, weeping and urging them to keep their eyes open and to recognize the wolves. "Therefore watch, and remember, that by the space of three years I ceased not to warn every one night and day with tears." (Acts 20:31)

Does this sound like Paul believed in an "open door policy" for perverts and wolves? Absolutely not! Would you let a cat burglar watch your house while you're on vacation? Would you let a convicted murderer have the keys to your gun safe? Why would you bring a person with a warped, perverted and dysfunctional mind into your church where your children and teenagers are? There is not a biblical precedent for that anywhere!

3. Paul the Apostle warned the church to beware of certain people.

"Finally, my brethren, rejoice in the Lord. To write the same things to you, to me indeed is not grievous, but for you it is safe. Beware of dogs, beware of evil workers, beware of the concision." (Philippians 3:1, 2) He warned them of three kinds of people in verse 2.

Beware of dogs. This is a metaphor for a man of impure mind, an impudent man. Paul warned them to be watchful of men with impure minds.

The second group was simply described as evil workers. These are those men that perform secret acts of evil on the weak and helpless. Their hearts and minds are evil; therefore, their deeds will be evil. Paul didn't exhort the church to change these men; he warned them to BEWARE of them.

The third group he warned them of were "the concision." This word means *to cut up or to mutilate*. These are men whose deeds destroy and shred the lives of people. Paul warned them to watch out for these men. He did not tell the church at Philippi to start a reform class. He didn't admonish them to pray for them, or to befriend them. He told the church to BEWARE of them!

Why did he do that? He explained his reason clearly in the next verse. "For we are the circumcision, which worship God in the spirit, and rejoice in Christ Jesus, <u>and have no confidence in the flesh</u>." (Philippians 3:3) There are simply some people you cannot trust!

4. The Apostle Paul boldly taught that certain people should be kicked out of the church.

"It is reported commonly that there is fornication among you, and such fornication as is not so much as named among the Gentiles, that one should have his father's wife. And ye are puffed up, and have not rather mourned, that he that hath done this deed might be taken away from among you." (1 Corinthians 5:1, 2)

Paul insisted that a man be removed from the church for the sin of incest. He was committing fornication with his father's wife. The sin was so egregious that Paul used the phrase, "and such fornication as is not so much as named among the Gentiles…"

The sin was so bad that even the unsaved heathen did not do that. Yet there was a man in the church of Corinth who was guilty of this terrible sin, and the people were *"puffed up"* or proud. They defended him and protected him, rather than weeping over the seriousness of the sin and putting him out of the church.

Imagine what Paul would have said about a man that was committing fornication with his own children? Or his own grandchild? Or his nephew or niece? Or the children of someone in the church?

He issued this harsh rebuke. "For I verily, as absent in body, but present in spirit, have judged already, as though I were present, concerning him that hath so done this deed" (1 Corinthians 5:3). Paul took the liberty to judge the situation from a distance; without even being there. Some decisions are simply not that complicated!

Many times you hear statements like, "Well, I wasn't there and I don't know all the facts, so I hate to weigh in on the situation." Paul wasn't there, but he heard enough to make a judgment call.

I find it interesting that Paul heard about this sin secondhand. He wasn't there. He didn't witness it. He didn't conduct an investigation. It was *"commonly reported"* and that was all Paul needed to render a verdict. And his verdict was "…that he that hath done this deed might be taken away from among you." Paul's advice was, "Kick him out of the church!"

He clearly commanded them in verses 4 and 5, "In the name of our Lord Jesus Christ, when ye are gathered together, and my spirit, with the power of our Lord Jesus Christ, To deliver such an one unto Satan for the destruction of the flesh, that the spirit may be saved in the day of the Lord Jesus."

The Apostle Paul's solution was to turn him over to the devil for destruction. Paul was not telling them to be patient with this man, or to work with him, or to try to help him overcome his incestuous desires. He told them to kick him out and let Satan do whatever he wanted with him.

The latter part of verse 5 indicates that Paul's opinion was that if the man was saved, he wouldn't go to hell. Regardless of whether or not he was a believer, Paul wasn't interested in welcoming him into the church. He wanted him GONE. REMOVED! "Your glorying is not good. Know ye not that a little leaven leaveneth the whole lump? Purge out therefore the old leaven, that ye may be a new lump, as ye are unleavened." (1 Corinthians 5:6, 7)

Notice the phrase *"purge out."* We find that phrase only one other place in the Scripture. Look at how God used it. "And I will purge out from among you the rebels, and them that transgress against me: I will bring them forth out of the country where they sojourn, and they shall not enter into the land of Israel: and ye shall know that I am the LORD." (Ezekiel 20:38)

Purge out means to run them out and keep them out!

Paul's rebuke of "your glorying is not good" was a direct hit on their unscriptural attitude. This pervasive trend that "our church is so inclusive" and "we welcome everybody" and "it's not our place to judge" philosophy is DEAD WRONG! Paul told them that a little leaven (sin) will eventually pollute the entire loaf of bread. Sometimes you have to do a little house cleaning and take out the trash.

Several times in my ministry I have, either personally or via a deacon or usher, simply asked someone to leave and never come back. If I get word that a sex offender is attending one of our services, I immediately send word that he is not welcome. I know that tweaks some people, but guess what? I don't have to keep an eye on that sicko from now on. He's gone. My children are safe, and I did my job of watching over the flock.

I remember years ago I had to put my foot down in a situation with a young man in our church. He had grown up in a good church and had been raised in a godly home. He knew full well how he was supposed to conduct himself, yet he found great pleasure in rebelling at every possible opportunity.

Long after he had left our church, he would randomly pull up on our church property at service time with his music blaring. Once he even opened the trunk of his car to reveal his hidden stash of booze to some of the teenagers. He was doing his best to entice the young people of our church to go against God's Word, to go against their parents teaching, to go against everything they had been taught about right and wrong. I heard about this potential negative influence and was troubled.

He strutted in the door one night and just stood in the back of the auditorium, trying to look cool. He had a smug look of defiance on his face. It was obvious that he was up to no good. He was no longer a member of our church. He didn't come very often, but when he did he made a splash.
I had determined the next time he came to deal with him. When I saw him that night, I walked back to where he was standing.

"What are you doing here?"

He looked at me and grinned.

"I'm just here."

"Not any more you're not."

"What?"

"You heard me. Leave."

He looked stunned.

"Leave?"

"Yes. Leave. And don't come back. You're not going to come in here and influence our kids any more. Get in your car and go. And I don't want to see you back here again."

He left and never came back. Was that the right thing to do? I do not feel that I had much choice. He had heard the truth and was a rebel. He was "a little leaven" and the Bible says if you don't get rid of it, it will "leaven the whole lump."

I'm not saying that some of our young people never experimented with booze after that, but I am sure of one thing. They didn't get it from him on our church property! He was a wolf. He had an agenda, and it was to use perverse words to draw away disciples unto himself. I had to put a stop to it. It was my job. I had no choice.

My church appreciated my vigilance. They knew I was doing my God-given responsibility to protect the flock of God from the wolves. You can't do that with a "Wolves Are Welcome Here" sign on the front door.

5. Jesus ran people out of the Temple with a whip.

The protective attitude that Jesus had when it came to His Father's house is on full display in John chapter 2. Jesus walked into the temple and found moneychangers.

The Lord has allowed me to take many missions trips around the world. Each time we land in a foreign country, our first task is to exchange our American money into the local currency. Many times the missionary will inform us that we need to be careful where we get our money exchanged because of the dishonest money changers. We have to exercise great caution to keep from essentially getting robbed during that exchange process.

As people came into the temple from all over the region, they had to get their foreign currency exchanged in order to purchase their sacrifices. These money changers were being dishonest about the exchange rate and were essentially robbing these foreign worshippers.

When Jesus saw what they were doing, He was livid! I love this story because it shows a side of the Lord Jesus Christ that many people do not want to know about.

The Bible says in John 2:13-17, "And the Jews' passover was at hand, and Jesus went up to Jerusalem, And found in the temple those that sold oxen and sheep and doves, and the changers of money sitting: And when he had made a scourge of small cords, he drove them all out of the temple, and the sheep, and the oxen; and poured out the changers' money, and overthrew the tables;"

Notice the premeditated response of the Lord Jesus Christ. He walked in and found these men doing this unethical and illegal activity in the temple. What did he do? He scrounged around, found some small cords, and then stood there making a scourge with them.

I can imagine Him as He looked around and watched this despicable behavior – the whole time making this whip. When He got it like He wanted it, He started swinging that whip and the Bible says He "DROVE THEM ALL OUT OF THE TEMPLE."

So much for the "Open Door Policy!" He was incensed. He was angry. He poured out their money. He threw tables over. He went ballistic over the sin taking place INSIDE HIS FATHER'S HOUSE.

Can you imagine the reaction of the precious Son of God if He had seen a man molesting a child? Imagine if Jesus had witnessed one of the priests sexually exploiting one of the little children who were there? Lord help us! He would have burned the place to the ground! All that these men were guilty of doing were cheating a little bit with an exchange rate. And look how Jesus responded.

What do you think Jesus would do today if He was a member or a pastor of a church where children were being fondled and raped and molested? I can only imagine the holy terror that He would rain down on that place!

Jesus didn't just run them out. He told them to STAY OUT. "And said unto them that sold doves, Take these things hence; make not my Father's house an house of merchandise." They had turned the house of God into a den of thieves. They had hijacked the house of God and made it into something dirty and self-serving and vile. Jesus would not tolerate that one minute!

Jesus was "eat up" with a holy zeal for the Father's house. "And his disciples remembered that it was written, The zeal of thine house hath eaten me up."

Keeping God's house clean was a priority. Keeping it safe and holy was important to Him. Kicking people out that came for the sole purpose of exploiting God's people was a task He didn't mind doing. He had no problem getting His hands dirty if it was a result of taking out the garbage.

We have to change the way we look at the church. I know the church is like a hospital. Sick and hurting people come seeking help and healing. I understand that. We go soulwinning multiple times in a week. Our church goes out into the highways and hedges and compel people to come in. We preach salvation messages often. We give an invitation for sinners to be saved and receive Christ every single service at our church. We are aggressive and confrontational in our efforts to evangelize.

But understand this: the church is an assembly of saved, baptized and unified believers. It is also private property. We have the right to restrict those who come in. All I am saying is that for too long, we've opened up our churches to the worst scumbags on the planet and then we wonder why our children are assaulted, violated and damaged for life. We need a cultural revolution in our churches in how we think about the local church.

It is not our house; it is HIS house. The flock is not our flock; it is HIS flock. He made pastors the overseers of HIS flock. We are commanded and obligated to protect them. If that means performing church discipline on a member, then so be it. If that means forbidding some to come in, then so be it.

God's Word is clear; Heaven is not open to certain people. I realize that the church and Heaven are not the same. I get that. But the point I'm making is I believe we have turned our sanctuaries into a sanctuary for the wrong people.

Revelation 21 teaches us that Heaven has walls and gates. Have you ever wondered why? It's not like someone can just walk in. Heaven is somewhere in outer space. We don't even know where it is. NASA hasn't found it.

It is very clear that an unsaved person, or a nonbeliever cannot just wander up to Heaven. I have given it a lot of thought, and the only answer that I can come up with is that Heaven has walls and gates to demonstrate just how exclusive Heaven is.

In fact, Revelation 21:27 says, "And there shall in no wise enter into it any thing that defileth, neither whatsoever worketh abomination, or maketh a lie: but they which are written in the Lamb's book of life."

John went on in chapter 22, verses 14 and 15, "Blessed are they that do his commandments, that they may have right to the tree of life, and may enter in through the gates into the city. For without are dogs, and sorcerers, and whoremongers, and murderers, and idolaters, and whosoever loveth and maketh a lie."

The local church was put here as a place for God's people to come hear the Word of God preached. A place to assemble and fellowship with each other. A place to grow in the grace and knowledge of Jesus Christ. A place to become equipped to win a lost and dying world to God. The church was not put here to cater to the unbeliever. The church is not to be a hunting ground for predators or a safe haven for those sick people who would hurt our little ones. We have to keep them out, and we have to be vocal about it.

We lock up our valuables. We put our jewelry and our guns in safes and lockboxes. We put deadbolts and locks on our homes. What locks have you put in place to protect your children? What security measures have you implemented in your church to keep your most valuable treasures – your children – safe from the wolves?

Are we guilty of protecting the offering plates full of money better than we are our precious children and young people? If someone in the church had a history of being a thief, would we make him the church treasurer or the head usher? Would he be entrusted to count the offering and make the bank deposits? Of course not!

Yet all too often, men with a history of sexual crimes or accusations of doing things immoral and illegal are made bus workers, children's ministry workers, school teachers and coaches. What is wrong with us? Why are we so adamant that we are to "love" and "restore" and "forgive" the guilty while at the same time leaving our helpless, trusting children and youth more vulnerable than ever before? Where is that type of "love" found in the Bible?

What love is this that we would risk our innocent to protect the guilty? What love is this that would cause us to put the feelings of the perpetrators over the feelings of the victims? What love is this that we would open our doors to the scandalous and isolate the suffering?

I've heard this until it makes me sick: "We believe in second chances." What about the ones who got molested? Do they get a second chance to live their lives without the horror of being abused? Do our little boys and girls get a second chance at retaining their virginity?

Our children only get ONE CHANCE to go through life without the nightmare of becoming a statistic. Once that opportunity is lost, it is lost forever.

1. Only 12 percent of child sexual abuse is ever reported to the authorities
2. Thirty percent of women were between the ages of 11 and 17 at the time of their first completed rape
3. Twelve percent of women were age 10 or younger at the time of their first completed rape victimization
4. Twenty-eight percent of men were age 10 or younger at the time of their first completed rape victimization

Source: https://www.nsvrc.org/statistics

These people who are soft on the pedophile need to understand; they do not interpret your compassion and forgiveness as a second chance to get their life right. In essence, it is a second chance for them to perfect their craft and hurt someone else. If anybody deserves a second chance, it is the victims.

30

An Environment of Transparency

"Like as a lion that is greedy of his prey, and as it were a young lion lurking in secret places."
Psalms 17:12

* * *

One of the greatest deterrents to sexual abuse in the church is an environment of transparency. When men with evil intentions know the light will be turned on them at the first whisper of misconduct, they will either control themselves or they will go someplace else.

An environment of transparency keeps people honest. It forces those with ulterior motives to re-evaluate them. Any pastor or church leader who shies away from transparency may have something to hide.

It has been my practice at every ministry I have ever been in to immediately reassess and establish very clear policies and procedures. It is my honest belief that self-imposed transparency protocols forces everyone to stay honest and above reproach.

Transparency in Finances

One of the things I look for to reveal the level of transparency in a ministry is their financial reporting. I alluded to this earlier, but I want to expound on this point for a moment.

Show me a pastor who is hiding key information involving the finances, and I will show you a pastor who is hiding other things. When you realize that money is a result of the faith and the generosity of the membership, you understand the need for transparency.

A pastor or leader who does not respect a church member's right to know what is being done with the money will not respect the members in other areas. I firmly believe that when a pastor implements policies and procedures concerning the finances of the church, he is building trust. He is revealing that he has nothing to hide.

I have found an astonishing correlation in men who have a sense of entitlement in the area of money, and a sense of entitlement in the area of sexual fulfillment. Many of these men who take advantage of the children or youth in the church also take advantage of the church in financial matters.

A major red flag in any ministry is extravagant and unnecessary spending. This is an indication of a low evaluation of valuable resources. It also reveals a disrespect for holy things. A church leader who wastes money will also waste people.

Corruption comes in many forms. Entitled leaders will search for multiple ways to satisfy their selfish greed. Sometimes it is in the form of wasteful spending. Sometimes it is in the exploitation of people. These type of leaders feel they are God's gift to the church in such a way that they are entitled to whatever they want to take.

Isaiah 56:11 says, "Yea, they are greedy dogs which can never have enough, and they are shepherds that cannot understand: they all look to their own way, every one for his gain, from his quarter."

In 2015, mega-pastor Creflo Dollar from Atlanta faced enormous backlash after asking his followers for $60 million for a Gulfstream G650. Televangelist Jesse Duplantis asked his followers in May 2018 to chip in so he could purchase a brand new Dassault Falcon 7X, which costs about $54 million. He said Jesus told him to do it. And he already had three planes!

Source: *https://www.washingtonpost.com/news/acts-of-faith/wp/2018/05/29/a-televangelist-wants-his-followers-to-pay-for-a-54-million-private-jet-its-his-fourth-plane/*

I could go on and on with the ridiculous examples of extreme fleecing of the flock that occurs around us. But that unscrupulous group is not the only ones we need to watch out for. There are a lot of unknown ministry leaders with that same mindset. They may not buy jet planes, but their mentality toward the people of God is sheer greed and entitlement.

It is disturbing to see church leaders squander the church's resources. They use the church's credit card for everything, paying for their own personal items with the church's money. They splurge and waste the Lord's offerings to satisfy themselves. This is an outward manifestation of some serious inner issues. This is completely contrary to the example that Jesus set in John 10:11 when He said, "I am the good shepherd: the good shepherd giveth his life for the sheep."

When Jesus fed the five thousand, all four Gospels make a point to tell us that they took up twelve baskets of fragments. Jesus set an amazing example of stewardship and avoiding waste. Considering the bread and fish were essentially free, it is even more impressive. Jesus multiplied those resources supernaturally and yet did not want to waste a single crumb.

Show me a waster, and I will show you someone with more serious problems. Show me a ministry whose leaders are allowed to pursue a life of luxury and grandeur, and I will show you a place that is setting itself up for a world of hurt.

Proverbs 16:18 says, "Pride goeth before destruction, and an haughty spirit before a fall."

Eliminate Opportunities

Crimes are solved when you can establish motive, opportunity and means. If a pastor or a church can reduce the opportunities for someone with bad intentions to operate, the safety of their people will increase dramatically.

As I laid out in chapter twenty-nine, keeping known sex offenders from entering the buildings is a major step. Keeping them away from activities and normal routines will prevent them from learning the best places and times to hurt someone. We know that these people have the motives and the means. We have to eliminate the opportunities.

My philosophy is simple. Eliminate the temptation, and you won't have to worry about sinning. You cannot lust if you do not look. You cannot steal what you cannot touch. You cannot hurt what you cannot reach. Put up strict boundaries around yourself and around everyone in ministry and you will eliminate a large percentage of wrongdoing.

As a senior pastor with more than twenty staff members, I am responsible for not only establishing the policies, but enforcing them as well. Many ministries have a handbook that covers most areas, but they do not oversee or enforce that handbook. If you are not going to enforce a rule, then you should eliminate that rule. Otherwise, you undermine your own authority and lose credibility with your people.

Make a rule and then stick with it. Make the standard high. Raise the bar. People will rise to the occasion. In these dark days, we need to elevate the standard for ministry workers and staff, not lower it. The people of God deserve to be served by people with character and integrity.

Many ministries have something similar to the old caste system. The pastor and his family are the top tier. They will even refer to the pastor's wife as "First Lady." I'm all about honoring God's servants, but Jesus said the first shall be last, and the last shall be first!

The Bible is clear that the pastor is worthy of double honor. What I do not find in the Scriptures is any man of God conducting himself like a celebrity. The Old Testament prophets would have rained down fire on some of these preachers today.

We have placed the pastor and his family at the top. Next is the pastoral staff, followed by the rest of the staff members and their families. Then you have those who work in ministry and hold leadership positions. Somewhere at the bottom of the pile is the rest of the church people. This type of church mindset is very unbiblical.

When this happens, many times there becomes a culture of people preferring one over the other. This is contrary to Scripture. God is no respecter of persons. The book of James chapter two deals in great detail with the seriousness of this matter. "But if ye have respect to persons, ye commit sin, and are convinced of the law as transgressors." (James 2:9)

For there to be a biblical atmosphere of transparency, the people in the church have to know that they matter. If a person has been a victim of sexual abuse and yet does not feel that she can say anything to anybody and be heard, something is wrong.

Every person in the church is important to God and should be important to the church. The stories of people approaching the pastor or church leaders with their story, and being cast aside like worn out shoes, is reprehensible. Jesus died for these little lambs! They matter!

God never intended for the church to be shaped like a pyramid. We are all members one of another. The body is fitly framed together. The people of God are to be united and of the same heart and the same mind. The leaders are to be the servants. The respect and honor for each other is key to a healthy church.

Paul the Apostle rebuked the church at Corinth for its lack of unity. He wrote to them in 1 Corinthians 1:10, "Now I beseech you, brethren, by the name of our Lord Jesus Christ, that ye all speak the same thing, and that there be no divisions among you; but that ye be perfectly joined together in the same mind and in the same judgment."

They had separated themselves in to cliques and groups. That atmosphere is a breeding ground for injustice.

Encourage the Reporting Incidents of Sexual Abuse

The greatest gift you may be able to give your church members is the knowledge that if they have a story to tell, someone will listen.

Too many times, the victims have been silenced. They have been rebuked for making accusations against "a good man" or "the man of God." People kick into overdrive to shut down any mention of impropriety.

If something bad happened, it needs to be confronted. It needs to be dealt with. If a person has been violated or witnessed something terrible, they should be encouraged to speak up.

From my pulpit on numerous occasions I have encouraged my people to come tell me if something bad happens to them. I promised them that I would deal with it. If they will come tell me, I can assure them that it will not happen to them again by that person.

I have stood with people against their own dad in a courtroom to show my support for their willingness to report his crimes against them. I received an email just a few weeks ago from a man who reminded me of the time I went to court with him. His dad was a leader in the church and was molesting his children. They had him arrested and he denied any wrongdoing. They all agreed that it had to stop. They asked me to go to court with them, and I did. They never forgot that.

An atmosphere of transparency in your church means encouraging children and teenagers to tell someone if they are abused. Establishing this type of environment will in and of itself be a deterrent. Pedophiles will not hang around a church where the victims are encouraged to speak out.

PART FOUR
Safeguards

✻ ✻ ✻

31

Common Sense Preventions

"For the oppression of the poor, for the sighing of the needy, now will I arise, saith the LORD; I will set him in safety from him that puffeth at him."
Psalms 12:5

* * *

The house of God should be as protected as our personal homes; maybe more. Most people today have security systems in their homes, yet we many times neglect the safety procedures on our church campuses. We fail to implement basic measures that could discourage predators. None of these suggestions are a guarantee that evil people will not accomplish their wicked agendas, but I assure you they will reduce the chances.

See Something, Say Something

"A prudent man foreseeth the evil, and hideth himself: but the simple pass on, and are punished." (Proverbs 22:3)

How many tragic incidents involving sexual abuse could have been prevented if people would have just taken the initiative to speak up? They saw a man follow a boy into the restroom and it looked odd to them. They noticed a man in the church holding little girls in his lap all the time. They saw and heard things that constituted a red flag, but instead of responding accordingly, they simply looked away.

Their aversion to accusations of unwarranted suspicion overrode their aversion to the possibility of sexual abuse. In their effort to protect themselves from possible criticism or rebuke, they failed to protect the next victim.

The people in the church desperately need to look out for each other. Why is it that we have been conditioned to "mind our own business" rather than protect the lambs in the flock? It is critical to follow your instincts.

Animals also have instincts. They have the ability to feel when something is not right. Unfortunately, we ignore our instincts far too often.

I am a deer hunter. I do not have the opportunity to hunt very often. But when I do get to spend some time in the woods, it is relaxing and enjoyable. I never cease to be fascinated at the alertness and caution of these beautiful animals.

Every step they take is made with a constant awareness of impending danger. They stop every few seconds and survey their surroundings. They hear and notice everything.

One of the greatest challenges for a hunter is to remain undetected by these amazing creatures. Even if you are fifteen feet up in a tree, their ability to scan with their peripheral vision makes it extremely difficult to get off a shot. They will bend their head down to eat, but then they look back up while they are chewing. Their ears move constantly. At the slightest sound or movement, they jump up and run away.

Their ability to communicate to the other deer in the vicinity is also impressive. They will raise their white tail like a flag to alert the others that danger is lurking. Many a deer hunter has gone home empty-handed because of the ability of the deer to detect predators. They never stop watching and listening. They never get too distracted eating to be on the lookout for danger.

Why can't people be more like that? Why is it when we see something that clearly doesn't look right, we ignore it? When we see that creepy man giving candy to the little children week after week, and it makes our stomach knot up, why do we suppress those feelings?

Do we honestly believe that God made the animals of the forest with a more sophisticated sense of right and wrong than human beings? We have been given the ability to discern good and evil, if we would just exercise it!

I must admit, women seem to outpace the men in the area of observation. Men are usually more trusting. We are also less inclined to pay attention to the little things.

Many times my wife has approached me with concerns that I completely overlooked. She noticed things I never saw. After she pointed it out to me, I had to agree that she was right. She has brought situations to my attention many times, giving me the opportunity to intervene.

Being proactive is far better than being reactive. As the old saying goes, "An ounce of prevention is better than a pound of cure!" I have gone to dads on multiple occasions, informing them that their child seemed to be receiving an abnormal amount of attention from the same person each church service. I was careful not to accuse the man in question of anything immoral or criminal. But I have no problem issuing a heads up to a father of a child that appears to be targeted.

Many times, to be fair, it would seem that evil intentions were not their original motive. But familiarity breeds contempt in many cases.

When a man in the church keeps attracting the same handful of children to him before or after the church service, something is not right. When you notice a person who loiters in the restroom, something is wrong. When children are surrounding a man for no apparent reason, that should set off alarm bells.

If a pastor is touchy-feely with the teen girls, someone needs to say something. I can assure you if my wife or I ever saw a man touching my girls, we would put a stop to it.

I have seen pastors who are "huggers." They hug the women and teenage girls, touching their arm when talking to them. They shake their hands and won't let go. They lean into them when they are speaking.

Mark it down. Something is wrong.

We must get to the place where we stop making excuses and stop squelching the nagging feelings in our gut. There is nothing wrong with a word of caution to the right person at the right time. If someone would have said something, the horrible scandal that hit our church recently would not have happened.

People recall knowing that Sarah Jackson had been given a cell phone by the church, but nobody asked why. People noticed she was being taken out of class at the pastor's request, but nobody asked why. Multiple people noticed her spending hours in his office, but not one person asked a single question.

That kind of blind trust and unquestioning loyalty cultivates the perfect atmosphere for sexual predators. Referring back to the situation here at my church, why didn't anyone ask why the pastor's wife was not in the pastor's office while he was supposedly counseling this sixteen-year-old girl? Why didn't anyone tell Sarah's parents about all these private meetings? Why did nobody ask why the door was closed for the entire time? Why did no one suggest they leave the door open, or include a third person for the sessions?

This ordeal had too many red flags, but nobody said a word.

Sexual predators have a specific and unique approach. They build trust. They build relationships. They cultivate the respect and awe of their victims. They also groom the parents in many cases to build trust and cover their tracks. It is sad how many parents refuse to believe their own children when told of sexual abuse. The pedophile has executed his plan perfectly.

Any keen set of eyes can detect when there is an abnormal relationship between men and other people's children. They can tell when a man seems to have an unnatural control over a teenager. How many women have noticed something strange occur, and then dismiss it as nothing? What would have happened if they had kindly asked the child or teenager if everything was OK?

I have been absolutely appalled at the number of emails, phone calls and text messages from victims that share with me how they told their mother they had been abused, and she did not believe them.

One woman shared with me and my wife that in ninth grade, her pastor put his hand up her dress. She told her mom, and nothing was ever said or done about it. It turns out the mother did not believe her daughter. This boggles my mind. This level of gross negligence in adults is inexcusable.

When people are being victimized, they will often give off subtle indications if people would only pay attention. I am not a sexual abuse victim expert by any stretch of the imagination, but I have been through this ordeal twice myself. It changes you. It affects your mind. It affects your body language.

Statistics show that a small percentage of victims show no outward changes, but many do.

- A common presumption is that children will give one detailed, clear account of abuse. This is not consistent with research; disclosures often unfold gradually and may be presented in a series of hints. Children might imply something has happened to them without directly stating they were sexually abused—they may be testing the reaction to their "hint."

- If they are ready, children may then follow with a larger hint if they think it will be handled well.

- It is easy to miss hints of disclosure of abuse. As a result, a child may not receive the help needed.

- Disclosure of sexual abuse is often delayed; children often avoid telling because they are either afraid of a negative reaction from their parents or of being harmed by the abuser. As such, they often delay disclosure until adulthood.

- Males tend not to report their victimization, which may affect statistics. Some men even feel societal pressure to be proud of early sexual activity, regardless of whether it was unwanted.

- Studies of adults suggest that factors such as the relationship to the perpetrator, age at first incident of abuse, use of physical force, severity of abuse, and demographic variables, such as gender and ethnicity, impact a child's willingness to disclose abuse.

- When children do disclose:
  o It is frequently to a friend or a sibling.
  o Of all other family members, mothers are most likely to be told. Whether or not a mother might be told will depend on the child's expected response from the mother.
  o Few disclose abuse to authorities or professionals.
  o Of all professionals, teachers are the most likely to be told.

- Historically, professionals promoted the idea that children frequently report false accounts of abuse. Current research, however, lacks systematic evidence that false allegations are common. Recantations of abuse are also uncommon.

Sources: https://www.nsopw.gov/en/ - *National Sex Offender Public Website and Office of Sex Offender Sentencing, Monitoring, Apprehending, Registering, and Tracking (SMART)*

Mark this down. Children and teenagers who are being sexually abused will many times let you know, one way or the other. People just do not pay attention.

One indication is becoming withdrawn and subdued. Children who are being molested will lose the sparkle in their eye and the spring in their step. The guilt, the shame and the fear will make subtle changes in their personality beyond their control.

If parents, teachers and church members were observant, they would pick up on this and ask if there's something wrong, pressing the matter until they got to the truth. They would look for anything in that child's life that could be causing it. No matter how hard these kids try to hide it, they can't.

Sexual abuse and sexual crimes inflict deep psychological scars. They are so deep that many victims will eventually attempt or commit suicide. The damage to the soul and spirit of a child is unfathomable.

The outward manifestations of being a victim are involuntary. Most of the time, even the victim will not realize the change.

When I spoke with our former school administrator recently, he emphasized this very fact. He told me he had noticed a change in Sarah during her senior year. It was subtle at first, but it became more and more noticeable as the school year progressed.

She became withdrawn. Whereas before she had been bubbly and happy, she became quieter and more reserved. He mentioned that she would cover herself with jackets and long sleeves when nobody else did. She wore her hair down over her face. These were all subconscious efforts to hide.

His words to me were heartbreaking. He told me that he knew something was going on, but he never knew what it was.

The point is, abuse changes children. It will usually involve some level of depression. If we are paying attention, we will see those changes. And if we see something, we need to say something.

Turn the Lights On!

One of the ways to reduce opportunities for predators to take advantage of children is to make sure the campus and the buildings are well-lit. Dark corners and dark rooms make perfect places for sexual abuse to take place. "And this is the condemnation, that light is come into the world, and men loved darkness rather than light, because their deeds were evil." (John 3:19)

Sexual predators often avoid well-lit places. I am amazed at how dark many of the older church buildings are. Their chandeliers and wall sconces are full of low-watt bulbs. The sanctuary and classrooms are dark. The whole atmosphere is dark.

People have different preferences, but I personally love a well-lit facility. Replace those low-watt incandescent bulbs with energy-efficient LED lights. The transformation is amazing! You will also save a small fortune on your electric bill.

At our church, we are constantly upgrading the lighting of our facilities. A few years ago, we added large, bright exterior flood lights all the way around our church buildings. Our parking lot looks like a shopping center at night. You can purchase super bright LED lights that are very affordable.

When we walk out of our church service in the evenings, our cars and sidewalks are well illuminated. This also serves to discourage vandalism.

The technology is also available to eliminate light switches by using motion detectors where light switches would normally be. When you walk into a room and the light automatically comes on, this prevents a person from being able to turn the light off. It is a good idea to put these type of light switches in stair wells, supply closets, restrooms, locker rooms, and any room off the beaten path where a sexual offender could take advantage of a child. The timers can be set to stay on a little longer than usual.

(The downside is these types of lights will go off if there is an extended moment of stillness).

The trend today seems to be moving toward churches becoming darker and darker. Many times, the only real lighting is pretty much focused on the platform area. It is so dark in many of these places of worship that people cannot see a songbook or a Bible. Worshippers are gravitating to these ministries with black walls, black ceilings, dim lights and minimal visibility. They have to put the lyrics to the songs on the screen, as well as the Bible verses for the sermon because the sanctuary is so dark. Those in attendance couldn't read a hymnbook or Bible if they wanted to!

I can't help but wonder how vulnerable children are sitting in darkened rooms for extended periods of time. There are strangers everywhere. When you take into consideration that 90% of sexual abuse is done by someone the victim knows, that makes it even more disturbing.

This type of environment is perfect for a pervert. They can do anything they like without fear of being seen. I am reminded in 1 Samuel 3 of the passage where the lamp of God went out in the temple (vs. 3). This is the same place where sexual immorality was taking place in the doorways (I Samuel 2:22). The Bible also says that the Word of the Lord was precious in those days.

I'm old-fashioned, but I believe the church should be well lit. Many churches today look like nightclubs. We know why the lights are turned off in those places. We understand why the dance floors and honky-tonks are shrouded in darkness. We know why pool halls and bars turn the lights off. But why are they turned off inside the church? Maybe these churches should rethink this particular setting.

Protect the children. Turn the lights on!

Cameras

One of the most effective ways to protect the flock of God is with security cameras. We have cameras all around the parking lots and in every corner of the buildings, – the hallways, stairwells, office area and the foyers. These cameras serve multiple purposes.

First of all, their existence is a tremendous deterrent. People act differently when there are cameras. Posting signage informing everyone that the property is under twenty-four hour surveillance will stop a large portion of unsavory activity.

We are currently in the process of upgrading our entire security camera system. This will give us greater capabilities to see and monitor the entire campus. We have purchased cameras with pan and zoom capabilities. We will not only be able to see a car driving onto our property, but we can follow them and zoom in on their tag number if necessary.

One of our offices is equipped with multiple screens located right over a secretary's desk. She can monitor the entire school with the split screens showing over a dozen cameras.

We are back to the subject of creating an atmosphere of transparency. Parents who walk into that office know that the safety and wellbeing of their children is a priority to us.

Secondly, security cameras record everything. We have used our security camera recordings on a number of occasions. They are in full color and timestamped.

This is good for assisting the police with complaints, and settling disputes that occur in the buildings. Video can be used to verify or disprove accusations. We have used it to clear up people's narratives of certain events.

We have recorded thieves moving stolen merchandise across our parking lot in the middle of the night. Law enforcement officials have gratefully utilized our security camera recordings to help them identify unsuspecting criminals. They never noticed they were walking right under our cameras.

Security cameras have the capability to do two things: catch the perverts, and clear the innocent. It eliminates the threat of false accusations when the coming and going of people is recorded. There's no greater alibi than a filmed recording of what actually transpired.

These security cameras have the capacity to store terabytes of footage for immediate reference in the event of an accusation. I highly recommend sufficient space to record at least a month's worth of footage.

The peace of mind that it provides to a church when there are security cameras is priceless. Our people respond immediately to any stewardship campaign that is initiated to upgrade our security cameras. The prices range from small, homeowner-type security cameras to state-of-the-art recording capabilities.

No matter which option you choose, just remember that the flock of God is priceless. Jesus shed His blood for the sheep. Do not let the cost of a security system blind you to the value of the little lambs in your church.

A Safety Team

No matter the size of your flock, you need a safety team. Most people do not realize it, but churches are the third highest target of terrorism. Churches are referred to as "soft targets" because of their extreme lack of security. Mass shooters and wackos target places where they feel they will face the least amount of resistance.

It is a sad fact that pastors and ministry leaders have failed to properly ensure the safety and security of their members. The shepherd's number one concern should be the safety of the sheep. The Psalmist David, a shepherd himself, alluded to the importance of securing the sheep in Psalm 23.

"Yea, though I walk through the valley of the shadow of death, I will fear no evil: for thou art with me; thy rod and thy staff they comfort me." (Psalms 23:4)

Stacey Shiflett

A couple of years ago I attended an all-day church security seminar with our church's head of security. We sat for hours, listening to lectures and watching videos. As the pastor, I feel it is imperative that I set the tone for the security plan at my church.

We mapped out a detailed security plan. Since I have a construction background, I personally built a security hub housed with multiple screens.

The parking lot, the entrances, the bathroom doors and hallways are all monitored carefully throughout every church service. The safety/security team can communicate to each other clearly and discreetly the entire time via two-way radio and earpieces.

We have men stationed throughout the facility and spread throughout the congregation. They are strategically placed to be able to respond to any and all threats, no matter which corner of the auditorium it may occur.

From time to time we will go to a church safety seminar or send some of our men to take refresher courses. It is always an encouragement to the team to discover that our church's security policies many times far exceed the average church. We strive to take this area of ministry very seriously. I do not want anyone being hurt or victimized on my watch.

One of the main things we learned from a retired FBI agent during one of the training sessions was the importance of responding to what he called a "DLR." This is an acronym for "doesn't look right." We heard story after story of tragedies that occurred because people ignored a "DLR." Something didn't look right, and they ignored it.

If a person looks sketchy, we check him out. If a person we have never seen before walks into the building with a backpack, we do not hesitate to confront him kindly and professionally and ask to inspect it.

We monitor every vehicle that comes into our parking lot. Our security team monitors the parking lot throughout the entire service. They walk outside and confront anyone they see loitering around people's cars during the service. We are always on the lookout for troublemakers.

Securing our people is a huge priority to me. I personally handpicked every member of my church's safety team. They are equipped and informed of my expectations.

There is not a church service where we do not have multiple armed personnel on site. It is not a secret but we do not flaunt it. Our church knows we have a capable and trained security team and they feel safe. Every flock of sheep need a few sheepdogs to ward off the wolves.

Terrorists and mass shooters are not the only ones who are discouraged by a well-organized security team. Sexual predators are as well.

Once the pastor has established a zero tolerance position, the effect of that will spread throughout the rest of the church's policies and procedures. It is absolutely essential that the church from the top down establish a clear policy of how to deal with sex offenders. The days of passive observation are over.

At our church, we are on the lookout for anyone that would do harm to our people. It is no longer sufficient to play defense. We must play offense; looking and scanning the crowd for anyone who has evil intentions.

Those on the church security team will adopt the mindset of the pastor. If the pastor is permissive and passive, his team will be also. Fear of confrontation is completely unacceptable. Hesitating to follow your gut will not work. The higher our tolerance is of potential threats the higher the rate of actual incidents will be.

My team cannot always clear every decision with me. I am on the platform during the service. I am involved in the music and usually the one doing the preaching. I cannot do their job. Therefore, I have clearly laid out my attitude, and my position and empowered them to make decisions on my behalf.

It is better to ask forgiveness than to get permission. I would rather them err on the side of caution. When they bring a situation to my attention, I simply tell them to handle it. They know what I would do and they do it.

My philosophy is quite simple. I would rather take the chance of offending a possible predator than to take the chance of them offending one of our little ones. Anybody who gets indignant and offended because a church is trying to protect its members is not worth worrying about anyway.

The church is there for the church. Outsiders are definitely welcome, but they are not entitled.

Recently, we had a man we have never seen before come into the service. He went up into the balcony area and set up a tripod with a camera. It immediately drew the attention of my security team.

The first problem was his hiding his tripod under his overcoat. I trembled to think of what weapons he could have concealed under there! Fortunately, it was just a collapsible tripod. He set up a camera and appeared to be preparing to video the service.

This was a "DLR" for sure. Our services are livestreamed on our church website. We post the video of our sermon on our church's YouTube channel. Each service is archived in its entirety on the church app "Sunday Streams."

His need for recording a regular service was obviously abnormal. It was not a children's Christmas play or a special event.

My security team brought this man to my attention prior to the service starting. We agreed that something was off with this guy. I told them to handle it. They approached him and asked him not to record the service. He not only turned off his camera and took down his tripod, but he left the service. We found out later that he was there to harass and intimidate one of our church members who is a Maryland state senator. I commended the security team for their proactive measures.

If something doesn't look right, do something. The more eyeballs you have on a situation, the less trouble you will have.

The Second Law of Thermodynamics apply to everything – even church ministries. Without continual attention and energy, things tend to disorder and decay. We have periodic meetings with the security team to keep everyone alert and on top of their game.

Preparedness is a deterrent. Any security protocols are better than none. The lambs in our flock should be safer at church than anywhere else in the world.

32

Implementing Ministry Policies

"And they shall teach my people the difference between the holy and profane, and cause them to discern between the unclean and the clean."
Ezekiel 44:23

* * *

It should go without saying, but I will say it. Anyone who volunteers to serve in any area of ministry involving children should be required to submit to initial and subsequent periodic background checks. Every person, no matter who, without exception must comply with this policy. It is not just for insurance purposes, although that is a valid reason.

Companies that insure churches and ministries usually require basic background checks for those in certain areas of ministry. In most cases, they will not cover a lawsuit involving sexual misconduct if the person was never screened. The church can be held liable for negligence by not having a mandatory background check policy. But the insurance company's mandate should not be the main reason for doing this.

We are back to this problem of people in our churches simply not wanting to know. Willful ignorance is inexcusable. Not asking questions and not screening applicants for ministry so you can plead deniability simply will not work. We must take this seriously!

From the nursery workers to the teachers in our Sunday school classes, everyone needs to be investigated at the most basic level prior to being approved for ministry. People can be deceptive. They can misrepresent the truth and sometimes they do. A person's eagerness to serve the Lord in ministry cannot negate the church's responsibility to do its due diligence. You will be shocked many times at what you discover!

Of course, the policy of requiring a background check usually discourages people with a record of sexual crimes on from even pursuing ministry opportunities. If they know their secret will be discovered, they simply abstain from moving forward with their plans. Sometimes, they are bold enough to submit to a background check and hope their personality and abilities will cause you to make an exception. You cannot do that!

Years ago, I ran a background check on one of my key bus ministry workers. He had gotten involved in the children's ministry without ever turning one in. As soon as I realized that, I asked him to submit to a criminal background check. When it came back, it was fourteen pages long.

The things in his past totally prevented him from further serving in that ministry. He was great at bus ministry, but his criminal record disqualified him from serving at our church in any ministry involving children. I asked him to step down and he did. He was one of the best children's ministry workers I have ever seen, but he did not pass the background check. As I stated earlier, God has been merciful to protect me in my ignorance. My current position in this area is much more rigid than it was in the past. It is my prayer that pastors and ministry leaders will re-evaluate their current policies and make the necessary adjustments.

If you do not INSPECT what you EXPECT, you will never have people's RESPECT. It is essential that every ministry have a clear list of requirements. Whether your church has twenty people or twenty thousand, every area of ministry and service should have a basic form with the requirements and policies of that ministry.

Some churches have a ministry handbook that contain each ministries' policies and procedures. This is a great idea. It is time consuming initially, but it will alleviate a lot of problems down the road. It also saves an enormous amount of time when the church is approached by new members about ministry opportunities.

We encourage people to get involved and serve the Lord within the local church. When they volunteer, we need to make sure they understand the ramifications of their commitment to serve. Not everyone will meet the basic qualifications.

Let me be very clear about this. A person with a criminal background of sexual abuse should be forbidden for life from working with children. Some leaders will only limit working with children to those that have a record of sex crimes involving children or minors. I take it further than that.

A person who has any kind of sex crimes in his past is banned from working with children at my church. The fact that this occurred prior to their coming to Christ is irrelevant. Just because they were lost and now they are saved doesn't change it. It may be under the blood of Jesus Christ, but I am not putting a registered sex offender in my Junior Church ministry! I am not going to allow a man who has raped someone sit on the church bus beside my children – not in a million years!

I am not taking any chances. I will not even allow a person who has been accused of it to work with children. Just because a court of law did not have enough evidence does not mean he did not do it.

If I have to choose between hurting the feelings of a potential ministry worker by saying no, or take a chance on them hurting a child later on, that is not a difficult choice for me.

Taking the High Road

I admit it. Many of my ideas are old-fashioned. I have been laughed at most of my life for some of the self-imposed boundaries in my life. That's OK. It works for me so I will continue to observe them. "See then that ye walk circumspectly, not as fools, but as wise." (Ephesians 5:15) This section will deal with some suggestions on how to raise the bar and further protect ourselves from sin and scandal. If the ideas in this section are too strict or seem ridiculous, feel free to skip it. In this day in which we live, I don't think we can be too careful.

When it comes to implementing guidelines, God encourages it. Especially when it comes to protecting one's self from immorality. In Hosea 5:4, God said, "They will not frame their doings to turn unto their God: for the spirit of whoredoms is in the midst of them, and they have not known the LORD."

The word "*frame*" here means to construct or build. The word "*doings*" means their deeds or practices.

God's rebuke for them came in a time where the spirit of whoredoms were in their midst. He reproved them for their failure to implement protective measures. God's will was for them to set up practices that would point them back to God and away from the wickedness of their day. It is a wise practice to keep one's self pointed toward God and His holiness rather than the permissiveness that has pervaded our society.

The unbelievers scoff at us for our attempts to live clean and right. The question is, just how clean and right do we want to be? How holy is too holy? Can a person live too far above reproach? Can a child of God be too consecrated? Is it too much trouble to ask God's people to consider taking the high road?

Sexual immorality is glorified in the television programs and movies in our day. We must look for ways to shield our hearts and minds from the spirit of lust that is in our midst.

My wife and I love working with the young people in our church. Even though I currently have three full-time assistant pastors, my wife and I for the past several years have fulfilled the role of the youth pastor. We plan all their outings and banquets. We host many of the teen activities in our home. I enjoy directing the youth choir and teaching them songs.

We load all the teens on a church bus every Wednesday afternoon and take them soulwinning. Together, we have walked up and down the streets of Dundalk inviting people to church and spreading the Gospel of Jesus Christ.

My wife and I take them skating, bowling, to the mall and out to eat. Kids love to eat! I'd love to have a dollar for every hour I've spent with my teenagers at a Taco Bell or a Chick-fil-A. I could retire!

I spend more time with some of these teenagers than their own parents do. They have no bigger fan at their soccer or volleyball or basketball games than my wife and me.

Many of them come from broken homes and are longing for love and affection. Guess what? They will not get that kind of affection from me. The teen girls in my church will not get their need for hugs met by this pastor! I will not lay a hand on them. The only thing I will do is shake their hand, or the occasional fist bump. I believe it is unwise for a man to hug a teenage girl or a woman who is not his wife.

I do not pay them compliments about their looks or their hair or their clothing. I shower my wife and daughters with compliments. I will not do that to another woman. My only exception would be an elderly lady in the church. Even then, the embrace should be discreet. I see men taking another woman in a full, frontal embrace. Beware!

I see men in some churches walking around and hugging all the women and girls. I was at a church once when they had what they called a "love offering." That was when everyone went all over the church hugging each other. Men hugging other men's wives, and visa-versa. And trust me when I say that some of them were taking full advantage of the opportunity!

You mark it down. That is trouble waiting to happen.

An attitude of permissiveness is a slippery slope. Strict policies need to be in place to protect the pastor, staff, and leadership in a church. Men in the church should not be allowed to touch and feel the women and kids in the church. When you throw in the added dynamic of many men and teen boys' secret addiction to pornography, anything is possible.

Bad things happen when the flames of sexual lusts are allowed to burn without control. No wonder so many children and teens find themselves the recipients of unwanted sexual attention. Someone needs to step in and discourage this type of behavior. In doing so, a possible sexual crime can be stopped before it happens.

It is amazing how people seem to be so quick to excuse these touchy-feely men. You'll hear statements like, "He doesn't mean anything by it." How in the world would you know? Are you a mind reader? You have NO IDEA what is in that man's heart or mind.

Paul the Apostle warned the church at Corinth of the importance of this very thing. "Now concerning the things whereof ye wrote unto me: It is good for a man not to touch a woman. Nevertheless, to avoid fornication, let every man have his own wife, and let every woman have her own husband." (1 Corinthians 7:1)

I'm talking about taking the high road. I'm discussing policies and procedures that will keep pastors and staff members from falling into immorality or worse.

Please! Keep your hands to yourself! These men who can't keep their hands off of the women and the girls need

Wolves Among Lambs

to be rebuked for their carelessness. Someone needs to pull them aside and issue a stern warning of the dangers.

Solomon warned in Proverbs 6:27, 28 about the risks of careless behavior when it comes to the opposite sex. "Can a man take fire in his bosom, and his clothes not be burned? Can one go upon hot coals, and his feet not be burned?"

Men who are in the ministry many times see nothing wrong with taking a woman other than their wife out for a meal. Staff luncheons and working lunches with the secretary are a death trap. Don't do it! Take the high road.

I don't mind giving little children a hug in their parents' presence, but I am extremely careful even about that. Sometimes a parent tries to force their child to hug me if they pull away. I always defend the child's right to not hug me. The last thing I want to do is teach children that just because a man is trying to hug them that they have to comply.

Any man that would force a child to hug him is doing great damage to that child as well as to himself. He may actually be creating a persona to be feared and avoided.

On the other hand, some little children crave attention and affection from a man. Maybe they do not have a dad or a father figure in their life. Their pastor many times becomes their only male role model. The amount of influence he has in their life is unbelievable. Sometimes it's another man in the church that they turn to for male attention.

Regardless of their need for love and affection, we cannot cross that line. Our policy at Calvary Baptist Church is for a man not to be with someone else's child alone under any circumstances.

For years, our family has maintained the highest possible policies. We will not travel alone in a vehicle with a member of the opposite sex. Period.

The men on my staff and I will not provide transportation for women and girls if they are alone. There are too many risks involved. The opportunities for temptation can be too great. Furthermore, it is impossible to defend yourself against a false accusation.

If everyone adhered to these guidelines, there would be far less teen pregnancies. There would be much less infidelity. There would be far fewer cases of sexual abuse in the church. As far as I can tell, the benefits are far greater than the little bit of inconvenience these rules may incur.

Neither I nor our men will take one of our teen girls home after an event without one of our daughters or our wife with us. Again, my philosophy is to eliminate the possibility for sin by eliminating the opportunity to sin.

My parents and my wife's parents raised us both this way. We dated for a year and a half, and not once did we go on a single date alone. We were accompanied by a chaperone every time. There was always someone present with us when we left the house. That was perfectly fine with me.

Grace and I enjoyed a great dating relationship completely free of the temptation to indulge in unbiblical and immoral behavior. We had our own firewalls in place. We could not have been able to commit sin, even if we had wanted to!

That's called taking the high road. I highly recommend it.

We have continued those same dating practices with our children. My oldest daughter has been dating a young man for over three years. They have never been on a date alone and they have never been in a car alone.

You may ask, "Don't you trust them?" The answer is NO! I don't trust myself, much less anybody else. Our carnal flesh is capable of anything. Don't make the mistake of trusting your flesh, either! "Watch and pray, that ye enter not into temptation: the spirit indeed is willing, but the flesh is weak." (Matthew 26:41) There are many parents today raising their grandchildren because they trusted their own children too much.

I require any woman who communicates with me via text message to include my wife in the text. If she fails to do that, I remind her of my policy. I do not worry about embarrassing her. If done correctly, it will neither embarrass her nor make her feel accused of anything improper. Then, I will either show my wife or I will screenshot the conversation and text it to her.

My wife has the security code to my cell phone as well as my computer. She has full access to everything and anything I have. If all the men in our churches had these practices, it would eliminate most, if not all, of the sexual abuse and immorality in our churches.

It seems that many people want to see how close they can get to immorality and survive. That is very foolish. Satan is a powerful force. None of us are a match for his tactics. If we give him an inch, he'll take a mile. Paul admonished the believer in Ephesians 4:27 by simply saying, "Neither give place to the devil."

Counseling Policies

One of the many responsibilities of a pastor or staff member is providing counsel. There is a wide range of reasons why people would need counsel. It is extremely important that a pastor and his staff have policies in place to protect everyone involved during these times.

If a pastor is approached by a woman for counseling, there should be normal operating procedures that have been clearly laid out. Under no circumstances should the man of God take a woman or girl into a room and close the door. "Abstain from all appearance of evil." (1 Thessalonians 5:22)

The moment he does that, he immediately waives all right to the presumption of innocence. Whether he does anything wrong or not, he's toast. Because of his negligence and carelessness, he failed to protect both the person he was counseling, as well as himself. If she walks out the door and makes an accusation, whether it is five minutes later or five years later, he has absolutely no recourse. His failure to have a firewall that protects everyone involved has made them all vulnerable.

My office door has a glass window from top to bottom. I will not even close the door when talking with a woman in my office, and I have a glass door. I leave the door open. I sit on one side of the room and she sits on the other.

The transparency protocols in place are there for my protection as much as hers. The last thing I want to do is to give some wicked woman with an evil heart the opportunity to say I did anything inappropriate. I value my testimony and my reputation far too much to be careless in this area.

I will not talk to a woman about her marriage without my wife in the room under any circumstances. If I need to talk to a woman by phone about her marriage, I will do so only with my wife in the room and the speaker is on. There is no way in the world I am going to talk to a woman alone who is having problems getting along with her husband! I will not counsel her alone anywhere, including the parking lot, the car, a restaurant or her home.

Women in that condition are so vulnerable. We must be very careful. Take the high road!

Counseling teenage girls who are going through a crisis is risky business. They are extremely emotional. Many times they are unstable, making their recollection of conversations and events a bit unreliable.

It is unwise for them, and for yourself, to try and deal with them without a third party. If their parent or my spouse are not available, I will bring in a teacher or a secretary.

Satan does not fight fair. He will use an emotional, crying child or young person to cause you to lower your guard. That initial contact that was intended to comfort can easily take a carnal and indecent turn.

If a woman or teenage girl repeatedly seeks my counsel, I will usually refer her to my wife. In many cases they are in need of attention. If that is the case, I immediately delegate that to my wife or another lady.

Sometimes, women feel that no one but their pastor can help them. I don't agree with that. Titus 2:4 and 5 admonishes the older women to teach the younger women. The older women are encouraged to help the younger women with their marriage and parenting, among other things.

I keep my counseling sessions with women and teen girls extremely short. I've yet to hear of a topic come up in a counseling session that my wife, or another godly lady in my church, could not help them with. I have told my church on numerous occasions that I do the bulk of my counseling three times a week from the pulpit. If a person is not faithful to those services, I will rarely spend a lot of my time counseling.

Beware of the traps of Satan that come attached to counseling sessions! By their very nature many times they have an intimate and secretive element to them. That is a recipe for disaster if one is not careful. Remain aloof and keep a distance. Don't get too comfortable with an emotional and vulnerable woman. What started out as innocent ministry can quickly turn into an emotional or possibly physical relationship.

From time to time, ladies on my staff need to discuss matters pertaining to their work or schedule. They are always welcome to come speak with me in my office. My door is always open – literally and figuratively. Many times, I remain standing and they do as well. Furthermore, I make sure another staff member is nearby to monitor the time of entrance and exit. They insure that my door is open and that nothing takes place.

These are policies I have implemented to protect my testimony. In doing so, I am protecting those who walk through my door.

PART FIVE
Hope and Healing

* * *

NOTE: *This part is written to help survivors of sexual abuse find healing. Therefore, I will address this portion of the book to the victim personally. It is written in a way that even the youngest victims can understand. I would love to sit down with each one of them and comfort them in person. Maybe this book will be a substitute. If just one person is helped by these next two chapters, it was worth all the hours it took to write this book.*

* * *

33

Victory for the Victim

"But thanks be to God, which giveth us the victory through our Lord Jesus Christ."
1 Corinthians 15:57

* * *

If you have been a victim of sexual abuse, I want you to pay attention to this section. Sexual relations affect people in ways that are both psychological as well as physical. There are emotional responses attached to sexual activity. When people are forced to engage in sexual behavior against their will or without their consent, it creates the wrong kind of psychological emotions.

God created sexual activity to strengthen the bonds of marriage. It is supposed to be an expression of pure love between a man and his wife.

Sexual intimacy within God's guidelines builds relationships. Sexual abuse destroys. Pure and biblical sexual expression brings pleasure and fulfillment to the marriage. Sexual abuse brings terror, pain and guilt to its victims.

Regardless of how you feel right now, you can get past this. In spite of what you have experienced, it is possible to put this nightmare behind you and move on. It does not have to define who you become. It does not have to haunt you for the rest of your life.

Whatever happened was bad and it was wrong. It should not have happened to you. You did not deserve to become a victim. Believe me when I tell you that you can get victory over this terrible occurrence.

Let me share with you just a couple of ways that can happen. I know this from personal experience.

Tell Someone

I cannot emphasize this first point enough. Finding the courage to speak out will be your biggest obstacle. Realizing the seriousness of what happened to you and making the decision to confide in someone you trust is extremely important. There is no way you will be free as long as you keep it to yourself.

One of the most difficult things you will ever do is tell someone what happened to you. The longer you wait, the harder it will be. The most liberating day in the life of a victim is when he or she musters the courage to tell someone. Keeping the secret of another person's criminal conduct brings a bondage that is stifling.

If you have been sexually abused in any way, you are a survivor. You are here, and you are going to make it. But you can do more than just survive. God wants you to thrive.

Find someone you can trust and tell them. If you don't say something, your abuser will only do it again to someone else. Chances are, you were not their first victim. If the last person they had hurt had told someone, it may not have happened to you. You have to find the courage to speak out!

Those of us who have been sexually abused in some way struggle to tell someone for a number of reasons. I know because I struggled with these same things at one time.

Satan is a master deceiver. He desires to keep victims bound in the chains of sexual abuse. He wants to take what happened to you and use it to ruin your life. You will have to overcome these lies, and with God's help, find healing.

Here are some of the thoughts you may be struggling with.

1. What happened to me is my fault.

One of the most powerful ways that a sexual abuser controls his or her victim is by somehow convincing them that they are to blame. They not only make them feel like they are "in on it," but many times blame them completely.

Many times I've seen the child molester blame the child. The church leader who engages in sexual relations with a teenager in the church will blame the teenager for making him do what he did.

There are many people in our churches who will blame the victims for what happened to them rather than the actual abuser. They make it harder for a young person to come forward because of their haste to blame the victim. Instead of blaming the pastor who molested the teenage girl in the church, they blame the girl for seducing or "bringing down" a good man.

Sexual abusers know how to project the guilt of their sick behavior onto their victims. They know how to connect the abuse they've caused to the stigma of the crime. Because sexual abuse is such a violation of a person's privacy, it is the perfect crime to commit.

If a person broke into your house and stole your jewelry, you would immediately call the police. If a person hijacked you in the street and stole your car, you would flag down the first car you saw and get their help. But when a person invades your body and steals your innocence, our first reaction is to keep that secret. Someone breaking into your garage or your home is bad. But when a person breaks into your underwear and takes what does not belong to him, keeping that crime from the police is only making the matter worse.

Sexual abuse is a robbery. Sexual offenders are thieves. They rob people of so many things. They cannot get away with it! If it happened to you, then you are the only one that can tell.

2. I feel so guilty.

Guilt is a powerful emotion. Satan uses guilt as a powerful way to control and ruin people's lives. Many victims of sexual abuse feel so guilty that they attempt or commit suicide. The weight of their guilt is more than they can bear. It was guilt that caused Adam and Eve to make aprons of fig leaves and hide from the very presence of God.

But if you were sexually abused, you are not the one that should be feeling guilty. You did not cause this. You must stop blaming yourself and realize just how bad you were treated. Whether you were a child, a teenager or a grown adult, you cannot live with the guilt of the crimes committed against you.

When I was molested as a teenager in my sleep, I struggled with guilt. I felt I must have done something wrong, that in some way I made that man feel that he had my permission. I struggled with guilt for so many aspects of my abuse.

I felt guilty for not waking up sooner. I felt guilty for not jumping up immediately and making a scene. I felt guilty for so many things that were beyond my control. But I was asleep. I had no control over what happened. All I could control was what I did afterward.

I cannot imagine how bad it must be for those who are victimized when they are not asleep. If I felt guilty, and I did not even know it was happening to me, I cannot begin to imagine just how terrible you must feel for what you have been through. Guilt is just a tool of your abuser to keep you from telling anyone. He knows how to recruit your emotions and make you a partner in his crime.

3. I am afraid.

Fear is one of the biggest reasons victims of sexual abuse remain silent. Their abusers have managed to convince them that bad things will happen if they tell someone.

Well, guess what? Bad things will happen when victims tell what happened– but not to the one who was abused. Bad things will happen to the pervert who took what did not belong to him. Bad things will happen to the sick individual who could not control his wicked mind.

One of my favorite Bible verses is 2 Timothy 1:7 where we are reminded, "For God hath not given us the spirit of fear; but of power, and of love, and of a sound mind."

The paralyzing effects of sexual abuse are impossible to explain to someone who has never experienced it. It is not a figment of your imagination. Fear is real. It keeps people from being able to think clearly. It makes bad things seem far worse than they really are. Fear makes a person do things they never thought they would do.

Fear does not have to be a way of life. God is able to help you overcome your fear.

The victims of sexual abuse are many times threatened by their abusers. You have been told, "If you tell anyone what happened to you, you will be sorry." Children live in secret pain in order to protect themselves and their families. The truth is actually the opposite. Telling someone may be the only way to protect yourself and your loved ones. So many victims think they are the only one, not realizing there are many others. How many children have suffered sexual abuse from their parents, right along with their brothers and sisters? It is not until many years later that they realize they were not the only one.

It is time to stop being afraid, and make your abuser afraid. It is time to take the fear they heaped upon you and turn it back on them. Let them know how it feels to be afraid. Once their secret is out, everyone will know what they truly are. You have the power to make that happen. Stand up for yourself and stop being scared of your abuser.

Abusers are cowards. They do not have the courage to face you if you will simply stand up and tell someone. Sexual abusers prey on the weak and the helpless. They take advantage of people who cannot defend themselves. Stop being afraid, and make them afraid. "Hear my voice, O God, in my prayer: preserve my life from fear of the enemy." (Psalms 64:1)

4. Nobody will believe me.

This is probably one of the most troubling dilemmas I have ever been in personally. When I encountered sexual predators in my life, I struggled with how to tell someone. My biggest fear was that I would be made to look like a liar.

Many times, a sexual offender uses this as a way to keep you from talking. He reminds you that nobody will believe you if you tell. He tells you that he will swear up and down that he did not do it. That nagging suspicion that he may get away with it keeps so many victims from telling anyone.

Just be careful to always tell the truth. If you spread false accusations or lies, it will destroy your credibility. No one will believe anything you say later on, even if you are telling the truth. Once you lie one time, it will be impossible to get people to believe you. Always tell the truth!

Sometimes the circumstances are so bizarre that we find it almost impossible to believe it ourselves. The facts do not match up with the person.

How could a parent do this to his own child? How could a church leader do this to his own people? The mind-blowing truth is enough to suppress anybody. It is all so confusing and unbelievable.

Yet, it happened. You are not dreaming. You are not imagining it. He did it. He abused you. He cannot get away with it. You MUST find someone you trust and tell them.

Someone will believe you. Even if the person who abused you is well-liked or well-known; even if he has a high position of authority; even if he swears on a stack of Bibles that he did not do it; you have to tell someone. And someone will do something to protect you and others from that sexual predator. If the first person you tell doesn't believe you, tell someone else. Don't stop until your story is told!

5. Why did God allow this to happen to me?

So many times, we look for someone to blame other than the actual abuser. Many people end up blaming God for what happened to them.

God's Word tells us in Matthew 5:45, "That ye may be the children of your Father which is in heaven: for he maketh his sun to rise on the evil and on the good, and sendeth rain on the just and on the unjust."

God lets the sun rise and set on good people, as well as evil people. He sends rain upon the godly and the ungodly. Because of Adam and Eve's sin in the Garden of Eden, sin entered into this world. From that time until now, sin has been a plague upon society.

Bad things happen to good people all the time. People who reject God and His precepts do evil things to other people. Good people are robbed and murdered. Good people are injured in car accidents and suffer from cancer.

And unfortunately, good people get sexually abused.

Don't blame God. Blame your real enemy.

The Real Enemy

In spite of your desire to focus on your abuser, he is not your real enemy. Mankind's greatest enemy is Satan. Ever since God created man and woman in the Garden of Eden, the devil has sought to destroy God's creation. It was Satan who deceived the woman, Eve, in the Garden. He tempted her to sin, and she did.

Satan is the mastermind behind every hurt, every tear, every broken heart and every misery ever experienced by humanity.

One of the ways that God helped me through my time of sexual abuse in 1990 was by reminding me that Satan was my enemy. Jesus reminds us of the devil's evil intentions in John 10:10, "The thief cometh not, but for to steal, and to kill, and to destroy: I am come that they might have life, and that they might have it more abundantly."

Though I was hurting and angry, I allowed God to show me from His Word that I should focus on fighting the devil, not other people. If I get distracted fighting everyone except my true enemy, I am falling right into his trap.

The person who hurt you is being used by Satan to destroy you. But what he does not know is that Satan is destroying him also. He uses people against other people.

Notice what Paul the Apostle said in Ephesians 6, "Put on the whole armour of God, that ye may be able to stand against the wiles of the devil. For we wrestle not against flesh and blood, but against principalities, against powers, against the rulers of the darkness of this world, against spiritual wickedness in high places."

The main thing I want to tell you is this: Satan is not going to be content trying to ruin your life. His plan is not to simply cause you pain and torment in this life. He wants to see you spend an eternity in torment.

The next chapter will show you how you can know for sure that will never happen. I hope and pray you will read it carefully.

God loves you and wants to help you heal. Will you allow Him to do that?

34

Ultimate Healing

"Have mercy upon me, O LORD; for I am weak: O LORD, heal me; for my bones are vexed."
Psalms 6:2

* * *

God loves those who are hurting, broken and hopeless. There is no situation so bad that God's love and grace cannot fix it.

Jesus came to heal those with broken hearts and broken lives. He said, "The Spirit of the Lord is upon me, because he hath anointed me to preach the gospel to the poor; he hath sent me to heal the brokenhearted, to preach deliverance to the captives, and recovering of sight to the blind, to set at liberty them that are bruised." (Luke 4:18)

God hurts when we hurt. He longs to restore you. He came to heal the brokenhearted, to deliver the captives and set at liberty those that are bruised. If you a survivor of sexual abuse, God can help you experience healing you never thought possible. He can not only save your life, but He can save your soul.

You have a choice. Either you can spend the rest of your life worrying about what needs to happen to your abuser, or you can focus on your own needs. Are you willing to let God take away the pain and hurt? Would you allow Him to do what only He can do in your life? Will you turn your attention inwardly for just a few moments and examine your own spiritual condition?

Has life become a burden, and no matter how hard you try, you can't enjoy anything? You look around and you are overwhelmed with the vanity of it all. Relationships are falling apart. Peace of mind is nowhere to be found. You try to portray an image of happiness, success and control, but inside you feel like screaming and quitting. But you keep on trying, because that is what you are supposed to do.

People are depending on you and you feel like a failure. People look to you for answers, but you have no clue. Life has eroded into a mere existence. You feel like you are letting the people you love down. You feel like God has let you down. People you trusted hurt you. The pain is deeper than you ever imagined. You are so tired of being afraid, confused and guilty.

Do you find yourself wondering why you're here and what it is all about? Is this all there is to it? Does it get any better? Is there any hope to actually having a life?
There is one guaranteed solution. Once you understand that Jesus Christ, the Creator, made each of us with a natural

desire to know Him, things begin to make a little more sense. He created every one of us with a void and an emptiness that only He could fill.

Without that personal relationship with God, a person's search for fulfillment never ends. Their life deteriorates into a series of one futile effort after another. Depression, extreme frustration – even thoughts of suicide are common at this point.

This is why so many people become addicted to the wrong things. They turn to alcohol, drugs, sex, crime, money, and every other option as a substitute for God. They are searching – longing – hungry for that feeling of satisfaction and completion.

But that feeling will not happen until God takes His rightful place as the Lord of your life and is in total control. Then, all of those feelings of doubt are replaced with confidence. Sadness is turned into joy. Turmoil is replaced with peace. Guilt over past sins is gone and God's forgiveness takes over. What used to be dread is now turned into anticipation and excitement over the possibilities that only God can provide.

God's Word tells us in 2 Corinthians 5:17, "Therefore if any man be in Christ, he is a new creature: old things are passed away; behold, all things are become new."
God is able to help you start all over. He can give you a new life and a new purpose. He is waiting for you to call out to Him! King David testified of this in Psalm 34:6, "This poor

man cried, and the LORD heard him, and saved him out of all his troubles."

The message of the Gospel can change your life. Jesus died on a cross and shed His blood for your sins so that you could have life. Not just eternal life in Heaven, but He wants you to have an abundant, meaningful life here on earth.

History bears witness to the multitudes of changed lives; lives that were transformed by simply placing child-like faith in the finished work of Christ on the cross. He loves you.

Though some people are hesitant to admit it, there is one basic need we all have in common. Somewhere down deep inside of every person is a desire to be loved. God created us that way. Some may pretend it doesn't matter and they can survive without anyone loving them or caring, but it does matter. We all need love!

The good news is that since God made us with a need to be loved, He decided to meet that need personally. One of the most familiar portions of Scripture is found in John 3:16, "For God so loved the world, that he gave his only begotten Son, that whosoever believeth in him should not perish, but have everlasting life."

The unbelievable truth is that He loved us when we were so unworthy of His love. How could a holy God love sinners? One thing is certain if we are honest – we are all sinners. The Bible is clear on that. "For all have sinned, and come short of the glory of God." (Romans 3:23)

Because sin is such a horrible problem, God demands a high price for the forgiveness of our sins. Our good works aren't enough. Church membership, baptism, giving money and good deeds will not pay the debt we owe because of our sin. God requires death as a payment. Romans 6:23 tells us, "For the wages of sin is death; but the gift of God is eternal life through Jesus Christ our Lord."

This is how He demonstrated His great love for us. He sent His own Son to die. Romans 5:8 tells us of that great love. "But God commendeth his love toward us, in that, while we were yet sinners, Christ died for us."

God's love for us was so powerful that He allowed a mean and hate-filled crowd to hang His perfect Son, Jesus Christ, on a cross. How could anyone ever doubt God's love after that?

No matter who you are, or what you have done, God's love for you is unchanging. He wants to forgive you of every sin you've ever committed and He wants a personal relationship with you. The Bible is clear; He loves and welcomes everyone!

2 Peter 3:9 says, "The Lord is not slack concerning his promise, as some men count slackness; but is longsuffering to us-ward, not willing that any should perish, but that all should come to repentance."

God is standing with open arms to welcome and forgive every one that asks Him. Revelation 21:6 says, "And he said unto me... I will give unto him that is athirst of the fountain of the water of life freely."

In order to be forgiven, you have to realize that God is waiting for you with open arms, and the decision is up to you! If you die in your sins and go to hell, you cannot blame anybody but yourself! God loved you enough to send a Savior to die on the cross for you. He also loved you enough to give you the opportunity to hear the truth.

If you want His forgiveness and you want to accept Him as your Savior, then you must get serious with God. Don't let anything or anyone discourage you from making things right with God! Today is the day of salvation. Please do not put it off! Let God heal and change your life today! Today could be the greatest day of your life. Every sin you've ever committed could be washed away forever if you'll just ask Him.

If you don't think your sin is very important, then one day you will die in your sins and you will stand before a holy and righteous God. Then it will be too late. Those who have heard the Gospel will not have a single excuse. After a person dies, it is too late to accept the gift of God's salvation. "And as it is appointed unto men once to die, but after this the judgment." (Hebrews 9:27)

Dear friend, Jesus loves you and died for you. Please don't reject His precious gift of salvation. Jesus promised us that He will not turn anyone away that comes to Him for healing and salvation. "All that the Father giveth me shall come to me; and him that cometh to me I will in no wise cast out." (John 6:37)

The greatest love in the world is the love between the Creator (Jesus Christ) and those who accept Him as their personal Savior. Will you receive Him today? He wants to show His love to you! He died for you. He rose from the dead and is extending an invitation to you now to be saved.

Why don't you kneel right now where you are and ask Him to become your Lord and Savior? I promise that you will never be the same. Pray right now and tell God you know you are a sinner and that you want His forgiveness for all your sins. Ask Him to come into your heart and save you and help you to live for Him. Repent (turn from your sins) and put all your faith and trust in Jesus Christ.

He is the only way you will ever be forgiven of all your sins. He is the only way you will ever get to Heaven. He is not the best way; Jesus is the only way!

"Jesus saith unto him, I am the way, the truth, and the life: no man cometh unto the Father, but by me." (John 14:6)

If you pray and experience God's healing through faith in Jesus Christ, your life will never be the same. I hope you will take a moment and contact me so I can rejoice with you.

Other Titles by the Author

The Exceptional Man
The Life of an Ambassador
A Place Called Calvary
Dare to be Different
The Gift of Salvation Made Simple
Fifty Shocking Facts about Tongues and Healing
Biblical Baptism
Deputation
Was Jesus Really God?
Much Is Given
Notes & Nuggets Series – Volume 1 – The Family
Notes & Nuggets Series – Volume 2 – The Church
Notes & Nuggets Series – Volume 3 – Revival
Notes & Nuggets Series – Volume 4 – Prayer
Notes & Nuggets Series – Volume 5 - Preaching
Notes & Nuggets Series – Volume 6 – Wisdom
Notes & Nuggets Series – Volume 7 - Purpose

To see all the books and sermon resources, go to

SUREWORD
PUBLICATIONS
surewordpublications.com

Visit the website

WOLVESAMONGLAMBS.COM

for additional victim resources.

You can also contact the author with your prayer request, testimony of God's healing grace or comments.

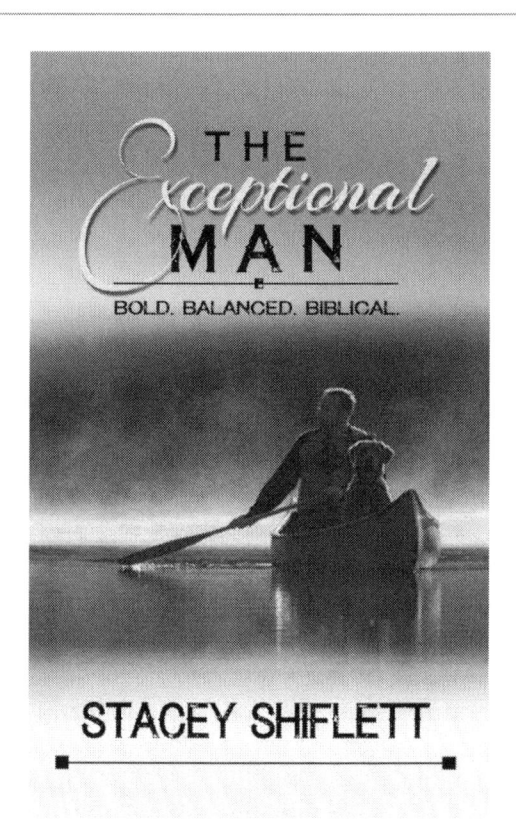

The Exceptional Man

God is searching for a man. Not just any man will do. This man must be different – a man He can use. A man that is fully qualified to lead our families, our churches and our nation back to God. A man that will step up to the plate and assume his God-given responsibilities in his home and church. A man that will discover God's purpose for his life. He must be bold in his demeanor. He must be balanced in his deeds. He must be biblical in his doctrine. A bold man is a strong man. A balanced man is a sensible man. A biblical man is a Spirit-filled man. A man that is all three is The Exceptional Man.

Paperback – 210 pages

Available at Amazon and surewordpublications.com

PRINCIPLES OF GROWTH
LESSONS FOR NEW CHRISTIANS

STACEY SHIFLETT

coming soon

EIGHT PRINCIPLES
THIRTY LESSONS
DISCIPLESHIP
WORKBOOK

SUREWORD PUBLICATIONS
SUREWORDPUBLICATIONS.COM

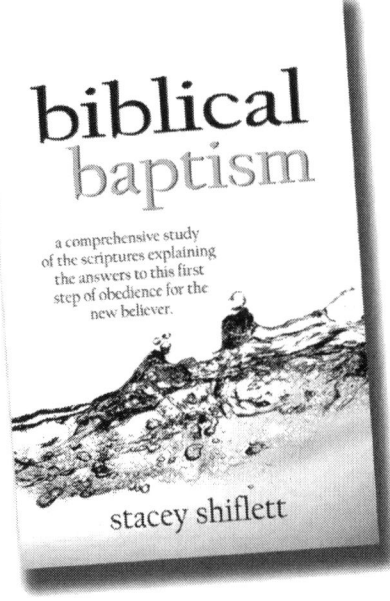

Made in the USA
Middletown, DE
05 March 2019